The Complete

TIME MANAGEMENT SYSTEM

CHRISTIAN H. GODEFROY
& JOHN CLARK

PIATKUS

First published in Great Britain in 1990 by
Judy Piatkus (Publishers) Ltd of 5 Windmill
Street, London W1P 1HF

First paperback edition 1991

British Library Cataloguing in Publication Data
Godefroy, Christian H.
  The complete time management system.
  1. Personnel. Time. Allocation
  I. Title   II. Comment avoir plus de temps. *English*
  331.25

ISBN 0–86188–990–8
ISBN 0–7499–1044–5 (Pbk)

Phototypeset in 11/13 pt Lasercomp Plantin
Printed and bound in Great Britain by
Butler & Tanner Ltd, Frome, Somerset

The Complete TIME

MANAGEMENT SYSTEM

This book is dedicated to:

Paul Meyer, master of time, who showed me the path.
Louis Robert, who pointed out many gaps in my organization.
Marcel Cools, who taught me the importance of thought before action.
Marc-André Poissant, my generous and genial colleague in the art of simplifying life.
John Clark, who revealed many of the TMS formulas.

And to you, Dear Reader, without whom this method would not see the light of day.

Thank you all!

CONTENTS

* Take the time to work, for it is the price of success.

* Take the time to think, it is the source of strength.

* Take the time to play, it is the secret of youth.

* Take the time to read, it is the seed of wisdom.

* Take the time to be friendly, for it brings happiness.

* Take the time to dream, for it will carry you to the stars.

* Take the time to love, it is the joy of life.

* Take the time to be content, it is the music of the soul.

(Original Irish Text)

INTRODUCTION: HOW TO HAVE MORE TIME

Certain chance encounters have a profound effect on your life. I'll never forget meeting Marcel Cools, self-made millionaire, owner of 21 businesses (among them two savings banks).

First his eyes, piercing, deep blue, a world of intelligence and concentration.

Then his voice, his gestures, calm, calculated, but carrying extraordinary force.

'Christian,' he told me, 'mastering time is the only key to success.'

'What do you mean?'

'You see, everybody has the same twenty-four hours to work with. But some make use of each second, while others fritter them away. Time is a precious commodity, the basis of life. Without time, you can't do anything!'

'And how should time be used?'

'The first secret is the simplest. It has three points:

1. Decide what needs doing most.

2. Forget everything else.

3. Put everything you have, body and soul, into this activity.'

'Seems easy enough!'

'Christian, do you have any worries?'

'Of course. Why?'

'The second point shows you how not to worry, or suffer from stress. Are you short of time?'

'Yes, I'm always late with my work.'

'The first point teaches you to say NO to useless activity, and frees you from the mental blocks that prevent you from succeeding. Are you efficient?'

'Yes, but not always.'

'Once you have mastered the third point, you'll reach a level of efficiency you never would have believed possible. Your resources are infinite. With this technique, you will be able to use them at will.'

Marcel C. has taught me many things since that conversation took place. I owe my success in life to him.

When I say that, I mean without his advice I would have toiled away, body and soul, without enjoying the passing moments at all.

Do you want to have more time? Do you want to become master of your own time, instead of being a slave (even if you're not always conscious of it)?

If you do, this method will reveal all the secrets of mastering time. I wrote it in honour of that meeting, which was a turning-point in my life, but also because every day I meet ambitious, intelligent, hard-working people, who are not achieving the success they deserve.

Are you in a similar situation? Maybe you realize there's a problem, but don't know what to do about it? The Complete Time Management System is more than an information session on the subject of time: I hope it will be a guide, and a companion for the rest of your life.

Christian H. Godefroy
Perros-Guirec, 20 November 1989

PART ONE

THE SECRETS OF TIME MANAGEMENT

1

MASTERING TIME:
THE KEY TO YOUR SUCCESS

'If only I had a bit more time ...'
   'I'm sorry, but I'm already late ...'
   'So sorry, but I'm already overloaded ...'
   'Call me next month, I haven't got a moment to spare ...'
   'Damn! Another weekend down the drain because of this stupid report. And I promised we'd go to the country ...'

How many times have you had to make these kinds of excuses?
   How many times have you heard other people saying these things, at the office, at home, in a restaurant, or elsewhere?
   Too often. Much too often!
   Did you know that 43 per cent of people in industrialized countries complain about not having enough time? (On the other hand, and this would be worth analysing, only 27 per cent would like to have more money at their disposal ...)
   So rest assured, you are not alone.
   Do you lack time? Are you often overloaded, irritable? Do you often feel trapped by time passing too quickly? Well all right, that's normal, at least for the moment. But after reading this method, and applying the techniques it contains, your situation will undergo a complete change: you will be master of your own time, you'll have enough time to do everything you like, you'll be up to date, you'll work faster and more efficiently, and you'll have a lot more time for leisure. Are you ready? Let's go!

Do you know how people who are noticed, who always end up succeeding brilliantly, manage their work? They are simply able to do a lot more things, in a lot less time. And that's not all: not only do they do more things, they do them better. It sounds incredible, doesn't it?

And these super-gifted people take longer holidays too, and more frequently. Why? Because each one of them dominates the situation, because they know how to control their time, and exploit it to the full.

Why are you so often overloaded with work?

Have you asked yourself why? Not really.

Well, invest a few seconds of your precious time and ask yourself:

Why am I overloaded?

Stop reading, and think about it. Write your answers down.

Is one of the reasons that you have too much work?

What does that mean exactly ... having too much work?

Are you saying that you're busier than the President of IBM? Or of Sony? Or of the United States?

How is it that these people can find the time to get away to their country houses, to take regular holidays, to spend time with their families, their children and grandchildren, to read volumes?

How do you think the President of Sony, Akio Morita, manages to have so much leisure time and, according to him, work as little as possible?

Do you have to be terrifically lazy in order to be master of your own time and have a brilliant career?

If you're not doing what you want to do, and feel overloaded, it might not be because you have too much work. If that were the case, how would other people manage seemingly superhuman workloads every day?

The secret of the two directors

Recently I had to meet two company directors. One heads a small publishing firm, with eight employees. The other is in charge of more than 4500 employees.

One of them let me have an appointment for the following morning. The other wasn't available until two weeks later.

Which one do you think was the more readily available? You guessed it! The director of the company with 4500 employees. His secretary made it clear that he could only give me fifteen minutes, and that he would greatly appreciate my being on time, but that he could meet me the next day. With the other director, I had to try three times just to get an appointment, and when I finally did succeed, it was only for two weeks later.

You might think, 'Well, that's normal. The director of a small company doesn't have as much help, and has to do everything himself.'

Not true! The director of the large company has at least as much work to deal with as the other. And furthermore, if he were suddenly called in to replace his opposite number in the small firm, he would quickly become as available as before ...

And it's for this reason that he became the director of such a large company. For this reason and no other.

Because he learned how to make himself available, by trusting his co-workers and delegating responsibility to them, and so keep himself free to make important decisions, to take advantage of lucrative opportunities, etc. In short, *because he learned how to manage and invest his time*. As for the director of the smaller company, as long as he doesn't learn how to manage his time:

1. His company will not grow as he would like.
2. He will probably never become the director of a larger company.
3. He will not overcome his 'incompetence threshold'.

According to the 'Peter Principle' everyone tends to reach their incompetence threshold, which means the hierarchical level past which they cannot progress. According to Professor Peter, people should stop at the level immediately below, and refuse any promotion which would bring them to that level.

Luckily, human beings can improve

A person who really wants to improve can raise his or her incompetence threshold almost infinitely ...

One of the best ways to do this is to use The Complete Time Management System. Thousands of American businessmen have demonstrated that this is without question one of the essential keys to success.

In the best-seller *The Success System That Never Fails*, William Clement Stone writes:

> Over the years, these companies have had amazing success with this method (selling life insurance directly by a sales organ- isation). But today, few businesses still apply the formula. Why? Either these businesses do not want to be profitable, and usually end up losing money. Or the system doesn't really lead to success. Or, if it does, because the secret has been lost ...
>
> Who are the exceptions? Precisely those groups of companies that I direct. Once again, the question is 'Why?' Simply because I have perfected a system which infallibly leads to success, a system which allows me to sell as many insurance policies in a week as others sell in a month, because they have no method. The reason is simple: *I economize my time.*

How do American Congressmen get re-elected?

In *Getting Things Done*, Edwin C. Bliss, one of the great American specialists in time management, explains:

> I became interested in ways to manage time a few years ago, when, as the assistant of a US Senator, I was struck by the similarities in working methods of the most outstanding members of Congress.
>
> *They were all using techniques which resulted in maximum profit from minimum time invested.*
>
> *They had learned how to concentrate on important issues, and put aside everything that wasn't.*
>
> Those who didn't learn how to do this were not re-elected!

You aren't a Congressman, you don't have as much to do, your responsibilities are more modest.

But what would happen if, like Congressmen, you:

1. Applied techniques resulting in maximum gain from minimum time invested.
2. Learned to concentrate on things that are important, and put aside everything else.
3. Learned to delegate responsibility, etc.

You would acquire a winner's attitude; you would start acting like a successful business person; you would be noticed; you would be ready to take advantage of new opportunities, deal with important responsibilities, achieve what you've wanted for so long.

A miracle? Not at all. Who or what can stand in your way if you use methods perfected by those who have already reached the top of their social or corporate ladder? Like them, you will become a winner, by managing your time.

Your days will no longer seem like chance journeys on a stormy sea, with an uncertain destination. You'll know exactly what you will be doing during the week, the month, the year to come. You will even have a master plan for the next five years.

But first ... to work!

Can you spare a minute?

Tell me, do you know exactly what you'll be doing this week? That's right, tell me NOW! Not really? Well, let me help you. Here are a few questions to guide you:

1. What are your objectives for the week?
2. What would help you reach your monthly objective? Your annual objective?
3. What is your MAIN objective?

If you have any difficulty answering these questions, the following chapters will help you.

Why do you need the complete time management system?

Would you like to earn more money, take more holidays, buy more things you like, be more relaxed, more creative, be successful in your personal as well as in your professional life? In short, would you like to be a SUCCESS?

Yes? Well, what's stopping you? Ah ... you've tried, you're still trying, but there are problems?

All right, what problems? Do you think that they have nothing to do with the way you manage your time? Are they because you are always overloaded with work? Can there be any other reason?

Let's say that your boss is a tyrant. And, in your opinion, lazy. Instead of doing the work a boss should do, he comes into your office every half-hour with something 'urgent' for you to take care of. And that's on top of the work that's already been piling up for three weeks because you haven't had the time to deal with it.

You are not the one who needs time organization ... your boss does!

But what if you discovered the secret that would 'pace' your boss, so that you wouldn't have to lose any more time trying to work out a conflicting workload?

What would you say to that?

Attract success

We often think that people who succeed must have had to sacrifice their personal lives in order to do it.

Not at all. With TMS you can – no, YOU WILL – reconcile the two. That's the way the method works best. It will make you succeed!

Thanks to The Complete Time Management System, you will be able to accomplish twice as much in half the time. You will amaze your colleagues, your clients, your friends, your boss, by becoming twice, three times, five times, even ten times more efficient than before. And that's only the beginning. The method has unlimited potential. Its resources are infinite.

Only you create the limits

Your spectacular transformation will be the envy of those around you.

Why? Because you'll be more relaxed, always perfectly in control of yourself, and much more creative. It's not unusual for users of The Complete Time Management System to discover whole new aspects of themselves that they didn't know about before.

The Complete Time Management System isn't a straitjacket. It doesn't constrain you. On the contrary, it's a gentle method, and the results are spectacular.

Free yourself

Very few people are really free. Rousseau in his *Social Contract* wrote: 'Man is born free, but everywhere he is in chains.' These chains have, for the most part, been created by man himself. He submits to them and tolerates them because of resignation, laziness, submission, fear, etc.

To think that people prefer being chained up to being free!

Actually, most people don't have, or don't acquire for themselves, the tools they need to get organized and conquer freedom.

That's right: conquer!

Freedom, like happiness, must be conquered.

The first condition is that you have to WANT it, to desire it, and to desire it with passion.

Ask yourself this question: do you really want to be master of your time and conquer that freedom which seems to escape most people?

Yes?

Bravo!

Because now that you've chosen your path, your life will begin to transform itself, even as you read these pages.

You've taken the first step towards a new life

That's right, without even knowing it, you've just taken the first step towards a new life. A new life where freedom and self-fulfilment will soon replace frustration and the feeling of always being over-loaded – missing out on opportunities that other, highly successful people seem to seize.

The second condition for conquering freedom is to use the appropriate tools, because, unfortunately, the best intentions in the world aren't enough on their own – even though I have often observed that if you really want something, you usually end up getting it ...

The fact that you are now discovering The Complete Time Management System is no accident. Nothing happens by chance. Never. We have met today because of your desire for success and freedom.

And I'm very pleased. You've done your part, and I can assure you that I'll do mine, by revealing all my secrets and techniques – the same ones that have helped managers, directors and presidents of major corporations become what they are, out-distancing their colleagues who are no less gifted, but who are simply less organized.

Some people refuse to apply The Complete Time Management System, saying they don't want to become slaves of their planning. Get ready: you're in for a surprise!

You waste 97 per cent of your time

An American expert, Dr De Woot, conducted an in-depth study of the working time of corporate executives. The results of this study are very surprising for people who haven't had any contact with time management. De Woot shows that for all executives with no previous time management training (who are still the vast majority):

- 49 per cent of their time is spent on tasks that could be done by their secretaries;
- 5 per cent of their time is spent on tasks that could be delegated to subordinates;
- 43 per cent of their time is spent on tasks that they could have delegated to colleagues;
- Only 3 per cent of their time is spent on tasks at their own optimum performance level.

You read correctly: executives who haven't taken time management training courses *spend only 3 per cent of their energy on tasks and responsibilities suited to their talents and abilities*. In other words, *they waste 97 per cent of their energy* through ignorance of the techniques of time management.

How then are these executives supposed to distinguish themselves, succeed, overcome their workloads, be ready to seize opportunities and assume new responsibilities? It's practically impossible.

Consider how much the company loses out in this situation. It's like paying for an extra secretary for 49 per cent of the executive's working hours, and for an extra colleague for $43 + 5 = 48$ per cent of the executive's working hours.

If the executive is paid £50,000 a year, and the secretary and colleagues an average of £25,000, the company loses about £24,250 per year per executive (which comes to more than £30,000 when you include the employer's contributions to national insurance, company pensions, and so on).

From these supporting figures, you can see that you have an amazing tool in your hands for increasing productivity. You will also have the time in which to show the techniques you have learned to your colleagues and friends.

What about leisure time?

You will also be able to apply these techniques to your daily life and, even better, to your leisure time. You will get more out of it, and have more of it.

Good. But to do all this you first have to learn the techniques.

How? You don't have the time? You're too busy? I beg you, spare me a minute and listen to the 'Busy Man's' paradox.

The busy man's paradox

Some time ago, a friend of mine, Denison Woods, bought a VHS recorder that could, among other things, make high-speed duplicates of video cassettes.

He brought it home, unpacked it and wanted to use it right away.

The machine was accompanied by an instruction booklet, but Denison said, 'It's not worth the trouble. I've already got a VHS recorder, this must work the same way. After all, I'm intelligent. No problem. And I haven't got the time!'

Without wasting any time, he started trying to copy the first cassette ... without success. Same for the second try. He fiddled a bit with the buttons ... still no good. So he started all over again, step by step, trying to prove that his 'intelligence' would work. Nothing happened. He got angry.

After half an hour the 'stupid machine' still wouldn't work, despite his imaginative and 'intelligent' efforts. He finally decided to read the instruction booklet. In three minutes the machine made its first copy.

Take the time you need ... to win!

What happened to Denison was silly: all he had to do was press two buttons at the same time. But he didn't think of it, and he might have gone on for hours before finally stumbling on the solution. He might have become so angry that he broke the machine in the process.

Convinced? It's the same thing with The Complete Time Management System: *invest your time learning the techniques, and you will profit from them all your life.* It would be hard to find a better investment.

All the more so because of three facts:

1. *You can't buy time*
   Time is distributed equally and democratically to all of us. Its inequality only results from the way that it's managed or wasted.

2. *Time cannot be saved up*
   It runs on uninterruptedly: you are older every second. You can't stock up on time.

3. *Time cannot be stopped*
   Lost time can never be recovered. This is certainly the cruellest of laws ...

Can you still reasonably refuse to take advantage of the benefits of The Complete Time Management System? Are you ready to invest some time in TMS?

Let's get started!

**The word ORGANIZATION
comes from the word ORGANON
which means HARMONY.**

2

MANAGE YOUR TIME BETTER

How to manage your time

Time management isn't taught in schools, despite the fact that those who know about it are convinced that it's one of the most important elements for succeeding in life.

It's a shame: most people only have a very vague idea of what time is all about. They are unaware of their own relationship to time, so they don't know if they're using it well or badly.

What about you? How do you manage your time?

The easiest way to find out is perhaps to look at what constitutes bad time management. Here are the twelve classic symptoms of bad time management:

1. Continually overloaded schedule; working more than 55 hours per week; frequently working at evenings and weekends; hardly ever taking holidays.

2. Unable to meet deadlines; constant delays; always having the feeling of catching up.

3. Lack of depth in dealing with problems.

4. Hasty decisions, despite the risks they involve.

5. Fear of delegating work, or of accepting others' initiatives.

6. Always favouring short-term gains over medium or long term; always 'putting out the fire' ... dealing with daily crises.

7. Inability to refuse any new task that might be presented.

8. A two-month waiting list for people who want appointments (even one month is excessive, unless you have a very important position, like Head of State, and even then ...)

9. The feeling of not being in control of the situation, of losing sight of your objectives and priorities.

10. Being a perfectionist.

11. Stress and burn-out.

12. Little or no time for the family, social life or leisure.

Do some of these symptoms apply to you?

For more accuracy, I've drawn up the following checklist (based on the work of Edwin C. Bliss):

TEST   Yes No

1. Have I decided on the goals I want to achieve in my life

2. Have I decided on my short-term objectives, say for the next six months?

3. Have I done anything today, *anything concrete*, that will help me attain my short-term goals? My long-term goals?

4. Do I have a precise idea of what I want to accomplish during the next week?

5. Do I know precisely which hours of the day I am most productive?

6. Do I do my most important tasks during those hours?

7. Do I evaluate my performance at work according to the results obtained (objectives) rather than according to the sum of my activities (working methods)?

8. Do I set up my priorities according to importance rather than urgency?

9. Do I delegate tasks to my subordinates?

10. Do I delegate interesting work as much as routine work?

11. When I delegate a task, do I consider the *power* as well as the *responsibility* it entails?

12. Have I found a way to prevent my subordinates from delegating tasks they find too difficult to their superiors?

13. Have I taken any measures recently to prevent useless documentation (publications, reports, etc) from appearing on my desk?

14. Have I gone through my files to eliminate all useless information?

15. During meetings, am I someone who can clearly sum up a situation, underlining the main points of discussion, the decisions to be taken, and the tasks to be accomplished?

16. Do I use the telephone effectively to solve problems, turning to written documents only when they become absolutely necessary?

17. Do I put the time it takes to get to and from work to constructive use?

18. Outside office hours, do I take measures to free my mind from my work?

19. Do I make any effort to make non-urgent decisions more rapidly?

20. There's a crisis at the office: will I be ready for the next one by learning from the experience, and applying the measures necessary to prevent it happening again?

21. Do I take as much care in setting up deadlines for myself as I do for others?

22. Do I allot enough time for planning my work?

23. Have I been able to terminate certain working methods which I know to be completely inefficient?

24. When I'm on a business trip, or waiting to meet one of my clients, do I use the time efficiently, with everything I need to occupy myself handy in my briefcase?

25. Do I force myself to concentrate on the present, on the task in hand, rather than ruminating eternally on the failures and successes of the past, or worrying about the future?

26. Do I regularly update my agenda, to detect holes in the way I use my time, and avoid duplicating unproductive planning models?

27. Am I well aware of the *monetary value* of my time?

28. Do I regularly force myself to practise habits that will make me more efficient in the management of my time?

29. Do I apply the 'Pareto Principle' (see Chapter Six) when I'm faced with a number of different tasks which all have to be done?

30. In short, am I someone who is master of my own time? Am I someone who determines how my time will be used, rather than having it dictated to me by circumstance, or by others?

Now add up your points: give yourself one point for each 'yes'.

- **Between 25 and 30 points:** Congratulations! You are already an excellent manager of your time. You will certainly have found techniques mentioned in the questionnaire that you already know about, but its direct and complete form must have pleased you: you can refer to it as needed, and use it to perfect your own techniques, as well as to train others.

- **Between 10 and 25 points:** Not bad! You are already applying some of the important principles for using your time more efficiently. This method will now allow you to manage your time scientifically, resulting in more and better leisure time.

- **Less than 10 points:** Don't waste a second! Immerse yourself, body and mind, in the method, and be as conscientious as possible. You have a lot to learn, which means that your progress will be all the more spectacular.

This could be the moment that begins your new life – a richer and happier life where you will finally be able to give everything you've got and reach the goals you desire the most.

So now to work. You'll find all the tools you need in the following pages.

Practical exercise

You have just seen the main symptoms of bad time management, and you've answered a questionnaire which has certainly pointed out some of your weak points and shown you what you have to gain by using The Complete Time Management System. Let's go a little farther. Invest 180 seconds to answer each of these questions:

1. What are my weak points in terms of time management?
    (3 minutes)
2. What are my strong points?
    (3 minutes)

Be as frank as possible. Make your list as honest as you can. Do you have problems answering? Do it quickly.

Time Management: My Problems
Sample Response

I often start something and don't finish it. Something comes up, so I stop. I don't stop to consider whether the new problem is really important or not. I think the reason for this lack of discipline is my impulsive nature.

The result is that I don't stick to my list of priorities.

I have a tendency to overload myself with priorities. More precisely, I underestimate the time I think I'll need for each job, so that I can never finish what's on the list. I'm often frustrated at the end of the day, which also makes me feel guilty.

I let myself get sidetracked too easily, maybe because unconsciously I think that what I'm doing isn't really important. One thing's for sure, I have a lot of problems saying no, especially to friends and relatives.

I think people have a negative image of me. I project an image of always being available. The other day I did a few calculations, and found that I wasted at least 40 minutes a day on useless conversations (useless for me, anyway).

I have to share my secretary with my boss, and of course he always comes first. I must find a way to get things done on time.

Because of my tendency to do everything myself, to delegate as little as possible, and because of the fact that for my secretary I always come second, I end up doing a whole lot of little things that should really be taken care of by the secretary, or by an assistant.

That's actually a good idea: I should make a proposal to my boss, supported by cash figures, to show him that it would pay to hire an assistant for me. I could spend my time doing things for the company that are really profitable, which is why I was hired in the first place.

If my secretary is away or busy, I have to waste a lot of time finding files myself. We have to get together on this, she should at least explain her filing system to me.

I wonder how well she keeps it up to date, if it shouldn't be completely reorganized so that everyone could understand it and use it efficiently.

I often end up putting in 60 hours a week. When I started here, I didn't mind the extra hours at all. But I'm not a beginner any more ... it's been going on for too long. Five years, to be exact, and the long hours are wearing me out. Of course, the promotions did help, I've moved quickly up the ladder, but I ask myself if maybe I'm throwing away my life, if the price for this success is too high, if I've sacrificed too much.

Is this really success? Or am I just fooling myself? I have less and less time for my family. I feel my wife and I growing apart. It's as if she's 'disturbing' me all the time, when all she wants is a little attention. Yet I do love her. I should take a good look at my life while there's still time ...

Time Management: My Strong Points
Sample Response

I can get a lot of work done if I'm not disturbed. Unfortunately this doesn't happen very often. People are always arriving at the wrong time. I regain my concentration easily after an interruption (which is maybe why I tolerate interruptions in the first place, knowing that I won't have trouble getting back to work when it's over). What I forget is that each time I stop, I lose ten or fifteen minutes ... that's the serious part ...

I can deal with stress pretty well, even during a crisis. I exercise every week, to keep myself healthy.

I make a list of my objectives for every day. Even if I do tend to overestimate my ability, at least I make a list.

I take the time to think before making decisions. I don't let stress get the better of me. I try to have as much data as possible in front of me beforehand.

My reports are precise and to the point. (Come to think of it, that might be a fault. I wonder if the people I work with really read my reports, if I'm not wasting three or four hours every week writing them up. Someone said that the spoken word gets through, and the written word gets filed ... maybe I should think about being more effective, more direct.)

A hint for answering more easily

It's simple really. Just write down everything that comes into your head. If you have trouble (you may encounter definite blocks because you might not be willing to admit certain truths about yourself) try this little trick:

Pretend you're an expert on time management (which is exactly what you will be after working with this method!) and that the employee you have to evaluate is none other than yourself. The trick is to distance yourself, so that you can talk about yourself completely objectively.

The more accurate a picture you create of yourself, the more you will benefit from this method. Do you need more than three minutes? No problem. Take all the time you need. The deeper your intro-spection goes, the faster you'll progress.

Some preparatory questions

You're still not sure if you've defined your problem, if the picture you've painted of yourself is accurate? Here's a detailed ques-tionnaire that will help:

1. Do you spend your time the way you want?

2. Do you regularly work long hours? How many?

3. Do you bring work home from the office more than one night a week?

4. Do you regularly feel a lot of stress at work, even if there's no serious problem or crisis?

5. Do you feel guilty because you don't do as much work as you think you should? Or your boss thinks you should?

6. Do you set up short- and long-term objectives?

7. Do you like your work?

8. Does your work bring you satisfaction?

9. Do you take the time to stay in shape?

10. Can you clear your desk of papers in less than a minute (putting them where they should go, of course)?

11. Do you check if your colleagues respect their planning sched-ules?

12. Are there papers on your desk which aren't important, which have been there for some time?

13. Do you often get letters or memos starting with 'In view of the fact that we have not received your response to our com-munication dated . . .'

14. Are you often interrupted in the middle of important jobs?

15. Do you allow your colleagues to come into your office at any time of day?

16. Do you take more than two hours for lunch, when an hour would usually be enough?

17. Do you eat in your office?

18. In the past month, have you forgotten any appointments, any important dates or meetings?

19. Do you often put important jobs off to the very last minute, and then work like mad to get them done?

20. Is it easy for you to make excuses and put off things you don't really like doing?

21. Do you have enough time to get away for long weekends, and take those holidays you dream about?

22. Do you have enough time for your favourite pastimes . . . reading a good book, going to films or concerts?

23. Do you have enough free time?

24. Do you take pleasure in the 'here and now'?

25. Do you always feel you should be doing something to keep busy?

26. Do you feel guilty when you rest for a long time?

27. Do you read carefully everything that appears on your desk?

28. Are you way behind in your work-related reading (magazines, newsletters, etc.)?

29. Do you have to review or finish work you asked your staff to do?

30. Are you busy sorting out minor problems, which prevent you from dealing with your company's important objectives? Do you lose sight of your overall plan, of the way to improve your department? Do you have the time to re-evaluate your methods and make them more effective? In short, do you feel that you're *dominating the situation*, or that it is dominating you?

That should get you working. Now it's up to you!

You are your time

In the light of these two exercises, you should already have a much better idea of how you relate to time. And more than that, perhaps you know a little more precisely who you are. Because the way you manage time is an accurate reflection of your own personality:

> **Tell me what you do with your time,**
> **and I'll tell you who you are.**

The next step is: how to develop better habits for using *your precious time*.

3

HABITS THAT SAVE TIME

The amazing power of habit

In the preceding chapter you became more aware of your relationship with time. That's the first step. Now we're going to see how the way you relate to time – your strong as well as your weak points – is discreetly but firmly determined by a single force: habit.

'Habit,' said Pascal, 'is a person's second nature.'

That's great, as long as you're talking about a positive habit. Most habits are so deeply ingrained in us that we're totally unconscious of them.

And, worse still, we end up believing that life is meant to be that way, that there's nothing we can do about it, and that we just have to accept it.

For example, haven't you been resigned for a long time to never being able to meet your deadlines; always being late, because that's just the way it is?

Or to staying late at the office a few nights a week, even though you swore never to do it again?

To accepting that extra job once again, while your colleagues wriggle out of it for various reasons, because you're really the only person who can handle it?

Situations like these aren't new to you, are they? In each case, the force of *habit* is at work.

**'Bad habits are easier
to abandon today
than tomorrow.'**

Judah Leib Lazerov

Interior messages that direct you

Behavioural analysts explain that many of these 'habits' are the result of restrictive messages that have been integrated into the deepest recesses of our minds since childhood. They have distinguished five types of restrictive messages, which they call 'drivers':

1. 'Be perfect': If your inner voice is always saying that 'you should do better'; if you often use the expressions 'Of course', 'Obviously', 'Clearly' . . .
2. 'Make an effort': If you keep repeating 'You should try harder' to yourself; if you often say 'It's tough', 'I can't make it', 'I'll give it a try', 'I don't know'; if you have an impatient character . . .
3. 'Try to please': You keep saying 'You're not nice enough' to yourself, and to others 'That's very kind', 'Do you think you could', 'You know best' . . .
4. 'Hurry up': You always tell yourself 'You'll never make it' and keep saying 'What do they want from me?' and 'Faster, faster!'
5. 'Be strong': You repeat to yourself 'You've got to hide your weakness'; and to others 'It doesn't matter' and 'No comment'. Your expression is impassive, hard, cold.

The results of these constricting messages? You structure your time in order to obey them, so in fact you are their slave.

The tortured worker

The classic example of this is the workaholic – the person who is prodded by one or more of these 'drivers'. Workaholics never feel good, they don't feel useful, they don't think they're worth anything, while at the same time they're always overloaded with work. They throw themselves body and soul into what they call 'their' work, for which they sacrifice all.

This kind of behaviour is the most unhealthy imaginable: feverish activity will never allay the fears and anguish of the 'tortured worker' (because the roots of the problem lie elsewhere). Their spirit is stifled by 'work'; they will never be able to take the necessary steps to gain perspective and extricate themselves from their rut. (And, even worse, these tortured workers hide behind their constant activity to avoid having to ask themselves uncomfortable questions, which would allow them to come face to face with their problem.)

Where do these messages come from?

These 'drivers' come from your parents.

- If they told you to 'Be Perfect', it's because they were rarely satisfied with themselves.
- If they told you to 'Try Harder', it's because the only things they thought had any value were those that were difficult to achieve. They never finished what they started, and failed to realize their dreams, except with great difficulty and hardship.
- If they said 'Try to Please', it's because they generally accorded more importance to the opinions of others than to their own.
- If they were always telling you to 'Hurry Up', it's because they never had enough time for themselves.
- If they told you to 'Be Strong', it's because they were afraid of being weak.

Think about it: what are your 'drivers'? Think about your childhood, and write down what you remember of what your parents told you.

Maybe you don't think these drivers are so important? In the opinion of most behavioural analysts:

**We spend 80 per cent of our time
responding to drivers!**

If there is one thing you should remember from this whole method, it's this: free yourself from your drivers. It will save you an enormous amount of time.

What to do?

You have to replace the restrictive messages in your mind with PERMISSIONS. Give yourself permission to BE YOURSELF!

Here are some 'permissions' you can repeat to yourself:

BE PERFECT
I have the right to be myself.
I have the right to make a mistake.
To err is human. I am human.
The search for perfection leads to paralysis.

TRY HARDER
I have the right to stop what I start.
I have the right to win.
I have the right to achieve.

TRY TO PLEASE
I have the right not to be responsible
for the feelings of others.
I have self-respect and consideration for my feelings.
I assume responsibility for my own feelings.

HURRY UP
I have the right to live in the present.
I have the right to take my time.
I have the time to achieve what I want.

BE STRONG
I have the right to express my feelings.
I have the right to be close to someone.
I have the right not to be strong.
I have the right to be open to others.

What about other habits?

Here's a little puzzle that will convince you of the amazing force (because it's unconscious) that habit exerts on our lives.

Look at these dots. Using only four straight lines (don't cheat – it makes the whole exercise futile!) and without lifting your pen off the paper, try to join up all the dots, without going back on a line twice.

Ready? Go for it!

O   O   O

O   O   O

O   O   O

The answer is on the next page. Don't look too soon, and no cheating!

Did you do it? Excellent!

If not, don't worry. Maybe you gave up too easily (most people need about an hour to find the solution). Or maybe the force of habit is too strong in you.

You started with the premise that a line has to have a beginning and an end, so that you stopped each line on one of the points, and were unable to imagine a rectangle that went beyond the one formed by the points.

The solution is easy ... when you know it. It's simply a question of not being afraid to cross the mental barriers which result from habit.

The solution:

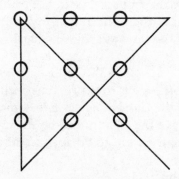

There's yet another solution, and one that needs only three lines: since the points are thick, you could start a line moving towards the right at the top of the top left point, so that it angles slightly down and passes through the middle of the top middle point and the bottom of the top right point. Then you extend it far enough so that the next line, moving back in the opposite direction, will pass through the middle three points in the same way, and so on. Another winner!

What are your bad habits?

You now understand what an (often negative) influence habits can have on you. The puzzle demonstrated clearly that habits prevent you from seeing things differently, and more important to our purpose, from

behaving differently!

It's time for a change.

You have now cleared the first step.

The second consists of identifying clearly and precisely those habits that are blocking your performance, and preventing you from realizing your full potential.

Don't underestimate the importance of making an objective and lucid 'inner inventory' of the habits you want to change. This method is much less effective without it, and as it's so easy to do, it would be a pity to skip over it.

Here's what to do:

1. Make a note of the habit you want to change. Write it down.
2. Write down your aim in changing the habit.

Don't forget to mention a precise period of time. Your resolution will be more tangible. You'll feel more obligated to do it, which will help you to succeed.

An example? Let's say you decide to reorganize your filing system. If you don't put a specific time limit on the job, you might end up putting it off indefinitely and the objective, although important, will never be achieved.

You should say, for example: 'Starting today, I will take the necessary steps to get an efficient filing system installed, and in one month, by 14 April, the system will be completed.'

NB: Don't forget to indicate the specific stages of your plan of attack. It's of capital importance! Set a date for each step: it's usually the simplest and fastest way to succeed.

3. Make a list of all the disadvantages caused by your bad habits.
4. Make a list of the advantages which changes would bring.
5. Do not leave anything out, especially at the beginning.

Be hard on yourself, especially at the beginning. If you find yourself getting lax, make sure you get back on the right track.

6. Exaggerate a little at the beginning.

For example, if you're regularly late for meetings, force yourself to arrive fifteen minutes early for a whole month.

A happy medium will soon establish itself. You sometimes have to exaggerate in one direction in order to get back to a balanced state.

7. Involve other people.

Speak to your secretary about your objectives, for example. Ask for help to achieve your goals. There's another advantage to this; by telling people about your aims, you commit yourself to them.

Don't give yourself the opportunity to back out. If you do, people will see you as someone who can't be taken seriously.

Find a role model

One of the best ways to acquire good organizational habits is to choose a role model.

Obviously this doesn't mean making yourself into a cheap imitation. But don't forget that when they started out, most great people – people who have achieved exceptional success – were ordinary folk just like you and me. They were, for the most part, gifted with this faculty, one could even say this strange virtue, which is the virtue of *admiration*.

While striving to reach the summit, most of these successful people chose a role model, someone they wanted to imitate – and surpass.

Maybe you've heard the famous line by Victor Hugo who, at twenty years of age, exclaimed: 'I will be a Chateaubriand or nothing at all!'

Well, he might not have become a Chateaubriand, but he did become Victor Hugo. He did exactly what I'm suggesting you do: he chose a role model.

Your role model doesn't necessarily have to be someone famous. Not that it shouldn't be. But the problem with famous people is that it's so hard to get close to them. We can only observe them – unless the famous person happens to be yourself! – through the generally distorted view of the media. We know them only through hearsay.

Your role model could very well be your boss, an especially brilliant colleague, a friend, your father ...

In *Roger's Rules for Success*, Henry C. Rogers wrote a fascinating passage on the subject which I quote below:

Find the time to do everything

You might find a solution by watching people you admire. Your boss? Your wife? Your best friend?

Speak to them. Ask them questions. Observe them. Discover their secrets.

There's an old dictum that says:

'If you want something to get done, give it to someone who's busy!'

Every day, all around me, I see the proof of this statement.

What's their secret?

They have organized their lives better than we have. They don't waste time. They don't spend three or four hours a day watching TV.

They've learned how to do the important things first.

They've planned out the 24 hours of their day so that they have enough time to do everything they want to do.

And company directors are the best examples of the fact that the busiest people have time to do extra jobs, as long as they coincide with their main objectives.

What about you? Are you one of those busy people who will always get the job done?

If not – or at least not yet – who, from the people around you, could you choose as your role model?

All right, time to stop reading for a moment and make a list of at least three people who seem gifted – not a natural gift, but a talent that was cultivated and developed – with a superior sense of organization, and who could therefore serve as your role model.

Now that you have your list, answer the following questions:

1. What qualities for organizing time do these people possess?
2. What personality traits accompany this heightened organizational ability (for example, very relaxed, energetic, active, a balanced life with plenty of attention given to family and leisure etc.)?
3. What qualities do I need most in order to (intelligently) resemble these people?

And finally, ask yourself the following question, which is perhaps the most important:

Why am I not like them?

It's certainly not because you lack qualities or ability. No, not at all.

It's simply because you don't have their sense of organization. That's their only advantage. And The Complete Time Management System will give it to you, too.

In the light of this, how much value do you place on your 'hourly rate'? What I mean is, for how much would you sell your time, if I asked to buy some? Go on, figure it out ... we'll be discussing this at length in the next chapter.

'The word Perfection spells P-a-r-a-l-y-s-i-s.'

Winston Churchill

4

Make Your Time Pay!

What is your real hourly rate?

Studies of the lives of successful entrepreneurs, well-known politicians and business people have invariably shown that they all developed excellent time management habits.

One was common to them all. Which one?

That's right, the habit of regularly evaluating, and therefore of being continually conscious of, *the precise value of their time.*

Do you do the same?

Have you developed this habit to its highest level, a habit which is so essential to success?

Doctors, psychiatrists, lawyers, consultants, anyone whose performance is remunerated in relation to the time they spend with their clients, is particularly aware of this attitude towards the passing of time ...

What about you? Do you know how much a fifteen-minute phone conversation costs you?

Money is by no means the only standard used to measure the value of time, but evaluation in money terms often reveals more than a few surprises.

A £50 letter

You don't work for your salary alone. You don't start a business only for the profit you plan to make.

Not at all. But financial compensation and hopes of profit are objective factors which motivate everything we undertake.

Writing a letter costs me £100. What about you?

One day when my secretary was absent, I had to go to the post office myself to post an urgent letter. When I returned, I asked myself a question that I should have asked before going: 'Could I really afford to take care of that job?'

I did some calculating. Just the time it took to post the letter and come back cost me £50. That's right, fifty pounds to go and post a letter. Did the urgency merit the expense? After thinking about it, I had to admit that it didn't. So I'd been 'had' by my own impatience and lack of judgement.

I noted the incident in my diary, which I keep with me all the time, so that in future I'll know just how much a trip to the post office can cost.

We usually try to cut costs in more tangible areas like production, energy, salaries, etc. But we'd be better off if we first evaluated the costs of what we and our colleagues do, of the time it takes to do all the jobs that we are assigned: a goldmine of profit and productivity is right there for the taking if we would just evaluate our everyday, routine activities rationally.

To come up with a realistic evaluation of what an hour of my time is really worth, I have to take a number of expenses into account. You should do the same.

And if you include write-offs for fixed costs and other overheads like office rental and equipment, communications, etc., the margin for lost income can be very high.

Some specialists even say you should consider your secretary's and all your colleagues' salaries when evaluating your own performance rate, including any extra benefits they may receive.

What if we calculate your hourly performance rate, just to see what it really is?

Twelve points for evaluating your hourly rate

As they say, 'Time is money'. In the following exercise, you'll find out that your time really is money.

Be prepared for a surprise when you work it out:

1. Your annual salary.

2. Your other revenues (including social benefits, which can represent up to 33 per cent of your salary).

_____

3. Your professional overheads (rent, equipment, heating, electricity, etc.).

_____

4. Miscellaneous costs (agents' fees, conferences, trips, etc.).

_____

5. Annual costs related to your function.

_____

6. Value of your weekly rate (divide your annual salary by 47, or the number of weeks you work in a year).

_____

7. Value of your hourly rate (divide the preceding amount by the number of hours you work a week).

_____

8. Your rate per minute (divide the preceding amount by 60).

_____

9. Annual salaries of your staff (all of them).

_____

10. Extra benefits of your staff.

_____

11. Additional personnel-related costs.

_____

12. Value of your actual hourly rate (add lines 1, 4, 9 and 11, divide by the number of weeks you work a year, and then by the number of hours you work a week).

_____

A little surprised by the results? Your time is worth a lot more than you thought. A lot more!

Be aware of your hourly rate

A friend of mine is a teacher. He gives private courses, at a fixed rate. Since his wife doesn't work, and they have two kids, he complained that he wasn't able to pay for a cleaner to come in once a week and clean the house, which would cost about £20.

'I don't see what the problem is,' I said.

'The problem is that we don't have enough money. My wife doesn't work, and I don't make as much as you do.'

'Why don't you try teaching one night a week?'

I don't know why, but my friend had never thought of that.

He made a few enquiries: he was lucky. He called an old colleague, who just happened to be looking for an English teacher to replace one of his staff.

He started the following week, teaching one night a week, for three hours, and earned £20 an hour.

Which means he increased his income by £60 per week, or about £45 after tax. So he could not only hire a cleaner, he had an extra £100 to put in his pocket every month.

Obviously, this is just an example. But it shows that we can often free ourselves from doing disagreeable work by putting in an extra couple of hours doing what we like. Think about it!

How much does a useless telephone call cost you?

Knowing the real value of your time will free you, and will make your time more profitable, more productive. It will also help you rationalize your use of time.

Have a little fun. Using your hourly rate as a base figure, make a few calculations and work out just how much the following activities cost:

1. A fifteen-minute coffee break;
2. A document that takes you five minutes to find;
3. A useless twenty-minute telephone call;
4. An unexpected job that takes half an hour;
5. A job that takes two hours that your assistant could have done, remembering that he earns 30 per cent less than you do.

Have you worked it out? Surprised?

And these are only daily losses. Add them all up and multiply by five. What do you have now?

Well, that gives you an idea of what you're losing every week ...

Go all the way. Multiply your weekly figure by 47 (or the number of weeks you work a year). The amount is enormous, isn't it?

That's what you've been losing every year, all because you were negligent or unconscious of just what a few minutes of lost time really costs. And that's only an average. At the end of his course, one of my students established what I would call a record. He discovered, using this method, that he'd lost more than £30,000 the previous year!

A sane and realistic approach to your overall time

I hear you object: there's more to life than money. And you haven't actually lost money, it's only potential theoretical money we're talking about.

That's true.

But this money you lost, this time you wasted, could have been converted into fun and extra income – both of which are very real and enjoyable.

This doesn't mean that in future you should count every minute that passes in order to convert it to pounds or dollars. That you should become a machine, cold and calculating, a person who never takes a few minutes off simply to talk to someone ...

Not at all. It means that you should acquire a sane and realistic approach to your overall time, which will allow you to make it as profitable and valuable as possible. It can give you a lot more leisure time, for example, or time to be more creative, to prospect for new ideas, etc.

OK? So with this rate in mind, ask yourself, as often as possible:

What is the most productive use for each hour of my day?

Let's work together once again.

Evaluate your most recent tasks according to your hourly performance rate. Make a table as shown overleaf.

For each task, ask yourself the question: 'Could I delegate this to someone who "costs" less than I do?'

We'll see later on, in Chapter Seventeen, that a job should always

Task	Time	Rate	Cost
1.			
2.			
etc.			

be given to the person on the lowest level of the corporate hierarchy who is still able to accomplish the task efficiently.

When a job is delegated to someone whose level is too high, for example a director instead of a production manager or foreman, the risks of loss are considerable.

Unless the director in question knows the principles of The Complete Time Management System, that is, and makes sure that he in turn delegates the task to someone who will be working at his or her optimum level.

Evaluate your hourly rate regularly

Each time your income increases, each time you are rewarded by promotion, don't forget to recalculate your hourly rate.

The conclusions to be drawn will quickly become evident.

For example, there may be some jobs that you cannot allow yourself to handle any longer, because they just cost much too much.

Up to now, you've probably been doing your paperwork and accounting yourself, instead of delegating it to a specialist. This has required some hours a month. But now you might find that with your increased income, the £30 or £40 a month fee that a specialist charges is a real bargain, since your time is worth double that.

A good accountant will usually save you money, so don't hesitate to use one.

When we start out, we tend to want to do everything ourselves, to economize. That might be OK in the beginning, but the habit can rapidly become destructive.

You must re-evaluate your hourly rate constantly. And if you find you're not earning enough money, why not concentrate all your energies and time exclusively on activities that pay most. The results will be astonishing. I guarantee it! You will achieve miracles.

Ask yourself the following question as often as possible: 'What would happen if, instead of a half or a third, I spent ALL my time working at my optimum level, without wasting a minute?'

It won't take long to find out . . .

How long do you live per day?

What I mean is: how much really free time do you have for yourself each day?

I'm listening . . .

All right, let's work it out together.

Basic needs demand at least 40 per cent of our time:

We use
● 8 hours to sleep (including going to bed, falling asleep and waking up);
● 2 hours to eat (cook, etc.);
● 1 hour for personal hygiene (getting dressed, washing, shaving, etc.);
● . . . that's already 11 hours.

After basic needs come subsistence needs: housing, medical care, food, heating, clothes, family support, etc. In other words, you have to work to live.

This takes an average of:
● 8 hours a day working;
● 1 hour's transport (average time);
● . . . which makes 9 hours.

Added to the 11 hours we already have, that makes a total of 20 hours.

That's right, twenty hours. That's a lot, wouldn't you say?

How much time is left for you to take care of yourself, to do something other than sleep and organize your subsistence? To live?

Only four hours a day for living

If you don't really like your work, you're left with only four pitiful hours a day to do the things you do like – to take it easy, see friends, spend time with your family, to do what you want. To listen to music, learn Italian, read a good book, go swimming or play golf . . .

Only four hours a day to really live!

In fact, my figures are not quite exact. The real situation is even worse because these four hours don't really belong to you. There are your children, who demand time and attention. It can be pleasant to spend time with them, but it can also be stressful.

Some days you're unwell or tired, you have a headache or you just feel down . . .

It's lucky we have weekends!

But what if I can't be free, even at the weekend? What if I'm so tired after my week? Or what if I have things to do, like fixing things around the house?

The most expensive pastime in the world

And wait! There's more, the real '*coup de grace*'.

A survey conducted by the French magazine *Telerama* revealed that people spend an average of twenty hours a week in front of their television sets! Work it out: suppose you're 'awake' sixteen hours a day, you watch television $20 \times 52 = 1040$ hours a year, which, divided by 16 (number of waking hours per day) equals 65 complete waking days per year. Can you imagine what you could do if someone offered you 65 extra days of holiday a year?

Try to resist taking a look to see what's on TV. Just think that as compensation for that film or TV special that you missed, you've gained 40 or 60 hours of freedom. Yes, the freedom of leisure, with a bonus prize . . . a direct route to happiness.

You can't admire someone who sits in front of the television every night, out of habit or laziness, even if '. . . there's nothing good on again'. Or someone who watches anything just to escape, to stop thinking.

Choose freedom

Choose life, choose freedom and gain 65 days a year!

These figures should help you understand just why our 'Capital Time' is most precious, much more precious than our money. So much more precious because it's limited. And if we don't use it well, we destroy it little by little.

The following axiom might surprise you:

Your time is your most valuable commodity.

5

HOW TO MAKE USE OF EACH SECOND

How to increase your hourly rate

How?

The answer is by applying the great principles of psychology and organization, and by being conscious of the fact that we can almost always do twice, or three, five, even ten times as much in the same period of time.

To get there, we first have to ask ourselves a number of questions – and of course, find the answers.

Two criteria for evaluating time

Have you already asked yourself this question? If not, now's the time.

Take 180 seconds, and write down at least two criteria that you use – consciously or not, it's not important – to evaluate the time you estimate is necessary to carry out a task.

Criterion No. 1 _____

Criterion No. 2 _____

Here is a list of criteria most often used. There are two kinds: limits which are imposed on you from outside, and limits that you impose yourself.

1. For example, your boss comes into your office in the morning, gives you some documents concerning a business offer, and asks you to prepare a report for that same evening.

2. You have a routine job to do, like preparing the pay sheets, which you know takes about three hours to do. That's what it's always taken, since you got past the 'breaking-in' stage of your employment.

3. You are presented with a new job, at least in part, and you try to make a preliminary evaluation, based on different criteria.

    For example, you first try to locate probable problem areas, which will take time. You also try to find parts of the job that you've done elsewhere, that you know how to do already.

    Then you can make an estimate of the time needed. You can start by doing one hour of work and looking at what you were able to accomplish in that hour. Based on that you can set up a schedule.

    And you'll usually allow some time for a margin of error, for the unpredictable things that always seem to happen.

4. You can also consult a specialist or a colleague, who can help you make a time estimate.

Do some of your own criteria appear in this preliminary list? Surely they do.

Discover mental time

The most important fact is that you almost always base your criteria on your own past experience.

Why is this so important?

Because your past has been directed by the force of habit, which is usually as strong as it is unconscious.

This force has the following effect:

> **The time we allot for a given task
> is usually a mental limitation.**

Who says you 'really' need three hours to do the job?

Your own mind places limitations on your time. You've always 'thought' that you needed three hours to do the job, so the job takes you three hours to do.

Do you find it hard to believe that you establish your own mental limits for a given job?

Well, let me help you discover what 'mental time' is: that is, the time as it is represented in our minds, as we imagine it, as opposed to real time.

The next time your teenage son or daughter is in the bathroom and calls out: 'I'll be finished in five minutes!' make him or her respect those five minutes. Set your watch, or a stopwatch: 10, 15, 20 minutes later your offspring will come running out saying, 'Eight-thirty already! I had no idea . . .' (Unless you're the one who always says you'll be 'right there', and twenty minutes later . . .)

What seems longer to you, five seconds with your fingers caught in a door, or five minutes under a nice hot shower? A night of love and passion, or half an hour waiting in line at the bank?

When did it feel as though you had more time? At the start of your last holiday, or two days before you had to come back? Remember: at the beginning you wanted to do everything, try every-thing, you were full of plans; at the end, you were almost counting each hour of freedom, there were only a couple of things you still wanted to do . . .

Do you understand? There is an astonishing difference between mental time and real time. Real time is continuous, fixed. Mental time is flexible, extendable in relation to our needs, our desires, our emotions, perceptions, etc.

Beware of Parkinson

The concept of mental limitations brings us directly to Parkinson's first law:

Work expands so as to fill the time available for its completion.

Interesting, isn't it?

For example, if your boss gives you a week to do job X, you actually take about a week to do it.

Right. And if you have more time, if your boss gives you two weeks instead of one, you'll take two weeks to do the same job.

Relatively speaking, a result of Parkinson's first law is the following:

We always take as much time as we are given to do a job.

In his famous work, C. Northcote Parkinson tells of a marquise who needed a whole day to write a letter.

First it took an hour for her to go and buy the paper. She got home and started jotting down ideas for her letter, which took another hour ... Then she started making corrections, which took another hour.

Then she stopped for lunch. Another hour. After which she got back to her letter.

She read it over, but she wasn't satisfied. She started writing it again from scratch, which took half the afternoon. She had to hurry to get to the post office before it closed. But she couldn't find the address! How tiresome!

She searched frantically ... and finally found the address. She only had fifteen minutes to run to the post office, where she finally posted the letter.

And she went back home, exhausted but happy: happy in the satisfaction of a job done and a day well spent ...

Are you a Parkinson's marquise without knowing it?

'Whoever said that a marquise's life is easy?' she asked herself, 'People just don't understand ...'

Why did she need a whole day to do something relatively simple? Was she particularly slow?

No? She was slow, in a way, but that's not the real reason.

Was it because the letter she wrote was twenty pages long?

No, she only wrote two-and-a-half pages.

Well, was it because the letter was so important, written to some very important person, to the Prime Minister perhaps?

Not at all. The letter was to an old friend.

So why did it take her all day to write a simple, friendly letter?

Simply, *because of Parkinson's law*. The marquise had a whole day at her disposal, so it took her all day to write the letter. That's all.

It's precisely because a busy man has many things to do, that he can find the time to do many things, and also seems to be able to find the time to do a little extra.

Now I want to ask you this question:

'Isn't there a Parkinson's marquise in each of us, that we don't know about?'

If you're overloaded with work – and I know you are – isn't it because you *systematically take too much time to do what you do*?

And if you take too much time, isn't it because you think you NEED that time, and so extend your deadlines?

How to double your efficiency

When I started out, I had an experience that literally changed my life – and my income. A client asked me to come up with a fast concept for an ad campaign. It had to be ready the following morning.

Usually, people in the ad business are in a hurry. If they're not, they're not in the business long. But that particular day I was feeling under the weather. I had a cold. So I asked one of the best freelancers I knew to come up with something – fast! I explained what I wanted – actually what the client wanted – and made it clear that the job was extremely urgent.

A colleague interrupted me while I was explaining things to the freelancer. There was another emergency. He had to see me in his office for a few minutes. I excused myself, offered the freelancer another coffee. He asked if he could use my office while I was gone. Sure, why not? Every minute counts, I said to myself.

Twenty minutes later, I went back to my office. The freelancer was all smiles. He gave me back my chair, and showed me what he'd been able to do while I was gone: three pages, clean copy!

I read them, and was amazed!

They were excellent. They had to be touched up here and there, but I'd never seen a better first draft. I almost thought he had prepared the whole thing in advance, just to impress me. But that was impossible.

I asked him about it, and he told me that since he'd started making a living doing freelance work, he'd learned to write quick, clean copy the first time round.

Learn to write good clean copy at the first attempt.

Writing fast clean copy

He explained that he really didn't have any choice, that he was paid 'by the piece' and that he'd get poor fast if he worked slowly.

When I was alone in my office again, with that terrific first draft, I started thinking. I discovered that:

1. I was subconsciously programmed to believe that I could never write a perfect first draft.
2. I always took it for granted that you need two versions to get one good one.

You might object that even the greatest writers (Balzac, for example, who was notorious for making corrections, even on his proofs, to the great dismay of his publishers) need to make corrections.

But I say that Balzac must have surely evaluated what he could do in an hour, because he was regularly able to write 300-page novels in as short a space of time as two weeks!

My little run-in with the freelancer completely changed the way I write.

Obviously, when I have to write ad copy, I sometimes spend a few hours rewriting. But on the other hand, there have been numerous occasions when I've been able to use my first draft.

And that's not to mention all my correspondence, and all the reports I write.

In fact, I simply doubled my speed. Just by re-programming myself.

Double or even triple your productivity!

Do the following short exercise. You'll see how instructive it can be.
Ask yourself:

'What would happen if I had half as much time as I thought to do a job?'

Think about a job that you have to do regularly, and find a solution. Write it down.

There's only one correct answer.

The important thing is to lessen the amount of time you spend thinking. It's most often that part of the work that takes the most time.

There are different possible answers, but what we usually don't realize is that we rarely spend all the allotted time actually working: and if we work to an extended deadline, in fact only a small part of that time is put to really productive use.

So, if we have a whole day to do something, it's usually only in the last hour that we're really productive. It's almost always the most productive, and by far.

The first few hours we tend to spend doing things that aren't really important: we dawdle, we permit interruptions, we find all kinds of little ways to divert our attention from the important task at hand until ... there's hardly any time left.

If you only had twenty hours a week ...

Ask yourself the question: what if you only had twenty hours a week to do everything you have to do around the office, what would happen? (If necessary, you can use some of the solutions you found for the preceding question, 'What would happen if I had half as much time as I thought to do a job?') Write down your answer.

Did you come up with some interesting solutions?

One of the things you might have discovered is that you really wouldn't have to work harder. (Don't let your boss see this!)

For a very simple reason: because even successful executives use only half or a third of their time doing things which are at their optimum level.

If they were deprived of half their time, they could cope easily, by doing the things they really should be doing.

And what about you? Do you put all the time at your disposal to efficient use?

Let's get back to the exercise. You have half as much time available. What do you do? You have to take certain steps.

1. Re-evaluate the real importance of each task. And to do this, apply the following principle:

   Everything that isn't indispensable is useless.

And you must not hesitate to eliminate everything that is useless.

You will realize that numerous secondary tasks, and therefore useless tasks, are devourers of time.

2. Re-estimate the time that really has to be allotted for the tasks you have retained. In your evaluation, think about mental limitations!
3. Push this idea to its extreme. If you had, not half, but a third as much time, what would you do?

Has this exercise helped you to understand something? Are you going to do anything about it?

What's important to understand is that the people who succeed, who climb the ladder of success more rapidly than others, are always asking themselves the following question:

What can I do in an hour?

And above all, they find answers to the question because they know that you can do a lot in an hour. And they know that each hour is precious. An Arab proverb says:

**For those who know how to fill them,
each day has a million pockets!**

So imitate the real winners, and follow their philosophy:

1. Think regularly about Parkinson's Law

Take a deadline that you're used to allotting yourself, and cut it in half. Look at the results.

If there's still extra time available, go a step further. Play the game seriously, as if the situation were real.

Obviously if you've cut your deadline to the point where it causes you undue stress, then you've gone too far. It's normal to do this, don't worry. There's always a certain orientation period at the beginning.

Consider advancing your deadlines as a game. Take it seriously, up to a certain point, but don't forget that it's basically just a game.

Successful people are able to maintain a certain distance from what they do. Therein lies a secret about balance ... and success, because one doesn't go without the other.

Don't hold back: as soon as you can, cut back your deadlines by another 50 per cent. You will be agreeably surprised, both with your progress and with your newfound perspective.

2. Think about the 'Pareto Principle'

If you give yourself less time to do something because you're testing yourself, why not try out the theory of putting in only 20 per cent of your effort to obtain 80 per cent results?

The Pareto Principle, when applied to time, states that 20 per cent of your time determines 80 per cent of your production. Why? The answer is in the next chapter.

We have just seen, thanks to Parkinson's Law and the Pareto Principle among others, how to do a lot more in the same period of time. In fact, without being overtly explicit, we have got to the heart of the delicate problem of efficiency.

Are you looking for techniques, for 'tricks' that will make you more efficient? You will learn them in the next chapter.

**The more time you allot for a job,
the more time it takes to do.**

**Everything that is not indispensable
is useless.**

6

THE GREAT SECRET OF PRODUCTIVITY

Are you effective or efficient?

Peter Drucker, the famous management expert, writes:

> Results come from doing the RIGHT thing,
> not from doing things right.

In this sentence, there's a world of difference between effectiveness and efficiency. Someone who is efficient *does things right*. Someone who is effective *does the right thing*.

Do you understand the difference?

Give me three examples of efficiency.

Now give me three examples of effectiveness.

You're not sure you found the right answers?

Here's an example that should clear things up.

Mark, a friend of mine, had not yet understood the difference between these two ideas, when he was hired by a large publishing firm to publish twenty books a year. With a beginner's almost feverish zeal, he set out to meet his target.

And he did. He was pleased. He had 'succeeded'.

But as soon as the financial reports appeared at the end of the year, his illusions were shattered. His department had lost hundreds of thousands of dollars.

He didn't know what to think. He had attained the objective that was set for him, but he had also confused effectiveness with efficiency. He had showed himself to be very efficient, *but not effective*.

An interesting story about dollars

In the work entitled *Time Management Made Easy* the authors provide a very interesting example that illustrates the difference between effectiveness and efficiency.

> 'If I had a hundred banknotes in my hand – 98 one-dollar bills, and 2 one-hundred-dollar bills – and a gust of wind suddenly sent them flying all around the room, what would your strategy be to retrieve them?'

One important detail: you're not alone in the room, and the other person is just as interested in getting richer as you are . . .

Let's hear what the authors had to say:

'Where are the two $100 bills?'

Were you thinking about these two bills, even if they'd fallen somewhere at the other end of the room?

Maybe you'd only succeed in finding the two hundred-dollar bills, while the other person would get . . . all the others.

So at best, the other person gets $98, while you're left with $200, plus everything else you could pick up afterwards.

Don't forget your goals

Do you understand the difference now?

In fact, most people unconsciously get carried away by the search for one-dollar bills!

On the other hand, this isn't just a question of money. Whatever the goals you set for yourself, don't allow yourself to become obsessed with routine problems: you'll forget your goals. And you will not achieve them.

So now you understand: being EFFECTIVE is directly related to the CLARITY of your goals, and to your DETERMINATION to achieve them.

The secret of success

An American millionaire came up with a judicious definition of what being rich and poor means:

'Being poor means putting out maximum effort to obtain minimum results;

Being rich means putting out minimum effort to obtain maximum results.'

Which category do you fit into?

Have you heard this one:

Don't work harder, work smarter!

People who advance quickly, who get rich faster than others, who become popular and excel in their chosen field, all belong to the same category: they're the ones who use each passing hour to the full. By putting out a minimum of effort, they obtain maximum results!

In his excellent work *13 Fatal Management Errors and How to Avoid Them*, W. Steven Brown, President of the Fortune Group (controlling the most prestigious financial publication network in the US) talks about:

The secret of playing your cards right

'One of my clients said to me one day: "I'd like you to have a talk to the manager of one of my 28 departments. He doesn't seem to be cut out for our firm. In fact, it seems our company is the most boring thing in the world for him. His real vocation is playing cards."

'I asked him for more details, and he said: "Well, this guy spends about an hour and a half in his office every morning, and then takes off to the country club, which is just around the corner, where he plays cards for a couple of hours. He comes back to the office in the afternoon, spends an hour or so with us, and then goes home." '

After asking his client a few more questions, the author learned that the department this fellow managed was, according to all the reports, the most successful in the company, way ahead of the 27 others.

And what's more, everyone who worked in that department adored their boss, so that there was hardly any need for rotating personnel.

Nevertheless, despite the pretty picture, his client asked:

'Well, what do you think we should do?'

'I think you should just go ahead and find 27 other managers like this guy. He's the best you've got!'

This story, which is absolutely true, should make us stop and think . . .

Work can be a dangerous drug

Instead of aiming to be really effective (we'll look at the rules for being really effective later on), we try to take on a lot of work, and we put in long, arduous hours. We spend so much time working that we lose sight of our real objectives, and we forget to re-examine our methods.

The person who succeeds best is the one who is methodical, who knows the subtle art of finding ways to shortcut effort, who can inspire direct and indirect associates to do their best without close supervision.

Eliminate everything that isn't really profitable

Revise your daily activities regularly, and reduce to a minimum those activities which aren't profitable, which means those activities which do not really bring you closer to your MAIN GOAL, or which don't get you there quickly enough, in your professional as well as your private life.

Use a little imagination, and ask yourself what would happen if, from one day to the next:

> **You found you only had half the time usually available to do the same work!**

Well, what would happen? You would be forced to eliminate certain things, to delegate effectively, in short to sweep the deck!

Here's a short exercise that will help you do just that. You only have twenty hours (or thereabouts) to do everything that you usually do in forty.

Make a list of your unprofitable activities in one column, and a second column of ways to reduce or eliminate them.

The question concerns your private life, as well as your professional life. Obviously, in your private life you can allow yourself more time to think, and to relax. But one thing I've noticed is that people who don't plan their personal lives well don't plan their professional lives well either. This is only surprising at first glance. A person's organizational sense doesn't suddenly disappear when they walk out of the office. It follows you, because, as we've seen before, it's a question of habit.

Organizational skills are part of your personality. If you're an organized person, you get a lot more out of life. You have more time to do sports, to pursue cultural activities, to meet new people, etc.

The Pareto secret

The Principle is named after the person who discovered it at the turn of the century: Wilfredo Pareto, economist.

Pareto observed that 20 per cent of the population in Italy controlled 80 per cent of the material wealth. This proportion was extended and applied to other areas of observation by other specialists. They concluded that:

- 20% of your clients account for 80% of your sales.
- 20% of your clients make 80% of the complaints.
- 20% of the workforce does 80% of the work.
- 20% of a newspaper contains 80% of its news.
- 20% of a book contains 80% of its information.
- 20% of your priorities result in 80% of your profitable productivity.
- At home, 80% of the dirt is found in 20% of the total area.

The Pareto Principle can be applied to dozens of other areas.

You might say, why not 18 per cent or 32 per cent?

This is a general principle. A margin of a few percentage points is allowed. Nevertheless, the principle remains approximately true.

Think about it.

Write down some examples of how the Pareto Principle, or the 80:20 equation, affects your professional and personal life.

Take advantage of the Pareto Principle

You've no doubt already noticed: effectiveness and the Pareto Principle go hand in hand.

A person who is not aware of, or who ignores this principle cannot be really effective.

One of the most useful – and most ignored – applications of the Pareto Principle is the following:

20 per cent effort produces 80 per cent effect

For example, you have to write a sales letter or a report. In general, the first few minutes or hours will result in 80 per cent of the work, and will especially produce 80 per cent of the effect.

Some people even call this principle 'intelligent botching'!

When I started out, I had to manage a number of writers. The Pareto Principle applied perfectly to them. Not in the sense that 20 per cent of all writers do 80 per cent of the work!

No, what I observed was that most freelancers did the bulk of their work pretty quickly, and then spent hours and hours refining: non-productive hours, one could say, since they added little to the overall effect, while 80 per cent of the effect had been achieved with the initial 20 per cent of effort.

The trap of being a perfectionist

Perfectionists have a lot of difficulty accepting the Pareto Principle. It contradicts all their old habits.

Nevertheless, only low-productivity time is threatened by the application of the Principle.

For example, say you have to submit text for an ad campaign to a client. Your writer does a first draft, then a first revision.

And then he refuses to hand it over right away ... he wants to make some adjustments ... he will only submit work that satisfies him. But what these people usually forget about is the element of time.

The time factor is crucial; it is essential.

Back to our example.

What if our writer is allowed to polish his work as much as he likes?

He'll never finish at all! His excessive zeal for perfection will result in zero productivity.

A trick to combat endless polishing

I personally discovered a way to combat this tendency. Instead of trying to find the perfect style or approach, I pretend I'm sitting face to face with my boss or a client, and that I have to explain to them verbally what the concept is about, as clearly as possible.

This technique simplifies my communication problems enormously. Because you might have a problem writing, but usually much less of a problem speaking.

By writing the way you speak, you will avoid two problems:

1. The problem of correcting.
2. The problem of getting through to the reader, who will certainly appreciate your down-to-earth style.

This is one of the most practical applications of Pareto's Principle. If you imagine that you're explaining something to a friend or a colleague while you write, 20 per cent of your effort will produce 80 per cent of the desired effect (especially if you're someone who doesn't write with ease).

What's more, in this case you will surpass 80 per cent, and approach 100 per cent.

How to proceed

Use simple sentences and short words. Instead of saying:
'The currently inert market and progressive deterioration in productivity in our firm has resulted in an overall slowdown of sales . . .'
say:
'Sales have fallen 18 per cent. Why? In my opinion, for two reasons:

1. Negative general economic situation and above all . . .
2. Lower employee productivity.'

Doesn't the second example seem more effective and to the point? We will get back to this technique in a later chapter on effective communication.

Pareto's Principle is of great importance. We will refer to it often in our study of the Time Management System. But try to keep it in mind from now on.

There is one piece of advice in this book that you should always keep in mind:

Am I conscious of Pareto's Principle?

Keep asking yourself that question. Never forget the Principle. And don't hesitate to apply it wherever you can.

If it's been proved that 20 per cent of your clients account for 80 per cent of your sales, why not allot them a proportional amount of time?

How often do we allot as much and even more time to clients who bring nothing but trouble and frustration, not to mention monetary loss?

If you really want to enjoy life, and benefit from the reorganization of your time, ask yourself what would happen if:

1. You only accorded your bad clients the time they merit.
2. You forgot about them altogether, and concentrated on your good clients.

If 20 per cent of your employees account for 80 per cent of the work, why not think about reorganizing workloads – and even doing some reclassification?

In the same way, if 20 per cent of your activity produces 80 per cent of your results, why not reduce or actually eliminate the other 80 per cent?

Clearly, analysing your activities will be greatly simplified by continually applying the Pareto Principle.

Used intelligently, it will help improve your effectiveness considerably. But you can never be truly effective if you don't start at the beginning, which means knowing precisely what you want to do with your life, professionally, socially, in your family life, etc.

In short, if you don't know the secret that we're going to talk about in the next chapter ...

You'd better turn the page, quickly!

The aim is not to work more but to work better.

7

HOW TO MAKE YOUR IDEAS REAL

Choose your lifestyle

Why did you get up this morning?

Because you have to make a living? Go to work?

But why this work and not some other?

And instead of working, why not take off to the mountains, or to some island in the Aegean?

These alternatives might seem a little extreme, but many people have chosen them instead of a 'normal' existence. You might have done the same, had you been one of them. Because, in general, they didn't have anything more than you do at the start.

So who determines every event in your life? *The choices you make are your life.* I ask you again:

'Why did you get up this morning?'

Take a few minutes to think about this extremely important question. Write down your answer.

If you had trouble coming up with reasons why you got up this morning, it's time you sat down and did some serious thinking.

Knowing what you want

Knowing what you want, having a well-defined, long-term goal is the key to your dream life.

If you don't know why you do something, or a series of things, you cannot make progress, you cannot determine your priorities.

Your actions will not be coherent. In fact, for any action to be coherent, it must be part of a plan.

A person without a goal is like a boat without a rudder.

How are you supposed to know whether you should accept one job or another, or an offer of promotion, if you don't know where you're going, and what you want to do with your life?

Who would you like to be in five years?

Another way of defining your goal is to ask yourself these questions:

● What would you like to be doing professionally five years from now?
● What would your ideal day consist of?

Think about the different aspects of your life, and describe that perfect day. Which position would you like to hold in your firm? Sales Director? Chairman? General Manager? Why not Managing Director?

Would you like to change careers completely? Get into business, or the arts, or law? Would you like to start your own business?

What kind of lifestyle would you like? Would you like to travel a lot? Spend more time with your family, with your children who are growing up every day? Put together enough money to take a year off and not have to worry?

Have you finished the exercise? Does your ideal day resemble your yesterday? If it does, then your coherence level is no doubt very high. Your long-term goal is clear, and you know what you have to do to attain it.

If there's some discrepancy between your ideal day and what you did yesterday, but only because of a delay factor, then you're also on the right road. You have established goals, and your priorities are coherent.

But if, on the other hand, you're incapable of forming an idea of what a perfect day would be like in five years, or if your ideal day is completely different from what you're doing at the moment, then you should take steps to change your dream into reality.

One thing's for sure: if you continue as you are, if you don't do anything about it, you'll never live that ideal day. Things don't change by themselves. You must take concrete and decisive measures, which will in turn determine your precise goals in life.

Put your goals in writing

The best way – and the simplest – is to put your goals down in writing.

It's not easy to write, but it forces you to clarify many things. And it works for goal-setting, which is as important as your life itself.

For one thing, by having your goals down in writing, in as much detail as possible, you will be able to refresh your memory whenever necessary, and so always keep your goals in mind.

If your goals are a long way from what you're doing right now, the fact of reading them regularly will help you get to know them, and make them less inaccessible by programming your subconscious.

Transform your dreams into reality

If the way you described your ideal day is very different from what you're doing now, you may ask how you'll ever get there?

Will your ideal day always be a fantasy, a dream? Is it really accessible at all? Know that from the moment you believe you can attain your goal, you can attain it.

If you don't believe, then you can't mobilize your interior energy, you will not persevere in the face of adversity, you will not inspire people to join in your enterprise.

We live according to our inner beliefs

If you believe, circumstances have a way of fitting mysteriously into place so that your dream becomes real, because life is respectful of our inner beliefs.

In drawing a portrait of your perfect day, be aware that you really have to *believe* in it. You mustn't let yourself be influenced by other people's defeatist attitudes, nor by your own. Transform your interior self (learn to believe in your dream) by practising auto-suggestion.

That this technique is much more important than studies dare to indicate is demonstrated by the fact that most people will not undertake anything that they're not sure they can finish.

The same goes for your goals in life. If you're not fully convinced that you can attain them, you will do nothing to try.

If you do believe you can realize your dream, and still do nothing to achieve it, ask yourself this question:

'Do I really *believe* in my dream?'

Maybe you'll have to admit that you don't really believe. If so, take the necessary measures. Wouldn't it be better to stop nourishing a dream that you don't really believe in?

If, on the other hand, you do believe in your dream, what should you do to make it a reality?

Transform your goals into tasks

You simply start by transforming each of your goals into specific tasks.

For example, if you want to become sales director of your department in five years – you might get there a lot faster than you think, if you take energetic measures – first ask yourself the essential questions. What precise measures should I take? What advice should I seek? Who should I ask?

Should you take some courses to perfect your performance? If so, you can immediately transform this goal into specific action. Start your course (or courses) as soon as possible.

Should you update your computer skills, since your department relies more and more on computers to get the job done? Don't wait. And what about speaking in public, which is essential if you want to motivate your sales team ... you might need help in that area too. Get informed and start as soon as possible!

Don't hesitate – act

You see, it's simple. It's simple because you know what you want. If you don't, how are you supposed to know what steps to take to progress towards attaining your goal, and finally live that ideal day of yours in five years' time.

As soon as you have defined the concrete measures you must take to attain your goals, don't wait. Act straight away.

If you don't do this, question yourself. Are you really serious about your goals? If you are, and if you know precisely what you have to do to attain them and still don't act, then maybe you're playing a game with yourself.

Establish a clear primary goal, specific tasks, a rigorous schedule, and act immediately: the rest will follow very naturally ...

A question which assures success

Having a precise goal allows you to simplify your life enormously. It makes decision-making a lot easier.

The proof?

Each time you're presented with a choice, each time you have to make a decision concerning a job or an offer someone makes, ask yourself:

'How does this offer or this job get me closer to my goal?'

Or simply:

'Does this task get me closer to my goal?'

And link it to the following questions:

'How does this job get me closer to my goal?'

'Is the investment in time worth it?'

'If the time investment is too much, is there any other task or job that would bring me closer to attaining my goal more rapidly and effectively?'

And keep asking yourself Lakein's Question:

> **'At this moment, how can I use my time
> to best possible advantage?'**

You should ask yourself this question in relation to your goals. You're not making the best use of your time unless you're doing something that is bringing you closer to your goal.

And don't forget a last rule: we only excel at what we like. If you are used to accepting jobs that don't correspond to your personality, to your abilities and to your goals, you will not make progress, at least not in any decisive way.

Be selective

Do you know clearly what your goals are? Then you can easily be selective in the range of activities you do now.

At work, what are the jobs that really bring you closer to your objectives? And which are the ones that:

1. Don't get you any closer?
2. Take you farther away, by making you lose precious time and energy?

Once you have identified these activities, ask yourself what measures you can take to eliminate, or at least reduce them. Don't let yourself be paralysed by force of habit, or by the fear that your boss or your colleagues will disapprove of your will to change.

This may very well be the case. After all, they probably don't have any clear idea of what you're working for, what you're getting paid for. So take the time to explain to them.

Redefine your total function

You'll see: your motivation will surge upward, and your real potential will soon become apparent to others.

And you'll know exactly why you get up each morning!

But be careful. You can't completely eliminate all the activities that aren't directly related to your goal right from the start.

You should only start worrying when you find yourself spending hours, weeks, even months doing things that don't bring you any closer to your goals. And unfortunately, most people do just that.

Try to devote a certain number of hours each day to attaining your goals. Obviously you have to be realistic: you can't just drop everything. You have certain obligations, to your family and to others, that you cannot give up.

Take four minutes right now to define four goals that you would like to achieve over the next few years. And then translate these goals into tasks that you can start without delay. Write them down.

Finished? Good. Now you're ready to use the secret weapon all 'super-managers' possess:

**To realize your ideas, establish precise goals
and transform them into action.**

8

DISCOVER THE GREAT MANAGERS' SECRET WEAPON

The renowned American specialist Alan Lakein states that if managers who are moderately successful refer only occasionally to their working plans, those who are highly successful do so constantly.

What working plan? The one that defines the activities to accomplish in order to attain your goals.

How does it work? Try it!

First work for two hours with no strategy, no list of priorities, then work another two hours following a working plan.

You will no doubt observe the difference. When you have no working plan to follow, your workload seems insufferably heavy.

On the other hand, when you have a plan, everything becomes concrete, measurable. You'll know better where you stand, and what remains to be done. If you have twenty things to do, you will be able to estimate the time you need to do them.

In the same way, you can evaluate the importance of the task in hand.

What a pleasure it is to start crossing items off your list, things that are 'in the can'. Personally, it's one of my greatest satisfactions!

The first working plan you should draw up is your _strategic plan of action_.

Devise a strategic plan of action for your personal and professional goals.

What does it consist of?

A strategic plan of action is the list of all the projects and all the tasks you would like to accomplish, or that you should accomplish, in order to attain your goals, whether short- or long-term.

This list can be very long, and should be updated regularly. Each time you come up with a new project or activity, it should be added to the list.

Later on we'll see how these projects or activities are spread out and redistributed among your other plans, your weekly or daily agendas.

In your strategic plan, for example, you should consider projects like learning speed-reading, or taking a course in oenology (wine-tasting).

You should also note projects like restructuring your department, or setting a goal to raise your income by 15 per cent.

For easier access, and to avoid confusion, you should divide your strategic plan into two distinct sections: one concerning your personal goals, and the other your professional goals or activities.

Get a notebook and write down your strategic plan.

Maximize your strategic plan

Now, review each project or activity and ask yourself:

'Do I *really* feel like doing this?'

You will discover a purely mechanical advantage of your strategic plan: each time you consider a project or an activity you will become very clear and precise, and your decisions will be based on complete objectivity and awareness of the reasons for it. Moral? You will eliminate mediocre projects which are not certain to pay off, and therefore not interesting, and give more time to those which are worth striving for.

Ask yourself these questions each time:

'Do I really feel like doing this?'

'Am I ready to devote all the time and energy this task requires?'

'Does this really bring me closer to attaining my goals?' And always remember the basic principle of success:

'Everything that isn't indispensable is unnecessary.'

Have you refined your strategic plan as much as you can? All right, let's move on to short-term plans:

You must choose which of your strategic activities you will do every week, and every day.

Some experts recommend using two lists: a strategic plan and a daily agenda. Personally, as you are probably very busy, I would recommend a weekly agenda as well. Most managers like to plan their entire week in advance.

A weekly plan will give you a better overall view of what you have to do. In a way it represents a transition stage between your strategic plan and your daily agenda.

From strategy to day-to-day

How do you know what to extract from your strategic plan so that it can be transformed into weekly and finally daily plans of action?

When learning how to establish priorities, you should know that you always start by making a list of all the things you have to do, before determining their priorities.

Most people don't do it this way, and therefore forget many important things.

Establish your priorities

Establishing your priorities has numerous advantages.

Does it ever happen that at the end of a day you get that unpleasant feeling that you didn't do the things that were really important, or that you spent much too little time on them?

If you often find yourself in that position, then you haven't *established your priorities*, and so you just let yourself be led along by circumstances.

Without well-established priorities, we quickly lose sight of what is really important. We let ourselves get distracted by a horde of minor emergencies and problems that are really of secondary importance.

The advantages of having well-defined priorities are numerous. They will help you to:

1. Do things according to their degree of urgency and importance;
2. Keep sight of your objectives;

3. Avoid wasting time on futile or unimportant tasks;
4. Delegate all the tasks that should be delegated;
5. Concentrate on one task at a time;
6. Work with the Pareto Principle in mind (see Chapter Six).

How to organize your priorities

Classify your priorities according to the two following criteria, which are objective and easy to understand:

1. **Importance**
2. **Urgency**

All your activities can be classified according to a combination of these two factors. Always keep them in mind when establishing your priorities.

Some tasks are important, but not urgent. If it's April, and you have to prepare for a vital series of negotiations in September, the task is not urgent, despite its importance.

Do you understand? It breaks down like this:

Important and Urgent: these tasks should head the list. Their importance means that they have a high potential for profit, and that if you neglect them, the negative consequences could be considerable.

Important and urgent things usually start out by just being important.

Thanks to the Time Management System, you will soon be in a position to predict, and therefore eliminate, numerous emergencies.

Of course, unexpected emergencies will continue to happen, there's nothing you can do about that. Depending on what kind of work you do, they might even occur frequently.

But we will see how to deal with them and master them with maximum efficiency by learning to predict and identify them, and finally to prevent them by applying suitable measures.

Whatever they are, because they are important and urgent, these activities should head your list of priorities. You should also classify them according to their relative importance.

Think profit

The best thing to learn to do is to think profit.

Does this or that task have a high potential for profit? A medium or low potential? When establishing the importance of your activities, always ask yourself these questions.

Highly profitable activities usually demand more concentration and imagination. Yet you cannot dedicate more than a few hours a day to them. But do it! Don't neglect them! There's many a person who will procrastinate, who will put these tasks off for another day, because they are difficult.

These tasks do not *all* demand intense concentration. Some might just be unpleasant. For example, having to reprimand an employee for inefficiency, or having to restructure your department.

If a number of positions have become obsolete and are losing the department money, the task of eliminating or redesigning them is important. It might not take a lot of concentration, but on the other hand it might need a good dose of courage and cool-headed determination.

It's not always simple to make cuts: the profit potential of a given task is not always obvious.

A way to identify the most important problem

The consequences of certain activities are sometimes difficult to evaluate in terms of profit.

So ask yourself this question:

'If I could only solve one problem, or only do one last thing before going on holiday, what would I choose?'

This trick has often helped me clarify situations which seemed impossible to comprehend.

Why?

Simply because I didn't allow myself any choice.

Things become a lot clearer when you've found the most important thing to do, and put it at the head of your list of priorities!

Then ask yourself the same question, excluding your first choice. 'What would I choose to do if I could only do one thing before going on holiday?'

This is one of the easiest and fastest ways to establish your list of priorities.

How to manage your priorities

Maybe your strategic plan has a large number of first-level priorities, which means tasks which are highly profitable and at the same time intellectually demanding.

This doesn't mean that you have to keep filling your daily agenda with these tasks. In fact, experience suggests that you shouldn't spend more than 20 per cent of your time on these activities, in order to achieve maximum effectiveness and efficiency. But if you train yourself, you might reach a level of 25 or 30 or even 45 per cent.

And your progress will be spectacular!

As far as your other priorities are concerned, analyse them carefully before transferring them from your strategic to your daily plan. Ask yourself (twice!) if you could not eliminate them, or delegate them to someone else.

Final advice for planning

No more than ten items per day

Experience has shown that it's better not to programme more than ten items per day. Obviously, if we're talking about extremely brief activities, they can be more numerous.

A little at a time

Break down complex and demanding activities into more easily programmable sub-activities.

Learn how to estimate the time needed for each task correctly

To accomplish regularly what you have listed in your strategic plan, you have to be able to estimate precisely how much time each task requires: there's nothing more frustrating than taking three hours to do something that you thought could be done in half an hour!

Get into the habit of noting how much time different activities take, so that you can refer to them later, when similar situations arise. For new activities, find out if you have already done something similar, which you can use as a reference point.

To make it easier for you to estimate accurately the time needed for each task, I have designed this chart for you. It is one you will want to use on a regular basis. After trying it a few times, you won't be able to work without it because it will save you so much time.

Estimated time/real time

Job: _____

Estimated time for completion _____

Real time for completion _____

Difference: _____ hrs. _____ mins.

Rate of efficiency _____ per cent.

N.B. Your rate of efficiency is calculated by dividing your estimated time by the real time, and then multiplying by 100.

Date:				
Time	Estimated Time	Real Time	Activity	% Efficiency Suggestions

In a few lines, try to explain why there was a discrepancy between your estimated and real time, and make suggestions about how to cut it down next time.

For example: it's 10 o'clock. Robert estimated it would take 20 minutes to write a letter. Instead it took 50. Robert's rate of efficiency, in this case, is 40 per cent. Robert fell into the perfectionist trap. He took too much time polishing his letter. Next time, Robert should stick to the essentials and write it in 20 minutes. It is possible. Discipline and coherence should play major roles in the way you programme your time management.

N.B. Note the time that you start each task, because you will see that a bad estimate will have a negative effect on the rest of your day. When you come up with a bad estimate, try to evaluate it in the context of the rest of the day's activities, including any uncontrollable factors, instead of evaluating it all on its own.

How to be more effective

Have you already entered a number of activities on your chart? All right, now ask yourself a few questions:

Do you tend to allow too much, or too little time to complete your activities? Do you operate on the basis of over-optimism, or over-caution?

If you usually lack time, ask yourself if you've been strict enough about interruptions. Did you correctly evaluate all the elements, all the implications involved in completing the task? Remember this:

> **The accuracy of your estimate for a given task is inversely proportional to the number of people involved in accomplishing it.**

In other words, the more people involved in completing a task, the more chances there are for delays, the larger the delays will be, and therefore the more time must be allotted at the beginning.

For this reason, whenever you can delegate a task to one person instead of to a team, do it.

And when you evaluate a task, keep Parkinson's Law in mind.

Be ambitious, but don't overload yourself

Everyone likes to have full, productive days, and to leave work with the feeling of having accomplished something, of having done what was necessary.

And there's nothing more satisfying than, 17 or 18 hours after composing an agenda of ten daily activities, striking number 10 off the list. Don't do more than you set out to do. On the other hand (and I'm sure you've already guessed), don't fall behind.

You might, when you were in top shape, have added a little extra to your daily agenda, just to test your limits. No more of that! Use the extra time to savour your success – you'll find that it's one of the best motivational drugs.

Only programme 60 per cent of your time

If you want to get through all the items on your daily agenda, you should only programme 60 per cent of your time – some specialists even recommend 50 per cent. There are always unpredictable events in a day – emergencies, interruptions, fatigue, loss of concentration.

Trying to plan down to the minute is usually unrealistic, at best naive. For example, it would be foolish to set up four half-hour appointments in a two-hour period, without allowing at least a few minutes before each one to look over the relevant documents.

Revise your plan objectively

Get into the habit of reviewing your plan every evening. How did the day go? Did you do everything you were supposed to do? What things were not done? For what reasons?

Ask your secretary's opinion. What measures does she think should be taken so that you will be able to meet the requirements of your daily agenda?

Couldn't you ask your secretary to:

● Screen calls?
● Be firmer with unexpected visitors, even with colleagues who show up with 'important' matters to discuss?
● Handle the correspondence more independently, without having to consult you about every detail? In principle, your secretary should become your 'right arm'.

Once you've analysed your agenda, and drawn the obvious conclusions, transfer to tomorrow's list what you weren't able to do today.

Then work out the next day's agenda. This is the ideal formula. You'll be able to start your day on the right foot, knowing exactly where you're going.

LIST OF PRIORITIES

From _____ to _____ 19__

Goals _____

_____

_____

_____

Priorities for this period

Degree of urgency	Description of job	Predicted duration	Person in charge	Deadline

Finish each task before going on to the next

As far as possible, of course. Try to discipline yourself to do this. It will prevent you from getting too 'spread out'. It will also help you to avoid having to 'get back into' a file that you haven't worked with for a while: getting started, familiarizing yourself with the data, preparation of material, etc., devours large chunks of time.

It can happen that you badly underestimate the time needed for a particular job, so that you have to leave it and move on to something else which can be put off. Remember this: memory is what's left after everything has been forgotten! To help you I have given you a model List of Priorities (see opposite). Draw up your own model, based on your particular needs.

Checklist

First, let us review an important set of rules that will help you make incredible progress. That's right – incredible!

1. Programme no more than ten items per day.
2. Divide complex and demanding activities into more easily programmable sub-activities.
3. Learn to make an accurate estimate of the time needed for each task.
4. Be ambitious, but don't overload yourself.
5. Programme only 60 per cent of your time.
6. Revise your plan regularly.
7. Finish each task before going on to the next.

9

LISTEN TO YOUR INTERNAL CLOCK

At what time are you most efficient?

The study of bio-rhythms, the biological cycles of organisms, has shown that although each individual has a personal rhythm there are numerous similarities between all human beings.

Look at the statistical curve representing the flow of an individual's efficiency.

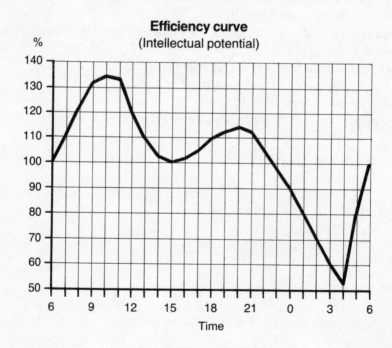

Efficiency curve
(Intellectual potential)

There are exceptions of course. Beethoven and Chopin wrote at night, Paul Valéry in the early hours of the morning, and Zola completed his four pages daily between 9 a.m. and 1 p.m. Each person has a unique rhythm.

But the general rule is that maximum productivity is achieved around 10 o'clock in the morning. Incidentally (and generally speaking, of course), this level is not attained at any other time of the day, whatever you may think.

After lunch, especially if it was copious and included alcohol, the curve gets pretty low. There is, however, a slight surge towards the end of the afternoon, between 4 and 6 o'clock at the office, which can be extended to around 8 p.m.

Determine your personal efficiency curve

Observe yourself over the next few days. At what point during the day do you feel you are at your intellectual best?

At what point does your energy peak?

By knowing your personal rhythm you will develop more efficiency:

- You won't devote your best morning hours to reading the mail, or writing routine correspondence, things that demand very little concentration and which you can very easily do at some other time of day, when your energy is lower.
- You will systematically reserve your high-performance hours for your most difficult tasks.
- You will not struggle with a difficult task when your energy is low, for two reasons. It will take you three times as long to do something half as good, and you will become frustrated – which is counter-productive.

Analyse yourself. Are you currently making mistakes because you aren't taking your biological clock into account? Can you be specific? What changes can you make in your schedule to remedy the situation?

Write down your observations and possible improvements. You will notice that you don't have to make drastic changes to put things right.

Be more aware of others

Find the right moment for yourself . . . and for others.

Obviously, you don't function alone. You have to take other people into account when making your plans. If you don't, the changes you hope to make will be somewhat artificial and may lead to nothing in the long run.

Try to include others in your planning when asking yourself what is the right moment for:

- Your creative thinking
- Meetings
- Appointments
- Supervising your secretary
- Routine activities

By knowing your own rhythms you can be more effective in managing your time in relation to others.

It will also help you to avoid getting impatient when things don't go quite as they should. You'll realize that it might be better to come back to a difficult problem when your energy curve is at a higher point.

How to manage your energy

When I have to go to an important meeting, or conduct a conference, I prepare myself in a very personal way: I always schedule a fifteen-minute walk before the encounter. During this preparatory walk:

1. I relax as much as possible, walking slowly and taking long strides. I fill my lungs with oxygen. When I get to the meeting I'm perfectly refreshed. Would you prefer negotiating with someone who's calm and clear-headed, or with someone who looks nervous and exhausted?
2. I visualize the encounter like a film in my head, unfolding as I would like it to happen. I arrive with a smile on my face, my client or the receptionist greets me with pleasure. I state my case logically and clearly, and everything is harmonious. When I leave, I shake my client's hand with a satisfied smile.

Often, people neglect this important aspect of the Time Management System. They forget that we are always dealing with other human beings: if you're relaxed, fresh and alert, your chances of success are all the greater.

The secret of always being ready

Despite the best-laid plans, the unexpected can occur. Emergencies arise, or jobs demand a lot more effort than we expected.

So how are we supposed to be always on top of things? The secret is simple.

Never over-extend yourself. Allow yourself frequent pauses, take time off regularly, have brief naps, plan your relaxation activities as seriously as you plan your so-called important tasks.

Working too long and too hard is valueless. We reach saturation point very quickly, without being aware of it. The average individual should not work for more than one hour at a time without taking a break. Why?

Simply because we tend to lose concentration after that time.

In his book *Master Your Own Time*, Lothar J. Seiwert cites the results of a medical study done on productivity over 60-minute periods of concentration, shown in the form of a graph.

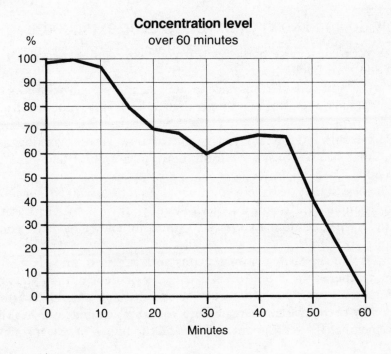

Concentration level
over 60 minutes

Optimum effect of taking breaks

Seiwert also emphasizes that breaks should not exceed ten minutes to produce an optimum effect. Therefore plan numerous *brief* pauses in your daily agenda.

Your schedule will not always let you stretch out on a couch for ten minutes after an hour of work, but you can always go and have a drink of water, or return a document to a colleague, making sure that you are not absent for more than ten minutes.

You can also switch to something easier, which is about the same thing as taking a short break. For example, if you're in the process of answering routine correspondence or reading the incoming mail, you can take a few minutes off to tidy your office or leaf through a magazine.

Ideally, you would get up and go outside for a breath of fresh air (maybe to buy fruit or some mineral water). Why not? But that's not always possible.

For this reason, you should always have a few easy jobs handy, to occupy you when the need arises.

How do you know when you're over-extended?

Does your conscience bother you if you take regular breaks? Or if you don't work long hours at a stretch?

Maybe you consider yourself to be a strong person with lots of stamina, so you can work for longer than most people without getting tired.

Be careful ... How are you going to know you're working too hard, that you're abusing your strength, if you don't take time to find out?

The best sign is definitely your mood. As long as you're in a good mood, patient, and as long as you carry out your work with a pleasant attitude, without forcing yourself too much, then you have not gone beyond your limits.

But if you are easily or, worse, constantly stressed, impatient and short-tempered, or if you feel exhausted or depressed, then you are definitely abusing your resources of energy. You should take the necessary corrective measures before you start abusing your health.

Remember the fable about the oak and the bunch of wheat stalks.

Because the oak is too rigid, it is destroyed by the force of the wind, whereas the wheat stalks – supple and therefore intelligent – bend with the wind and survive.

In the best-seller *In Search of Excellence*, by Thomas J. Peters and Robert H. Waterman, we find this superb analogy:

> If you put six bees and six flies in a bottle with a narrow neck, and place the bottle on its side so that the bottom is touching a window, you will observe that the bees will keep trying to find a way out towards the window until they die of exhaustion and hunger, while the flies, in less than two minutes, will have escaped through the opening at the other end. It's the bees' love of light, and their conditioned intelligence, that results in their demise in this experiment. They always see bright light as a means of escape and act accordingly, in this case *persevering for too long in a logical activity*.

If you don't want to end up like the bees, then please stop pushing yourself like a fool: change the scene, try something else. You will be making the winning choice!

Learn to put on the brakes

This is an extreme case, but I've seen it happen. One of my business associates, Fred, was in the process of setting up a new company. He gave himself, body and soul, to the enterprise, to the point where his wife complained that it was 'worse than if he'd taken a mistress!'

Fred worked late every night, and one night in January he had so much work that he left the office three hours later than usual. He was nervous and exhausted. He got in his car and started to drive home.

Ten minutes from his house he took a turning a little too fast, braked too hard and lost control. He left hospital three months later, and still has to spend five hours a week visiting a physiotherapist.

What a pity that Fred committed two errors before getting into his car that January night:

1. He overestimated his strength.
2. He didn't ask himself the questions 'Are all these hours of work really useful? Couldn't I do less and obtain the same results?'

I can answer both questions: those working hours could not all have been productive; and Fred could have worked less and obtained even better results if he had applied the principles of TMS.

Learn to put on the brakes. If you're tired, if you can't see your way out of a problem, if you're gnashing your teeth and getting frustrated – STOP! Take a break. Cut your working hours down to the bone. Take steps to define your objectives, establish your priorities, etc., until your new working plan fits in with the amount of time you have available to do effective, creative work. Then you will be ready to seize any new opportunity that might arise.

Your health can save you time

Look around you: some people always seem pale and unfit. Their complexion shows that they aren't taking care of their body. These people are often badly dressed. And these same people usually have a harder time getting promotions. Why?

You don't necessarily have to have a tan 365 days a year, but people who take care of themselves physically, through sports and a balanced diet, are generally more dynamic and succumb less to minor colds and other little maladies that limit activity. More dynamic and sick less often – why do you think they are chosen when a promotion comes up?

Their health makes them 10, 15, even 20 per cent more profitable for their company.

Health problems = lost time

Shall we work it out together? Healthy people are productive more often than their colleagues who easily become ill. Since they are more alert and clear-headed, they are more creative and better able to take advantage of opportunities as they arise. When work builds up, they are able to call on reserves of energy and don't get tired as quickly as their colleagues.

Do we really have to continue listing the advantages of being fit? And what about the personal satisfaction it brings, the ability to savour better the pleasures of life, and to offer the best of oneself to family and friends?

Try to see the funny side when you are continually bothered by fatigue. To combat it, think about the pleasure of waking up all fresh, alert, full of energy, aware of the beauty around you, ready for anything. Read a book on positive health.

Despite everything you've already learned here, are some of your projects just not getting off the ground?

Do you still often find yourself in emergency situations, which cause considerable delays?

If so, it's because you still don't know the secret of setting deadlines. You'll find out how in the next chapter.

Take a break every 60 minutes.
Respect your inner rhythm.

10

HOW TO COMPLETE
ALL YOUR PROJECTS

Many of your projects have been cancelled, or delayed considerably, or put off 'indefinitely', even though you thought they were worthwhile.

For example, why have you never begun to study another language, like Spanish or French; or taken a course in speed-reading, even if you've been thinking about these things for a long time?

Take 180 seconds and do the following exercise:

Write down at least ten dreams or projects that you've been wanting to do for a long time, but you always put aside to deal with later:

OK? Now, in 120 seconds, write down the main factor which prevented you from realizing each one.

Why is the situation like it is?

The answer is much simpler than you think: *you neglected to set a deadline for yourself.*

In other words, if you've put off learning Spanish for two years, it's simply because you never said to yourself: 'All right, six months from now I have to be speaking Spanish fluently, at least well enough to be able to work in our branch in South America.' (The job was available, but you didn't apply for it because you couldn't speak a word of Spanish.)

**If you want to do something,
set yourself a deadline.**

The starting point

That's the first step: you set yourself a deadline, a time limit, and you plan your activities around that date.

If you have to speak Spanish in six months, you must:

1. In one – or maximum two – weeks find the name of a school or teacher, and enrol. (The deadline for each stage has to be precise. It's not enough to say that you have to find a teacher quickly. 'Quickly' isn't precise enough, it will not force you to act. Avoid this trap!)

2. Arrange your schedule so that you have the time not only to take the course, but to do the necessary back-up work needed to make it worthwhile.

3. Find the money to pay for the course. (Find out about possible sponsorship from your company. Who knows, your boss might be interested in helping you take a course in Spanish, or computer training.)

4. Make sure your new schedule doesn't conflict with your family time.

   The deadlines you set will work wonders.

   As soon as you start using this 'key' for all your projects, you will be astonished to see how often your dreams become real.

   But be careful, there are always pitfalls.

Errors to avoid

1. **Misunderstood instructions**
   Make sure everything has been properly explained.
   - What does your boss expect? An oral report or a 30-page memo?
   - Do your subordinates know exactly what kind of work you expect from them?

2. **Inaccurate evaluation when setting a deadline**
   If you are put in charge of a new project, you might make a bad estimate of the time it will take to get it done. To avoid this situation:
   - Ask people who are familiar with this kind of work what a reasonable time limit would be.

or
- Ask the other people involved in the project to make estimates of how much time it would take.

Above all, make it clear that you want to know about any delays, so that you can adjust the project's schedule instead of having things all come down at once, with the risk of total failure.

3. Lack of information
- Are you certain of the steps to take to meet your deadline?
- Is your working plan adequate and realistic?
- Have the tasks been delegated clearly and precisely?
- Have you obtained, and (depending on the case) passed on, all pertinent information necessary for the completion of the project?
- Have you made sure that you're available at specific times, in case any questions should arise about the project?
- Have you encouraged an open-minded team spirit?

4. The 'Yes, Yes' Syndrome
One reason deadlines are frequently not met is that, instead of being frank about the situation, a subordinate who is already overloaded will keep saying that everything's 'just fine' when it isn't. The added work might interfere with their already heavy schedule, they might have other work which should be done first.

Explain clearly that you would prefer a justified refusal when delegating work, rather than excuses and long delays later on.

5. Setting a random deadline
Using your intuition to set a deadline leads to:
- either too much time to do the job
- or, on the contrary, not enough time.

In either case, efficiency is sacrificed.

GENERAL RULE:

**The deadline should be far enough away
to allow for complete and efficient work
and
close enough so that everyone involved
is kept busy and productive.**

6. Respect deadlines set by other departments
If you ask for a sales report for the tenth of next month, when

you know that accounts will not be able to start compiling figures before the eighth, then you're asking for trouble ... you know the report will be late.

So be realistic in setting deadlines!

7. Avoid perfectionism

Perfectionists like nothing better than to spend hours, days, even weeks polishing their work.

Outline precisely what the work consists of, and cut short any tendency to go beyond what is necessary and useful.

8. Put yourself under pressure

There is a positive and stimulating kind of stress when you have to meet certain time limits.

Pressure yourself only to the point where your activities yield maximum production in minimum time.

How?

- Instead of extending the deadline a few days, bring it forward. The aim here is to challenge, to create stress. A reasonable deadline can be brought forward by 10 to 15 per cent without creating undue stress. But not more than 15 per cent.
- Be aware of individuals' reactions: some people work well under stress, while others get nervous and panic.

Three techniques

1. Set a deadline for each job

- Don't get trapped. Do not accept any work from your boss that doesn't have a completion date. If your boss refuses, calculate your own estimate and set a deadline for yourself.

2. Be realistic

Take an objective look at your attitude towards deadlines.

- Do you get work done on time? (If not, look for the causes.) Don't let these mistakes happen again.
- Are you too much of an optimist? Are your deadlines too short?
- Are you taking all factors into account when you estimate your deadlines?

With a little experience, you will learn to estimate within a margin of error of about 5 to 10 per cent maximum.

3. Reward yourself when you bring the project in on time

Each goal attained merits a reward: so reward yourself at each opportunity!

This little game will boost your confidence and motivation ... Your colleagues, friends and family will notice. You will be someone they can 'count on'.

Checklist

Yes No

1. Have you got into the habit of setting deadlines? Even when your superiors don't?

2. Do you tell people in your team about your deadlines?

3. Do you set a deadline for each and every job?

4. Do you keep up-to-date notes about your performance vis-à-vis your deadlines?

5. Do you reward yourself each time you meet a deadline?

6. Do you make sure the instructions concerning a project are clear and precise?

7. Do you take the trouble to get informed about 'reasonable delays' when estimating deadlines for projects that are new to you?

8. Do you try to have all the pertinent information at your disposal when estimating a deadline?

9. Do you avoid the 'Yes, Yes' syndrome?

10. Do you refuse to accept any arbitrary deadlines?

11. Do you take other people's deadlines into account when setting your own?

12. Do you try to avoid being a perfectionist?

13. Do you apply, to yourself as well as to others, enough pressure to achieve maximum production in a minimum of time?

It sometimes happens, despite our good intentions and our commitment to setting precise deadlines, that we still can't get things rolling, or find a comfortable rhythm.

What's wrong?

How come we're stuck for so long, and the project, which we really think is a good one, just doesn't get off the ground?

The answer might be that, without being aware of it, we procrastinate.

What does that mean exactly?

Don't procrastinate: turn to the next chapter.

1. Set a deadline for each project.

2. Be realistic.

3. Reward yourself when you bring a job in on time.

11

DO YOU PROCRASTINATE?

Procrastination is a terrible sickness, Enemy Number One as far as mastering the organization of time is concerned. That's why I've written three chapters about it in this book.

Procrastination: an uncommon word which describes one of the most widespread diseases known to man. It is an insidious habit and in Chapter Three, when you were listing your bad habits, it must have appeared somewhere, in one form or another.

What is it exactly?

By definition, it is the tendency always to put things off until tomorrow.

At its terminal stage, since everything always gets put off, nothing gets done at all. Or if something gets done, it's not done well. After a certain incubation period (which usually isn't very long) the virus spreads, and you move from one crisis to another, and end up never finishing anything properly.

Are you a procrastinator?

Do this test right away!

(a) A little   **(b)** Sometimes   **(c)** Always

1. Are you the type of person who invents reasons, or finds excuses to put work off for later?   **(a)**____**(b)**____**(c)**____

2. Do you need to be under pressure to perform?
   (a)____**(b)**____**(c)**____

3. Do you neglect to take efficient measures to prevent delays on a project?   **(a)**____**(b)**____**(c)**____

4. Do you fail to exercise enough control over interruptions and unrelated problems that delay completion of a job?
(a)____**(b)**____**(c)**____

5. Do you sometimes feel you don't care about the job?
(a)____**(b)**____**(c)**____

6. When a job doesn't appeal to you, do you arrange to have it done by someone else?   **(a)**____**(b)**____**(c)**____

7. Do you just let some bad situations continue, instead of acting in time to correct the problem?   **(a)**____**(b)**____**(c)**____

How to stop procrastinating

Whatever the results of the test, you should know that in all likelihood you do procrastinate ... simply because the large majority of people do too.

How many students wait until the night before an exam to cram it all in, or sit up all night writing an essay?

Company directors prepare themselves at the last minute for meetings that are often very important.

A speaker hasn't written his speech three days before the conference, and has no idea what he's going to say.

How many job applications are posted after the closing date has passed?

A vicious cycle

What about you? Do you spend your life not doing what you want to do? Not respecting your deadlines, always waiting because other people don't respect their deadlines either. Do you know how the worst procrastinators behave?

1. *They want to do something,* and even make the decision to do it.

2. *They don't do it.* They don't follow up on their decision.

3. *They become aware (at least partially) of the negative results of not*

acting on their decisions. In other words, they suffer.

4. *They are gifted with an immense talent for inventing excuses for not doing what they should,* to stifle what they call their conscience.

5. *They become angry* and make new resolutions.

6. *They don't carry them out either.* They procrastinate even more.

7. *They keep repeating the same cycle* until a crisis arises that cannot be put off; then there's no choice but to finish what they started.

And the worst thing about procrastination is that it becomes a total way of life. We're not even aware of it, it's just a habit. But, unfortunately, a very negative one that engenders only stress, more problems, difficulties, letdowns, etc.

So stop procrastinating!

Would you like to know some techniques you can use to predict, prevent and combat procrastination? Here are five symptoms of procrastination that should always put you on the alert:

1. You let your mind wander. Instead of working, you daydream. You think about last weekend, or what you're going to do next weekend.

2. You voluntarily let yourself be interrupted by anything that comes up, a phone call (instead of having your calls screened) or a visitor (instead of having your door closed to everyone, during certain hours of the day).

   Not only do you let it happen, but you're usually glad of the interruption. It takes you away from the drudgery.

   Take it one step further, and you're subconsciously hoping for the interruption to occur.

3. You get sidetracked by the least little unimportant job, instead of doing what you really should.

4. You take long coffee-breaks, over-extended meals. You do a lot of things that you don't really have to do, like paying your phone bill in person instead of having it posted.

5. You insist on having all the information, all the documentation concerning a project, before writing a report or making a decision, even though you know full well that you can never have all the information at hand – and even if you wait until you have most of it, it will already have become outdated because all situations change in time.

Do you recognize one or a few of these symptoms in your own general behaviour? To combat them better, let's study them.

Fear of failure

This is one of the most frequent and subtle causes of procrastination. By not undertaking something, or putting it off day after day, you are subconsciously protecting yourself.

If you don't try, obviously you won't be able to fail. But at the same time, you won't be able to succeed either. Don't forget that.

This fear, which arises so frequently, and is so paralysing, often stems from a failure we experienced earlier on in life, which we haven't completely got over, or from a 'driver' which we haven't worked out: by procrastinating, you feed the driver that says 'Try harder'. (See Chapter Three.)

Be positive. Don't be afraid to take the plunge. Stop putting off the start of an activity or project. You should be acting today.

Identify your fears, analyse them as objectively as possible, and you'll see how they can vanish from one minute to the next. Be brave! You'll see just how easy and effective it is. Having failed in certain specific situations in the past doesn't mean that you're going to fail again. Life is constantly changing. Look at your previous failures as precious sources of information. Each project is a new ball game. Remember the words of Cicero: 'There's no shame in tripping on a stone. What would be shameful is to stop moving, or to trip over the same stone twice.'

Most successful people have failed at one time or another – often more than once – before succeeding. But they didn't let themselves get discouraged. They persevered.

You can do the same: act now! Without waiting any longer.

When is the best time to act?
N – O – W!

Fear of success

Pardon?

'I have an unconscious fear of succeeding, so maybe that's why I'm always putting things off.'

Strange as it sounds, don't you think that you might have some small fear of success? Or that you don't really want it? If you *really* wanted it, wouldn't you take all the measures necessary to get it?

Could you afford to continue to delay getting your priority projects moving?

Are you really motivated?

If you're not really motivated, you're going to let things drag on. So, how do you motivate yourself?

Usually, lack of motivation is hiding another problem. For example:

- previous failures that cause fear;
- a lack of self-confidence;
- and almost always: badly defined goals, never clearly visualized, never really desired.

All the successful people I have met have been able to speak clearly, simply and precisely about their goals. Once the goal is very clear, with no contradictions, success is inevitable, and seems to happen even faster than they expect.

What is preventing you from acting like them?

Tell yourself that any effort which does not advance you towards your goal, really and truly, is useless. Not only superfluous ... useless!

To help you clarify your goals, here is a little exercise:

1. What is your goal?

2. Do you really want to attain it?

3. How much time are you willing to spend daily to achieve your goal?

4. Do you deserve to attain your goal?

5. Do you still have certain internal fears, anxieties, hesitations or

DO YOU PROCRASTINATE? **105**

contradictions concerning your goal? If so (and we almost always do), what are they?

6. In your opinion, what is the biggest obstacle, interior or exterior – and generally it's interior – preventing you from attaining your goal? (Remember the story about the directors of the Ford company getting together with some bankers to discuss financing the Model T. Someone objected that it was ridiculous because there weren't any roads, and one of the directors answered simply, 'We'll build the roads!')

7. In your opinion, what's the best way to overcome this obstacle?

8. Are you ready to do everything in your power to overcome this obstacle and attain your goal?

9. If you answered no, ask yourself the following question: 'Do I really want to attain this objective?' If not, you're better off not wasting any more time and choosing another objective.

10. If you decide to choose another objective (which is not only permitted, but actually very astute on your part, since you will be saving time and energy), then get started on it right now!
Go on, I'm waiting . . .

Do you suffer from 'excusitis'?

There are some real excusitis champions around. They could all write best-sellers: 'How to Make the Right Excuse at the Right Time' with a list of a thousand and one of their most effective excuses.

The worst of it is that when we make an excuse, we start to believe it's true. It's a natural defence mechanism which protects our love of self – especially in the driver situation 'Be Perfect!' Your subconscious is very creative and skilful at fabricating excuses.

Be wary of those ping-pong rallies of accusations and excuses. Take the time to think it over, telling yourself that you too have the right to be wrong.

Each time an excuse or justification for late performance occurs to you, ask yourself the following question: 'Is this explanation just another excuse?'

People who have had spectacular success, who fulfil themselves through their work, do not tolerate excuses, either from themselves, or from their associates.

A goal with no deadline loses 80 per cent of its value

Have you been setting deadlines for each job, at least to get it started?

If not, delays, setbacks, complications will multiply. And what's worse, you'll be a target for failure, bad luck, a jinxed person ... and nothing you do will work out as it should.

A goal without a deadline is not a goal. You may have done everything necessary to get your project off the ground and finish it on time, but if you don't have a deadline, you risk ending up running around in circles, or watching things drag on interminably, especially if part of the work was delegated.

But be careful. Set reasonable deadlines. Take special care not to make them too long.

Some people say: 'I understand, I'll set a deadline.' But they choose a date so far in the future, that it means nothing. It's as bad as having no deadline at all.

All right, you'll say, but there are things I have to do already that can't be put off.

OK!

Subdivide those big jobs into smaller, less important ones, and give each of them a relatively short-term deadline. For example, I can say to myself that I'm going to finish this book in three months.

Then I would subdivide the method into two chapters per week, which would be my short-term objective.

Your subconscious always needs *precise* directions in order to function well. Things that are too distant in time become hazy, and generally don't materialize.

Be careful of chain reactions

A chain reaction starts when you fail to meet the deadline for a minor task. On it goes, until you have an overwhelming number of minor things to do.

For a while you could handle it, but now you're really overloaded. Your desk is piled with files, your agenda is full.

Your strategic plan has become so packed with data that you can't take it in at a glance any more.

What seemed like a long way to go three weeks ago, is now a crisis.

You only missed one little deadline. Now you're faced with a mountain. But it's your own fault.

This kind of thing doesn't happen to me any more, not for a long time. Precisely since I started watching out for chain reactions: and when I detect one, I don't look through my agenda for a free space of time, a holiday during the week, for example, or a free afternoon. No. Instead of laying on more stress, I take my daily agenda and my weekly plan, and compare them with my strategic plan. And then, I 'make cuts'. Which means I delegate tasks, cancel others, until my schedule – daily and weekly – is returned to its normal, easy, 'human' pace.

Would you like to know about a way to get your projects and jobs started more easily, to get things moving more quickly? What you need is a 'starter'.

Let a 'starter' work for you

Getting started is often the most difficult part. Even when you have a strategic plan, and precise daily and weekly schedules.

Do you have trouble getting started? What do you do with your car when it's cold out? *You turn on the engine!* Well, this is the same thing!

For example, take a writer sitting in front of a blank page. He waits for inspiration. Without a starter, the writer will just sit there, biting the end of the pencil, drinking coffee, listening to the news, checking the time, having a bite to eat.

With a starter, the writer will start writing whatever comes into his or her head, without stopping, without crossing out, precise, condensed . . . and bang! Suddenly the idea comes. And then another one . . . and so it goes.

The trick?

S –T –A –R –T !

Turn the key and get started, even if you're not ready. Tell yourself:

I MUST ACT NOW!

Without a starter, hours and days will go by without inspiration. With a starter, inspiration will come within a quarter of an hour, and you will continue with confidence.

How is this possible? When you get yourself into action, and are in the process of accomplishing whatever it is you're doing, the energy and creative juices start flowing: you tap into your own power.

As long as you sit at your work table and dawdle, nothing's going to happen. You'll feel you don't have the energy, creativity, determination, and above all the perseverance to get through the task in hand.

But as soon as you act, the energy starts to flow ... as if the energy came from your movement, while your immobility prevented it from flowing, from appearing ...

And it's an exponential phenomenon: the more you get into the work, the more the energy flows, the clearer your ideas become.

And soon, almost without noticing it, you've finished. You put down your pen, lean back in your chair, and bask for a while in that great feeling of satisfaction that comes with a job well done.

Two almost infallible techniques

A very important company director confided his technique to me for avoiding procrastination:

1. He mentally programmes the day, and visualizes the list of things he will have accomplished by the end of the day.

2. Each morning, the second thing he does is always the one he hates to do most. Why not the first thing? To get himself into a good mood first. After that it's easier to 'attack' the rest of the day. (Remember that the things you dislike the most are often the ones that teach you the most, in terms of personal development, perseverance, etc.)

Visualize the consequences of a delay

It might be easy to use a starter to get things going, nevertheless you might have trouble getting into the spirit of the 'game' and starting work.

There's a third technique: *make a commitment* to someone else, in a formal and irrevocable way. Bet money if you like, or take a solemn oath, that you will finish such and such a project.

If you place your self-esteem on the line ... you'll see: you will turn into a punctuality pro. Not convinced? Well, what do you think about this question: 'Do I really want to bring this project to an end?' (Or variations such as: 'Do I really want to succeed in this business? Do I really want the contract? The budget?' and so on.)

Answer sincerely, without hedging.

You might be surprised to learn that in many cases, the real, profound reason for your procrastination is that you don't want the project to succeed. Find the reasons!

Condition yourself mentally

On the other hand, if you really do want it, if your objectives are clearly outlined in your mind, leaving no room for hesitation, ask yourself the following question:

'If I really want this, why not do everything in my power, immediately, to obtain it?'

And then, visualize right away all the terrible inconveniences that would result if the project were delayed. That's right, all the negative effects and problems you can think of. Be precise and exhaustive!

Does stress stimulate you? Get you in high gear? Your ideas are clearer, you're full of energy. Good. Now keep visualizing until you feel the adrenalin ...

This will happen quicker than you think the first time. And very soon you will become conditioned to it: as soon as you want to start work, you can depend on your starter, on your power to direct your energies, and you will pass effortlessly into action. So much time saved, once again! The road to success opens before you ... It's up to you.

I WILL ACT IMMEDIATELY.

12

READ TWICE AS FAST

Read like John F. Kennedy

Do you know how John F. Kennedy, late President of the US, used to read?

Well, he read very rapidly.

He read at an average speed of 240 pages an hour, which is pretty amazing. Especially when you consider that the average individual reads no more than 60 pages an hour, which is four times less.

Did he have a natural gift for reading quickly? Maybe, but not enough of a gift to be able to do without a method. He took the bull by the horns, and mastered the art of speed-reading.

He wasn't the only US President to use speed-reading. Woodrow Wilson read even faster. He had the reputation of being able to read at the speed it takes to turn the pages. And we're talking about complex documents, full of numbers and details ... At cabinet meetings, documents were distributed so that members could look them over. Wilson always finished well ahead of the others, and spent his free time reading Greek authors – in the original, of course.

Did these men become President because they had mastered the art of speed-reading? Probably not. But this extra skill certainly must have played a role in their climb to the top.

'The mind of the poor reader loafs along, picking up very small units at a time, while the eyes of the excellent reader race over the lines, gathering an entire meaningful idea at each glance.'

N. Barton Smith Ph.D

Read as fast as the top directors

Imagine the advantage you would have if you could read two, three, or even four times as fast as others, or if you even went on to become what is called a 'page reader', like Wilson, who took in a whole page at a single glance.

We live in the information age, where knowledge means power. The more you know, the more you are able to assimilate, the faster you will rise in your chosen field.

Almost anyone can learn speed-reading, yet very few people take a few hours, or even a few minutes, to find out what it's all about.

This is another good example of the paradox of the 'busy person'. Not wanting to lose a few hours prevents them from saving hundreds, thousands of hours later on.

Are you a tortoise reader?

Do you have the feeling of being submerged in a pile of paper that seems to grow inexorably on your desk? Every time someone asks, 'Have you had a look at that report?' must you answer, 'No, I haven't had the time.'

If so, you might be one of those tortoise readers who take hours to read a newspaper, and who need a whole day to read a report that should normally take an hour.

Do you want to know if you really need to improve your reading habits?

Well, go ahead and do this little test, and you'll see clearly whether or not you're someone who can benefit from this method.

TEST   **Yes No**

1. Does reading the newspapers take you more than an hour a day?

2. Do you read literary and technical works in the same way, i.e. in a linear fashion, from the first to the last line?

3. Are you easily distracted when you read?

4. Do you move your lips when you read?

5. Do you hear the words in your head when you read?

6. Do you always read at the same speed, no matter what kind of text it is?

7. Is it difficult for you to grasp the overall concept of an article at first glance, from just looking at the titles, the captions, the bottom of the page, and the first and last paragraphs?

8. Is the idea of reading an entire chapter only when your first glance reveals something interesting, new to you?

9. Do you have trouble reading a few words at a time?

10. Do you read in such a way that you often have to go back and re-read a word or a phrase?

11. Would it be difficult for you to concentrate on the centre of each line, and to keep your focus there until you reach the bottom of the page, while reading the text?

If you answered 'yes' to most of these questions, then you can certainly make some improvement in your reading techniques, with the help of the Time Management System.

Learn speed-reading!

To end your reading problems, the ideal solution would be to take a course in speed-reading. Most people find that the results are astonishing.

If you're not convinced that you should take a speed-reading course as soon as possible, ask yourself how many pages you think you should read a week.

Usually the number is alarming in itself. Now calculate the time it takes you to read each page: usually it's one minute. Now do the multiplication.

You'll see that you spend at least one full day a week reading, and often two. If you could double your reading speed, you could save one whole day a week.

Climb the corporate ladder more rapidly

In many positions – usually the important ones – it's *necessary* to read and absorb massive amounts of information. Someone who doesn't read fast enough is putting a direct limit on their rise through the ranks. Or they end up putting in hours and hours of extra time to keep up.

But since there's a limit to the amount of time we can put in, these people will be quickly overtaken by their more adept colleagues.

The good news about speed-reading is that almost any individual who devotes a few days, with a minimum of perseverance, can succeed, and double their reading speed in a few weeks, no matter what their initial speed is.

Double your comprehension

'It's very nice to read quickly, but what about comprehension? Doesn't that suffer?'

Well, no it doesn't. Contrary to popular misunderstanding, people who read fast also read *better*. Everyone who learns speed-reading ends up with a better level of comprehension than they had before.

So there is a double advantage: reading *faster* and *better*.

Mastering speed-reading doesn't mean that you lose all sense of poetry, of literary style and feeling, and that you end up reading like a machine. If you want to re-read your favourite classical authors, or share a beautiful poem with a good friend, sitting by the fire, you will still be able to savour each page . . .

But why take three hours to read a boring technical report when it could be done in an hour?

Get rid of your apprehensions about speed-reading.

Escape the trap of traditional reading

- **spelling** Apply modern techniques for learning to read: instead of reading a word letter by letter, get used to reading the word as a whole.
- **reading word by word** This way of reading is already an improvement on the previous stage, but it's better to be able to read groups of words at a time.
- **speaking while reading** Whether you just move your lips, or whisper to yourself, or speak the words in your mind, this slows your reading down: you automatically read at verbal speed.
- **following the lines** By following lines with your finger or a pen, you slow yourself down.
- **re-reading** If you often have to go back and re-read a word or a phrase, you lack concentration. Don't confuse speed-reading with hurried reading. If you become aware that you're nervous, reduce your reading speed. If necessary, stop and take a break. You can start again when you have regained your calm.

An exercise to read faster

Take any text, and draw two vertical lines, so that the page is divided into three equal parts.

Start reading. Don't look at the first word, but instead at the group of words immediately to the left of the first vertical line.

Now move your eyes over so that you're looking at the group of words in the middle column, then in the right-hand column.

In this way, you read the line in three steps, by moving your eyes three times.

When this becomes easy, move on to step No. 2: divide your page into two parts, with one vertical line, and try to read each line by moving your eyes only twice.

When you have mastered this, try the next step: focus only on the dividing line, centre page, and try to take in a whole line at a time, without shifting your eyes.

If you practise regularly, you will, in a very short period of time, be able to double your reading speed. Don't forget to time yourself with a watch or stopwatch. You will soon be surprised by the progress you make, and the advantages speed-reading brings.

Avoid reading

'I don't understand,' I hear you say. 'First you tell me to master the art of speed-reading, then you tell me not to read!'

It's fine to read rapidly, but you will not make any progress – in fact, you risk getting bogged down – if at the same time, you don't learn to *be selective*. Choosing what you read is of prime importance when allotting time that is already limited.

How to proceed?

The first question you should ask yourself about a document, an article or a book is: 'Is it really essential that I read this document?'

If the answer is no, then don't waste a minute reading something you don't need.

You can also ask yourself the following question: 'What impact will this have on my personal and professional life?'

If you think the impact will be minimal or nil, why waste time? In any case, try to keep the amount of time you waste to a minimum.

Manage your reading

You should classify your reading in order of importance, just as you do for your correspondence. Better still, you can arrange for your secretary to do it.

You can set up four categories:

Waste

This includes everything that is not essential to your work, such as publicity and certain bulletins, etc.

To have to read

Ask your colleagues or subordinates to read certain articles for you, and give you a report on them. You can then decide whether it is important for you to read the material.

To be read later

This category makes an excellent odd-job supply. Once you have mastered speed-reading, you will be able, at first glance, to see what articles or parts of articles are important, and cut them out for later study. (If you can't cut them out, photocopy them.)

Must read

When you get to this category, start reading!
A few helpful hints:

1. To make your selection, first read through the contents page of the periodical or book under consideration (if there is one). Obviously, you should only read the articles or chapters that interest you.
2. Certain books have a summary at the end of each chapter, where you can find all the essential information. If you're in a hurry, you need only read that.
3. Generally speaking, the theme or main hypothesis of a work is contained in the first chapter. The following chapters develop this theme, and present examples and proof.

   It's often not necessary to read through them all. The conclusions are found in the last, or next to last, chapter.

A last trick: even when faced with a hefty tome of 500 pages or more, ask yourself the question: 'If I only had one hour to read this book, and then had to answer questions about it, what would I do?'

This is the same type of problem set for our mental limitations, which we discussed earlier.

N.B. You should be just as selective when buying your books. I've often fallen into the trap and, even after numerous recommendations, bought books that I found boring and entirely useless for my personal needs.

Again, before buying a book:

1. I always consult the table of contents.
2. I always read the first page. (If the book is protected in a plastic wrapper, I unwrap it. If the assistant doesn't want me to unwrap it, I don't buy it. It's usually difficult to get your money back once you've taken the book home and started reading, so you'd better be sure of what you're buying.)

I often base my decision about whether to buy a book or not on the first page and/or the table of contents. If I'm not impressed, I put it back on the shelf. I may have lost three minutes, but I've saved myself the price of the book, plus a lot of unwanted frustration.

Limit your reading time

If you have a lot of time ahead of you, your reading speed will naturally be affected. If you have a couple of hours in which to read ten pages, don't be surprised if you use all that time to do it. Remember Parkinson's Law ...

Impose limits on your reading time

For example, a report that took you three hours to read last week, should only take you two now.

Force yourself to finish what you're reading before a meeting, an appointment, or the office closes. In this way, you unconsciously force yourself to increase your reading speed.

Make reading an appointment

You will quickly sink under the load of reading that is essential to your work if you don't take care. But it is of the utmost importance that you keep up-to-date with everything that concerns your job. So?

Add a reading period to your diary, at least once a week.

In this way, you allow yourself the time to catch up on your reading, or at least to make a selection of what you should study more closely in the weeks to come.

Don't waste time

Take full advantage of your reading time.

If you're dealing with highly technical material, read more slowly. If not, *just glance over the text to select the important material.*

Limit memos to one page

Are you plagued by over-zealous and perfectionist subordinates, who submit voluminous reports for your perusal?

Take the advice of the famous Procter and Gamble executive: memos one page maximum.

Demand reports that are extremely concise and clear, never longer than a page (and do the same yourself).

Break your reading down

When faced with a lengthy text of highly technical material, which is nevertheless essential to your work, it helps a lot to break the material down, so that it can be assimilated more easily.

Read one section at a time, instead of the whole thing in one shot.

Assign a date limit for reading each section. With only this pressure, you will see an acceleration of 10 to 30 per cent in your reading speed.

How to master technical jargon

Don't be impressed by over-use of technical jargon. Learn to translate what the author means into clear, simple language. Excessively specialized language is often a disguise to hide an incomprehension of the subject, and does nothing to help others understand.

Nevertheless, if you have to get through a lot of technical reading, here are a couple of hints which should help you substantially reduce the time it takes:

1. Get to the point
Very often, the summary and conclusion contains all the information necessary for an understanding of the subject.

So look at these sections first. Later you can fill in the general ideas by a more attentive study of the chapters which you think are important.

2. Mark up the text
Don't hesitate to underline words or sentences that you have difficulty understanding, so that you can verify them later.

Also, use a fluorescent marker to underline passages which are important, so you can locate them easily for review.

N.B. A book is a tool, not a precious object. Use it accordingly.

When to read

When is the best time to read?

- First, during the 'reading appointment' which you took the trouble to list in your diary: you have an appointment with the authors.
- Next, whenever the occasion arises, as outlined in the section on odd jobs.
- Finally, after working hours, or over the weekend.

Consult the experts

Have you ever wanted to meet the 'top people' in your field, so that you could glean the latest, most up-to-date information concerning your work?

Over lunch, an hour or two of discussion with your colleagues will allow you to select those publications which contain the latest, most up-to-date developments in your field.

In this way, you will avoid the dilemma of someone who doesn't know where to find the answers to important questions.

Avoid post overload

Don't hesitate to ask your secretary to eliminate all the post that is not *of real interest* to your work.

CHECKLIST
Yes No

1. Have you been selective about the things you read? (Do you only read those publications which will help you attain your personal goal, or that of your company?)

2. Have you cancelled your subscriptions to all publications which you don't need to read?

3. Have you prevented a build-up of reading material by setting yourself a 'reading appointment' at least once a week?

4. Have you got into the habit of checking the contents page and the first and last chapters, before deciding whether you really need to read a book?

5. Do you assign certain reading to your subordinates and instruct them to submit a report, before deciding whether you must read the material yourself?

6. Do you organize your reading material according to subject? (Do you read everything you can about a particular subject before going on to something else?)

7. Have you subscribed to a publication which keeps you informed of the latest developments and other publications relating to your field?

8. Do you underline pertinent passages in an article or book, for easy access later on?

9. Do you glance through your reading material, in order to set up a list of priorities?

And now, if I told you that I know how you can find some free time, a lot of free time ... a whole lot, if you like ... would you be interested?

All right, let's move on to Part Two.

**Teach yourself speed-reading:
it's a vital key to greater efficiency.**

PART TWO

HOW TO SAVE TIME BY NOT WASTING IT

In the following chapters, you will learn how to save time by not wasting it any more. We will identify the main time consumers, and see how to eliminate them, or at least gain control of them.

Each chapter is useful, but some may be more useful to you personally than others.

Which ones?

I propose two tests:

● The first will enable you to identify the principal factors which cause you to lose time;
● The second will help you identify your main time consumers, so that you can better equip yourself to combat them.

TEST 1: Time loss factors

Identify your time loss factors from among the 42 following examples:

1. I accept too many jobs at the same time.
2. I pass responsibility on to others.
3. I change my priorities without having a valid reason.
4. I don't discipline myself.
5. I put off making decisions.
6. I am confused, disorganized.
7. I am too organized, too systematic, too particular.
8. I don't delegate jobs, or I do it badly.
9. I don't let my employees work on their own.
10. I don't establish my priorities.
11. I have not set standards for myself.
12. I am often tired.
13. I can't say no.
14. I rarely, or never, spend time planning.
15. I don't know how to set up a good working team.
16. I am often interrupted.
17. I lack the authority to carry out my responsibilities.
18. I don't have precise goals.
19. I have trouble concentrating.
20. I am not well informed.
21. I lack method when dealing with routine, daily problems.
22. I am not motivated enough.
23. I only take my 'managerial' position seriously when there's a crisis.

24. I like meetings.
25. I frequently change the order of my documents around.
26. I don't have a daily agenda.
27. I have old-fashioned working methods.
28. There are often conflicts in my schedule of activities.
29. I have personal conflicts with my colleagues.
30. I am insecure.
31. I don't communicate well.
32. I don't have a good filing system.
33. I am not in the habit of listing the things I have to do.
34. I often put things off that should be done today.
35. My personal life is too active.
36. I involve too many people in my decision-making.
37. I write too many memos, letters, notes.
38. Many of my projects don't get past the planning stage.
39. I make and get a lot of useless phone calls.
40. I often spend too much time on the phone.
41. I sometimes do useless jobs.
42. I write reports myself, that could be written by others.

TEST 2: Time consumers

In the following exercise, we will try to identify the factors that consume large amounts of your time, and are therefore a problem.

PART A: YOUR PROFESSIONAL LIFE

Planning
1. Inability to establish goals.
2. No daily planning.
3. Unclear and unstable priorities.
4. Unfinished jobs.
5. Crisis management: 'Put out the fire!'.
6. No set deadlines.
7. Inaccurate time estimates.

Organization
8. Bad personal organization: messy desk.
9. Work done twice.
10. Unclear responsibilities.

11. Numerous bosses.

Direction
12. Work done under my direction.
13. Routine details.
14. Inefficient distribution of delegated tasks.
15. Lack of motivation.
16. Irresolute action in face of conflict.
17. Inability to adapt to change.

Control
18. Telephone interruptions.
19. Unexpected visits.
20. Lack of discipline.
21. Too many conflicting or divergent interests.
22. Errors of inefficiency in my performance.
23. No standards, no rapport at work.
24. Incomplete information.

Communication
25. Meetings.
26. Unclear directives.
27. Inability to listen.
28. Teamwork.

Decision-making
29. Hasty decisions.
30. Indecision – procrastination.
31. Group decisions.
32. Perfectionism.

PART B: YOUR PERSONAL LIFE

1. Bad shopping plans.
2. No plans for the next few days' meals.
3. Doing things that other members of the family could or should do.
4. Diverse family appointments (doctor, dentist, piano lessons, etc.).
5. Driving kids around.
6. Inability to say no to exterior demands (volunteer work, canvassing for one cause or another).

7. Getting things and information for other family members.
8. Perfectionism.
9. Others.

Comments

If you analyse the negative time consumers in your private and professional life, you will see that they fall into two groups.

The first includes exterior consumers: telephone interruptions, visitors, etc.

The second includes internal consumers: lack of discipline, inability to delegate, indecision, etc.

Most of us tend to exaggerate the importance of the first category, which makes us also tend to blame others for our problems, thereby placing ourselves in a position where we can do nothing to act and complete our projects.

It's better to make mistakes and to repair them – by learning from them for future experience – than to place all the blame on others, or on external elements. This only serves to reinforce the situation.

13

THE MOST IMPORTANT AND THE SUBTLEST TIME CONSUMER

Dr De Woot's study on highly placed executives in the United States (see Chapter One) came up with a very interesting statistic: on average, an executive is interrupted every eight minutes in his or her office, and the interruption lasts three minutes. This can be due to an unexpected visitor, or because the calculator's not functioning properly, or a phone call, etc.

If you add the fact that it takes at least a couple of minutes to re-establish concentration and get back to work, you'll start to see the real situation: over a 13-minute period, the employee spends five minutes on unexpected and usually unprofitable activity, which comes to 40 per cent of his or her time.

Now do you see why some people advance so quickly, while others sit and vegetate? Just by managing your time and limiting interruptions, you can save up to 40 per cent of your productivity. That's enormous. On a basis of only 40 working hours per week, that comes to 752 hours per year, which is 94 working days.

No wonder people who refuse to be masters of their own time, and let themselves be guided by whatever comes along, get left behind. By applying just a few principles of time management, you can easily double – yes double – your productivity and effectiveness.

Of course, there are some interruptions which are justified and even profitable, and the aim of The Complete Time Management System isn't to eliminate them completely – an artificial and potentially dangerous goal – but to reduce them, keep them under control, so that you can enjoy more hours of reflection, productive work, creativity, etc. The Complete Time Management System teaches you to:

1. Identify and eliminate your 'auto-interruptions'.

2. Effectively combat useless interruptions by clients, suppliers, or unexpected visitors.

3. Reduce considerably the time spent 'discussing' with colleagues.

4. Control and diplomatically handle situations arising from needless interruptions by your superiors.

5. Provide you with 'an hour of solitude' so that you can organize and plan your work better, and complete all your budding projects and pressing business.

Are you someone who is interrupted easily?

Interruptions are so much a part of our everyday routines that we often don't even notice that we've been interrupted dozens of times, while trying to do the same job. Do you want to become aware of the magnitude of this problem in your organization of time?

Keep a journal of interruptions

Since you cannot eliminate all interruptions during the course of a day, it becomes necessary to identify those that are to be tolerated and those that are to be eliminated.

Take an average working day, and note down the time, duration and subject of each interruption.

Then, to simplify things, set up two categories:

1. Useful
2. Useless

Interruption journal

Week of _____ to _____

Name _____

Call ☐ Visit ☐ Time_____ Duration _____

Reason _____

Evaluation _____

_____

_____

With your journal handy, set up the following list:

1. The most frequent interrupters (auto or external).
2. Among those, the ones who cause most loss of time.

Also distinguish between:

- *exterior interruptions*: unexpected visits, telephone calls, secretary, colleagues, etc.
- and *auto-interruptions*: distractions, suddenly abandoning jobs, daydreaming, making a phone call in the middle of an important job, extended coffee breaks, etc.

What should you do to permit only the 5 to 10 per cent of interruptions – internal and external – which are necessary and useful?

How can you keep your most frequent and time-consuming interruptions down to a minimum?

Don't see any visitors without an appointment

Make it clear to your secretary: no one is to be admitted who hasn't first made an appointment. Exceptions to this rule should be kept to a minimum, and only allowed under very special circumstances. You'll see, your secretary will become a valuable ally in your fight to manage your time.

You might have to tread a little delicately with your colleagues, but:

1. Gradually get them used to making an appointment if they want to see you. Be firm but polite. Let them understand that you have a very heavy schedule, and that you're just not available on demand.

2. If the interruption is unavoidable, keep it down to a minimum

by explaining to your colleague that you only have five minutes to spare because you're working on an important report.

3. Get your secretary to work with you on this. If someone persists in making needless interruptions, your secretary can act as a screen and explain that you're extremely busy and can't see anyone.

    And if the person still insists on seeing you, your secretary can cut the interruption short by coming into your office a couple of minutes later, saying that you have an important phone call that can't wait.
    Don't let your interrupter tell you: 'Never mind, it doesn't matter. I'll wait until you've finished your call.'
    Thank him or her kindly, and tell them you'll have to continue the conversation later on.

4. A good way to let someone important know that their time is up, is simply to stand up and smile.

5. Get into the habit of setting up regular meetings with all your associates. If a colleague calls or comes into your office unexpectedly, ask if the problem couldn't be discussed at the next meeting. Four out of five times it can, since only 20 per cent of interruptions are really important and urgent.

6. When you have to leave your office, walk quickly and decidedly through the corridors if you don't want to be intercepted.

    If necessary, you can even pretend to be reading something important . . .
    This doesn't mean to say that you shouldn't be pleasant and smile at your colleagues. On the contrary. But with a couple of words and a smile, you can tell someone you meet that you hold them in the highest regard, but that you're also very busy, too busy to stop and chat:
    'How are you?'
    'Fine.'
    'Me too. Feeling great . . .'
    . . . and just keep on walking. The important thing is not to slow down.

7. If a colleague arrives and says he absolutely must see you in your office right away, and that he objects to being kept waiting around,

go to his or her office. Why? Because it's much easier to leave someone else's office than to kick someone out of your own.

8. To live happily, live privately. When working on an important job, try to find an out-of-the-way place, like the library, or a conference room or an unused office.

Don't be a slave to your staff

In theory, the people who work under you are there to help save you work. Unfortunately, things don't always work out according to the textbooks. All too often, you have to intervene in their work, to help them with problems that they should be able to solve themselves. This is what the experts call 'retrograde delegation'. The job you delegated rebounds back to you. Obviously, you can't avoid this kind of thing completely: it's part of the normal training process.

But if it occurs too frequently, then you are not delegating correctly.

How can you avoid the trap of having work that you delegate come back to you?

The first step is to identify the ways staff members use to shift their responsibilities back to you:

1. We've got a problem!
2. Can I get your opinion on this?
3. Can we discuss this?
4. You're the only one qualified enough . . .

What remedies can you apply?

1. Insist that they always try to solve the problem themselves before seeing you. Delegate more often, and more carefully.

2. Ask them to save their questions for the regular meetings.

3. Don't let them get you to do the work, except in extremely exceptional cases. If you do, they will become accustomed to falling back on you whenever there's a slight problem.

    They should work on their own. Give them more instructions, suggest corrective measures and possible solutions, encourage them when necessary.

    And above all, don't hesitate: test them, ask them what they would do to solve the problem if you weren't around. The results are often surprising.

4. If the people who work for you have to make many minor decisions over the course of the day, set aside twenty minutes, at a convenient time, when these details can be worked out all together.

But get them used to being independent. Each one should assume responsibility and be able to make decisions!

Learn to say no

Of course you should be positive as often as possible. But this doesn't mean that you can't say no. So, if you feel like answering 'yes' to these questions:

- Are you afraid of disappointing someone who really needs help?
- Are you worried about the resentment people might feel towards you, if you don't listen to them?
- Do you think your refusal will result in their refusing you when you need help or advice?

Tell yourself that this stems from a lack of self-confidence.

Learn to say 'no!' It might be difficult at first, but there are many ways to say no:

'I'm sorry, I'm not available just at the moment ...'

'I can't talk to you any longer ...'

'Could you come back to my office at the end of the day?'

Learn to use these polite refusals more often.

Take time to think

Don't give an answer right away, when you are interrupted and asked for something. Say you need a few minutes to think about it.

Then call back, or better still have your secretary call back, and say that you're very sorry, but you won't be able to ...

Saying no is sane and economical

Some people don't dare say no, then they regret having said yes and suffer for it. This shows a lack of self-affirmation.

Don't forget that efficient time management continually demands making choices. Saying no is also making a choice.

Haven't there been many situations where you would have preferred to say no, but didn't dare? Try to remember the most recent, and then visualize the problems that resulted from your inability to say no.

A last word on the art of refusing: develop an opposite reflex to the one you have now. When asked for your time or energy, first think 'no', then 'maybe', and then perhaps ... 'yes'.

This is how most highly successful people think. If it works for them ... why not for you!

What if your boss interrupts you?

**Does your boss
make you waste a lot of time?**

Here are eight ways to prevent this in future:

1. Review, together with your boss, the list of things to be done, including the time limits for overall projects and for specific stages.

2. Ask your boss how much time he or she thinks the work should take.

3. Ask yourself if you honestly think you can do the work in that time.

4. Always bring along a number of minor things to do, like reading an article or a report, in case you have to wait before seeing your boss.

5. Ask your boss if he or she would like to discuss any new ideas over lunch.

6. Then ask some of your colleagues to develop these ideas and put together a file.

7. Make your own suggestions, eliminating all useless documents or procedures.

8. Learn to say no. A simple, clear, and convincing . . . 'no'.

But what are your present reactions when your boss interrupts you, or keeps you from working? Write them down.

All right. Now, in the light of what you've been reading in this chapter, write down the techniques you are going to try out, clearly and precisely, when the situation presents itself in future.

There are obvious interruptions, and then there are other, more subtle kinds of interruptions, which are due to your environment, your office for example. We'll get to those in the next chapter.

Learn to say 'NO'.

14

ORGANIZE YOUR WORK SPACE

What does your office look like?

Does your office look like it was hit by a tornado? Or is it like a minimalist painting, clean, almost untouched?

Can you clear your desk every night, or do the files just keep piling up?

Everyone has their personal style: 'Tell me what your office is like, and I'll tell you what kind of person you are.'

Beethoven wrote in a mess of books and musical scores, but he was lucky in that he could work in total solitude: he forbade any interruptions while working. Combined with his genius ... well, the result is his music, which speaks for itself.

But generally, a messy office creates a bad impression on visitors, colleagues ... and your boss!

And it can get depressing pretty fast. At least that's what the psychologists have discovered. Your environment actually has a direct effect on your mind, and on the minds of your associates.

What does your work space look like? Here are some questions to help you draw a portrait:

1. Is your work table always covered with all kinds of papers?

2. Do you need a special space for priority documents, and for projects that you mean to undertake?

3. When you sit down at your work table, do you feel negative about the work you're about to do?

4. Is your work table in such a mess that you hesitate, consciously or unconsciously, to sit down and get started?

5. Would you say that the physical environment of your office is dull and stuffy?

6. Do you think your work space is not conducive to clear, concise thinking, to being creative and efficient?

7. Do you often have difficulty taking notes while on the telephone, or do you get the phone wires tangled?

8. Do you have insufficient space in which to do your work?

9. Do you often find yourself searching for misplaced files or reports?

10. Do you dread people visiting your office?

Well, how many questions did you have to answer yes to? That many? Here is some advice, and a few techniques to help you change all that. First, close the door so that you're not disturbed – and so that no one sees you playing house!

Everything at hand

Excuse me, but which hand did you use to close the door? If the door was stuck, and you had to use both hands, never mind. What I want to know is whether you're right- or left-handed. It's important. Make sure that, if you're right-handed, your telephone is placed on your left.

Why? How are you supposed to make notes when you're on the phone if the receiver is already in your right hand? Pass it over to the left? Interesting. Do you prefer writing over or under the telephone wire?

So, if you're right-handed, your telephone, your computer screen, and your lamp should all be on your left (unless you prefer writing in the shadow of your arm on long winter evenings). On the other side you should place: a list of the people you call most frequently on the phone; your computer disks, paper, pens and a calculator, a tape recorder or dictaphone, and two clocks, with large numbers, one for you (your time is precious) and one for visitors (throughout the conversation you should let them know, discreetly of course, that your time is valuable).

Are you left-handed? Well, switch the objects around. You can draw a line down the middle of the desk, and use that to orient the placing of your equipment.

Do you have enough space?

Sit down and hold out your arms. I suppose they reach almost to the edges of your desk. The space in the centre of your desk should be completely clear ... totally empty ... that's the ideal working space. If you don't have enough room, move the phone, the computer screen etc. to a side table, which is placed at right angles to your desk. You should now have a sufficiently large space.

Very close by, within arm's reach, you should place a filing cabinet, one with enough drawers to file all your documents and classify them according to three criteria: urgent, important, and file/pass on. You then try to empty the urgent drawer first, important second, and file/pass on third ('pass on' means pass on to somebody else).

You should have a large wastepaper basket handy, or even a couple of them, if you have the space.

Now stand up. I hope you have a pivoting, reclining chair with smooth rolling wheels. It should be comfortable, and adjustable for height. All right? Perfect ...

Let's look at the rest of your space. In a convenient and accessible corner, plan to store all the office equipment items you may need (pens, stapler, markers, sellotape, glue, paper clips, folders, envelopes, etc.). Make sure you have enough stock so that you never have to stop in the middle of something important to fetch supplies. What a waste of time, running out to the stationer's for a roll of sellotape!

Is there a petty thief in your building? Do your pens and erasers seem to vanish into thin air? If you don't have any locks on your drawers, you should start a special drawer, labelled very discreetly, where you can hide your reserves.

Some advice on how to organize your work space

● Put your desk or work table in a place that doesn't lend itself to interruptions. Arrange it so that you're not seen from the door. You will not be inviting visitors, and at the same time you'll be less distracted. If your work station is in an open plan office, you can use dividers or a large plant as a masking device. Let your secretary act as a barrier: make sure her desk is directly in the line of oncoming traffic.

- Place your filing cabinet so that files are quickly and easily accessible.

- If you can, reserve a space for 'being creative' ... a couch where you can lie back and think. Try to place it so you can't be seen from the door.

- If possible, choose warm colours to stimulate your creativity (peach, beige, pale pink) or cold colours to help you concentrate (blue, turquoise, green).

   Avoid colours like lavender or yellow: they're not flattering and you won't look good. Bright red is known to make people nervous, so it won't help with your work.

- Don't face a window. Lighting should be indirect, and at best come from behind you, at shoulder height. If you don't have overhead lights, you should use halogen for indirect lighting, and a normal desk lamp. One will create a warm atmosphere, the other is for accuracy.

BOSTA (Buffalo Organization for Social and Technological Associations) conducted a six-year study, questioning more than 6000 white-collar workers in more than 70 companies. They found that it is possible to increase productivity an average of 15 per cent – that's right, fifteen per cent – just by providing employees with a well-designed office.

What does BOSTA advise? Simple. There are three factors to be considered:

1. **Personnel participation:** the best results were obtained when companies consulted their personnel about office design.

2. **Furniture:** the work space should be comfortable, and well equipped with communication devices.

3. **Need for privacy:** it is recommended that work spaces be enclosed on at least three sides by walls or dividers.

And nine parameters:

1. *The area of the work space:* an employee's performance can be affected by the amount of space he or she has to work in.

2. *Furniture*: the amount, the quality, the size and depth of the furniture, the way it's arranged, how comfortable the chairs are, etc. also affect performance.

3. *Windows*: the closer you work to a window, the more light you have, the better.

4. *Temperature and air quality*: problems occur especially when there are frequent variations in temperature and air quality (as well as in positive and negative ionization of the air).

5. *Lighting*: reflections, shadows, variations in intensity, etc. should be avoided.

6. *Noise*: Performance diminishes as noise levels increase.

7. *Personalization*: the addition of personal objects like plants, photographs, etc. are greatly appreciated.

8. *Colours*: opt for pastel colours and warm materials (woollen fabric, etc.).

9. *Sharing space*: many people prefer not to work alone, but too many people in the same space will multiply the problem of distraction and become a nuisance.

(Adapted from an article in *The Echoes of Industry*, 6 April 1988, p. 20.)

My own techniques for saving time

Here are a few more ideas that may help you:

- I buy duplicates of all my office equipment: pens, scissors, glue, etc. This saves me having to go out shopping if I've misplaced something, or if someone borrows something and doesn't return it.

- These items are hung on the wall, using hooks originally designed for tools. I do this so I don't have to go looking through drawers or boxes when I need something.

- My paper supply is arranged in a series of small drawers, similar to those used for nails, nuts and bolts, etc. (Yes, you guessed it ... I like to build things!)

● I attach my telephone to the wall, to keep my desk space clear.

● I have a small desk. This FORCES me to keep it tidy as I go along. When I did have a large desk, it was always in a mess.

● My wastepaper basket is ENORMOUS! And it gets filled up very fast. I think of it as my best friend.

My office is full of electronic gadgets of all kinds, which save me a lot of time. Sceptical? Wait till you've read the next chapter . . .

When you are sitting at your work table
everything should be within arm's reach.

15

DO YOU KNOW HOW TO TAKE ADVANTAGE OF NEW TECHNOLOGY?

Communicate at the speed of the electron

New technology can provide you with marvellous services, and help you save precious time. Use it! At least try things out, remembering that when the telephone – a device that you'd be hard pressed to do without – was invented, it was considered a 'gadget' that would soon disappear.

You should be careful when acquiring new equipment. You should first ask yourself whether you're making the best use you can of the equipment you've already got, if buying new equipment is really necessary.

Let's take a look at some equipment that can help you save time.

Use your tape recorder

A micro-cassette, or a simple portable tape recorder, can be a very practical tool: they don't cost much, they're light, compact, and can be taken almost anywhere.

Most business people have one (or a few) and wouldn't give them up for anything in the world. They come in handy on so many occasions – on the plane, in taxis or driving the car, at meetings, conferences, seminars, etc.

It's a little like a secretary who follows you around everywhere you go.

Here is some advice on how to use these little machines to gain time and profit, making them an excellent investment.

1. Carry a 'portable professor'

There are all kinds of courses offered on audio cassettes, from language and public speaking, to management and motivation. Improve your professional competence by listening to one of these courses whenever you have the chance.

2. The benefits of repetition

Do you know that you forget about 80 per cent of the things you hear during the course of the day? Repetition helps you retain the things you consider important to your job.

So, in order to remember the important things you pick up during your working day, tape them and listen to them again a few times later on.

Instead of re-reading reports and memos, you can tape the important parts and listen to them again whenever it's convenient.

3. Store personal memoranda

You can file the details of important interviews or meetings, the main points of contractual and/or commercial agreements, comments and decisions taken during meetings, etc.

4. Have a personal 'messenger service'

Instead of wasting time repeating the same instructions over and over again, tape them and circulate a copy in the office, among colleagues and subordinates.

In this way, you can be delegating different jobs while you yourself are attending a meeting.

5. Have a dictaphone

With this little machine, you can dictate notes, reports, memoirs and letters at any time of day or night.

It can also be used as a storehouse for new ideas, as they come to you (often at very odd moments). Circulate the tape among your colleagues, who can add their criticisms and thoughts on how to develop your ideas.

Quarter your correspondence time

Every week, you spend hours dealing with your correspondence. If you are from the 'old school' you might even write your letters yourself, by hand, spending long periods of time finding the right phrasing, the right tone, etc.

Result? You don't necessarily create a favourable impression on your correspondent (neither do you necessarily create a bad impression).

The truth is that *nine times out of ten, you're wasting your time*. Why? Simply because the person you're writing to just doesn't have the time to sit down and appreciate your prose. He or she is in a hurry, and only wants to know the essential information your communication contains.

My own experience has shown that it's usually better to be brief and stick to the point, which means sending *information*. In this way misunderstandings are avoided.

One of the best ways to do this is to use the tape recorder's little brother, the dictaphone.

Dictaphones don't cost a lot, and can save you a considerable amount of time. Strangely enough, studies have shown that four out of ten managers still write their own letters by hand.

The simple act of dictating your letters and having your secretary type them up will cut your correspondence time in half. Better still, proper use of a dictaphone will allow you to cut this time down to a quarter.

Not counting savings in material: according to my calculations, a letter dictated to a secretary costs 30 per cent more than if you use a dictaphone.

How to use the dictaphone

● Tell yourself that *anyone who can talk can dictate*.

● If you think your voice sounds horrible the first time you hear it played back, don't worry: it's just because you're not used to it. Accept it as it is. The more you dictate, the more self-assured you will become.

● Set your objectives and sub-objectives before you begin speaking. Stop between each sub-objective.

- Always begin by outlining what you're going to say in general terms, and state who you're sending it to.

- Imagine that the person you're talking to is there in front of you. Talk into the microphone as if you were speaking directly to them.

- **Don't stop.** It's easy to make corrections later, using a word-processor.

- To train yourself, you might want to start with a report or a memo that's already written, and practise dictating it. Compare your taped version with the typed version – look for possible points of confusion.

- Next, tape a résumé of an important article.

- Finally, make a tape of directives concerning an area of work that you are familiar with.

- Make sure that *you are not interrupted while dictating*.

- Make sure that your secretary is equipped with a playback machine.

Make your telephone answering machine a second secretary

A telephone answering machine can be the perfect solution, especially if you work at home, and you aren't able (or don't want) to pay for the services of a secretary.

Since I got mine, I've been asking myself how I ever could have done without it: my associates, clients and friends, who were a little sceptical at the beginning, now chastize me every time I forget to turn it on!

That shows how strong a resistance people have to new technology, until they realize just how useful these things can be in our lives.

A telephone answering machine allows you to:

1. Be contacted when you're not there.
2. Take messages without being interrupted when you have important work to do: it also filters your calls.
3. Listen to incoming messages being taped, and to answer if you

think the call is important enough.

4. Know who called while you're out of the office or not at home, since you can pick up your messages by remote control (I highly recommend choosing a model with this option). In this way, you can get your messages from anywhere in the world, as long as there's a telephone nearby. Fantastic, isn't it?

If you want your caller to leave a message, make your recording an exercise in communication: the quality of the initial contact will condition the results. Smile when you speak, be pleasant, natural, lively, talk clearly: then callers won't want to hang up instead of leaving messages.

Should you buy a computer?

The ads are very enticing these days. For the price of two television sets you can get a good word-processor. For a little more you can get a powerful PC machine, with a huge memory and a library of all kinds of programs, from accounting to video games.

What should you do? First, don't make any hasty decisions: the initial investment might not seem a lot, but it could lead you to further expenditure that can add up to a considerable amount.

So the problem is not really whether to buy one or not, but *to know what your needs are*, right now, and what you envisage in the near and not-so-near future. So:

1. What kinds of problems do you have now?
   - Not enough time to answer letters.
   - I often have to rewrite and/or retype the same material.
   - I have a lot of repetitive accounting work that I do regularly by hand.
   - I have a lot of trouble getting documents ready, collecting all the information I need, etc. in order to write a book, a thesis or report, to make plans, design models, etc.

2. What are your potential needs?
   - I'd sometimes like to experiment with the layout of my writing ... paragraph structure, page design, etc., just to see what it looks like.
   - I'd like to know just where my accounts stand at the end of

each month: I'd like to see a balance sheet, a list of debits and credits, etc.

- I would like to hand my printer a brochure or publicity memo that is camera-ready: it would save a lot of time, I wouldn't have to pay a graphic designer, and the brochure would look exactly as I want it to look.
- I would like to have an up-to-date file of all my clients, with statistics concerning their behaviour, so as to know them better and therefore serve them better; maybe also do some direct marketing, keeping them informed of new products and prices, etc.

3. What are your long-term needs, if everything develops according to plan?
   - I will not have the time to deal personally with as many clients as I'd like.
   - I will need programs that are more and more specialized; a large variety of programs for personal and professional use.
   - I'd like to link up all my offices/agencies/branches so that they all have the same information available to them.
   - All my billing and marketing, as well as my accounting, will be computerized.

It's up to you to answer these questions, and to decide what your present and long-term needs are. Be honest and realistic. And above all, keep a cool head on your shoulders. Don't look at this as a way of having fun.

How many people, out to start a small or medium-sized business, go and buy a computer first thing, because they think it's a serious move, it's professional, etc., even though they don't really need one to do a market study of their product or service?

How many people thought they got a good deal by buying an inexpensive micro-computer, only to find out later that:

- the machine is very limited in its capabilities;
- the machine is not able to answer growing needs;
- the number of available programs is very small, and what is available is not of a professional standard;
- the optional accessories (like extra memory chips, modems, mouse, interfaces, etc.) are very very expensive (when you can get them at all), or
- the company does not offer any after-sales service . . .

In other words, *take your time!*

Have you considered your needs and problems carefully? Let's move on to the apparatus itself.

Word-processing or accounting?

First, a slight clarification:

A word-processor is a program or a machine that allows you to make corrections easily, organize material, rearrange or restructure documents, to store them and have them at your disposal on command.

Since you are reading The Complete Time Management System, you can expect your functions and responsibilities to become more and more important in future.

Even though your present needs might only justify the purchase of a computer capable of word-processing, I would advise taking a look at some more sophisticated models. If you already have problems that necessitate the purchase of a word-processor, you might as well buy a personal computer that can do both word-processing and accounting.

Why? Because the price difference between a machine that does only word-processing, and one that does both word-processing and accounting, has become almost negligible.

Because in a year or two, when your job requirements have grown so that you need an accounting program, you will not appreciate being stuck with one that does word-processing and nothing but word-processing. Whereas a more sophisticated PC might only need a memory extension, or a graphic card to be able to fill your needs as your career develops.

But hold on a minute. Don't misunderstand me. I didn't say 'Go out and buy a sophisticated micro-computer', I said: 'If you already need a word-processor, you might as well buy a computer that can do accounting, desktop publishing, etc. as well.' There's a difference.

In God you should *trust*.
Everything else, you should *test*.

How to choose your computer

There are two main systems, more or less (these are the ones which will continue to dominate the market in the next few years): IBM and APPLE. You must have often heard the term 'Compatible'. This means compatible with IBM.

If you're not really adept with computers, if you think that a lot of people in your office will need computer training, if your needs are not very specific (or rare or unusual), if you're ready to pay a little more to have life simplified for you, then I would suggest that you buy an APPLE.

If you plan to be working with people who are already equipped with IBM, if you want to hook up a number of terminals, and augment the potential of your system as you go along, then I would suggest buying an IBM (or if you want to save money, an IBM 'clone' – a computer which is designed and built exactly like an IBM, is able to do the same things, but costs a lot less).

Compare the factors

Now compare:

The price of your set-up: this includes the main machines, as well as accessories like subsidiary terminals, printers, extra disk drives, hard disk, modems, graphic cards, connections, programs, diskettes, etc.

The programs available: make sure that the programs which are available suit your particular needs, and are accompanied by a detailed manual which is easy to understand. (Be prepared for surprises: why do you think bookshops are full of texts explaining how to use various programs?)

User friendly: the easier a program is to learn and use, the better. Factors like how fast it is, how clear the instructions on screen are, what books exist on how to exploit the program to the full, what courses are offered on the program ... all these are important to consider when choosing a system.

Reputation: are older models usable with new technology and programs? Often you just have to change a card or the 'mother board' in order to get an up-to-date computer. Make sure that the company you choose has such a policy.

After-sales service: consult relevant publications, talk to people about their experiences; it's extremely important to choose a name and a dealer that provide excellent after-sales service. Imagine yourself at work on a Monday morning, with your whole system out of order. If you rely heavily on computers, it can cost a whole week, for you as well as your associates.

Don't overlook after-sales service: you can't afford to. One more piece of advice on this subject: get into the habit of regularly making back-up diskettes, which means you store all your information on separate diskettes, which you leave at home or in some safe place other than your office: nothing is immune to fire, theft, negligence, etc., or just to some stupid mistake.

For example, on most IBM and compatible computers, all you have to do is try and 'format' the hard disk, the one where all your data is stored, to have it go up in smoke.

Then what do you do?

Buying a computer is a bit like buying a car: the final decision is up to you.

N.B. Before taking out your chequebook, ask your dealer for a little 'bonus': get him to throw in the word-processing program for free, ask for a 5 per cent discount, a few free disks and some free paper. You usually get at least some of what you ask for (the dealer market is very competitive), and anyway, it doesn't hurt to try, does it?

Ask people who know

The next time you meet someone whose work impresses you, ask them about their computer set-up, the hardware they have, and the programs they use.

Try to get them to let you in on some tricks, like making full use of the 'macro' options, etc. This will save you a lot of time finding out for yourself.

My favourite programs are:

- Xerox Ventura Publisher (desktop publishing)
- Wordperfect (word-processing)
- Corel Draw (types and drawing)
- Paradox (database)
- Quattro (spreadsheet)
- PC Tools (utility).

I recommend buying your programs through mail order companies: the service is reliable, prices are much lower than in shops, and the programs are not copy protected.

Should you get a fax machine?

These machines perform surprisingly well. In a few seconds, you can send a very complex, detailed letter, accompanied by a photograph or a graphic, to the other end of the world, for just the price of a long-distance phone call.

Fax machines (abbreviated from Facsimile) are booming all over the world. People are even buying them for their homes. In major cities, you can already find service outlets that will send a fax for you, just like making a photocopy in a shop (for a slightly higher price, of course).

Prices are still quite high, because most users are medium-sized and large businesses, but there are models available (which include telephone, telecopy and photocopy functions) for the price of a typewriter.

Personally, I couldn't do without my fax: ultra-fast, efficient, portable, modestly priced, it allows me to keep in touch, and to be reached by people, with unparallelled efficiency. And most models can also be used as simple photocopiers as well.

Employees are using fax machines more and more FOR INTERNAL OFFICE USE. They don't have to move around, delivering messages or memos personally; they don't even have to make phone calls ... they just send the information or the invoice direct. And unlike the telephone, the fax *doesn't interrupt you*. You can read the incoming information when you've finished what you're doing. You can also add a fax board to your computer. It will allow you to send faxes automatically at the date and time you wish, and to send the same fax to a group of recipients automatically.

All this technology saves us precious time, and among other things reduces the need for us to move around. But there is one form of communication that has been with us since the dawn of Man ... meetings!

That's what the next chapter's all about.

Why do something yourself when it can be done faster – and just as well – by a machine?

16

TRANSFORM YOUR MEETINGS INTO TOOLS FOR SUCCESS

Do you suffer from 'meetingitis'?

Meetings are essential: they are set up for direct communication, personal contact; they are indispensable for the establishment of a 'team spirit', and a sense of belonging to a company.

In meetings, misunderstandings arising from unclear memos, directives, reports, etc., which often lead to confusion, can usually be cleared up.

But usually, they aren't as effective as they could be. For example: how much time do you spend in meetings a year? Add up:

1. Conversations with another person

2. Personnel meetings

3. Directors' meetings.

   How much of this time is really productive?

How much does a meeting really cost?

Add up the number of minutes lost from:

- starting late;
- social chatter;
- digressions;
- etc.

... and multiply by the number of participants.

A recent study conducted by the American management consultants Booz, Alen & Hamilton concluded that 299 managers, at an average salary of $50,000 per year, spent *half their time* in meetings.

And that a large proportion of this time is wasted on:

- useless discussion;
- political manoeuvring;
- personal conflicts.

Exercise

Add up the hourly salaries of each of your colleagues
and
Multiply by the length of the meeting.

Don't forget to add travelling expenses (if some of the participants have to come in from elsewhere), time lost on conversation about other things, coffee breaks, etc.

You can make meetings pay

How?

1. In the role of chairperson, if you are aware of the *costs involved*, you will exercise firmer control.

2. You will share this information with the other participants.

3. You can display the cost per minute of each meeting. Participants will naturally become more disciplined if they know how much money their digressions cost.

What about a general rule?
Estimate the potential for profit of each meeting. Don't plan a meeting that will cost £10,000 for a potential profit of £1000.

To make sure that you don't call unnecessary meetings, ask yourself these questions, and try to answer them as simply as possible, without hesitation or rationalization, just with a yes or no:

1. Will the decisions taken at this meeting generate profits, if not now then at some point in the foreseeable future?

2. Are the meeting's objectives well defined?

3. Are there less costly alternatives, which might be faster and more convenient to all concerned, that could yield the same results?

What about the alternatives?

Very often we call meetings mechanically, out of habit, because that's what we've always done, and we think there's no reason to change.

But now that you're aware of the real costs involved in calling meetings (often quite high), you should ask yourself every time you're thinking about calling one, if there isn't an alternative method which would be cheaper in terms of time and money. And which would, in short, be *more effective*.

Here are a few alternatives that you might look into:

1. Information memos
   Instead of calling a meeting, circulate a memo which contains all the information you want people to know.

Comments and suggestions could be sent in the same way.

2. Suggestion notebook
   - First write the problem to be dealt with, or the goal to be achieved, in a notebook.
   - Place the notebook in a place that is accessible to everyone.
   - Let your associates know that they are welcome to add any suggestions, comments, etc. that they might have.
   - Make copies regularly, and have them circulated to the people concerned.

3. Have you thought about tele-conferencing? At a given hour, all participants call the same number. They can all talk to each other at once, as on a party line. Always appoint a chairperson if you want to avoid total chaos.

4. Computers also offer you an efficient way to conduct meetings without having to move, or waste any time.

Obviously, if a quick and important decision has to be made, it's better to use the telephone, telex, or a fax.

In the light of the different alternatives which we have just looked at, try to establish a list of those that could be useful in reducing the number of meetings you have to attend. And if you can come up with any others, don't hesitate to add them to your list.

Here's a table that will help you whenever the idea of holding a meeting occurs, either to you or to one of your colleagues. Also use

154 THE COMPLETE TIME MANAGEMENT SYSTEM

the chart for those meetings which have been going on for a long time, on a regular basis, and whose value or effectiveness have never been put in question.

1. Importance

- Why hold this meeting?
- What are the alternatives?
- tele-conferencing
- memo or message
- written report
- rapid decision
- integration with another meeting
- other
- Who should attend?

2. Preparation

- When?
- the best time would be
- because
- What are the objectives of the meeting?
- What subjects will be discussed?
- How much time will be allotted to each subject?
- Who will chair the meeting?
- Do you plan to deal with diverse topics?
- Have you organized a room and necessary equipment?
- Is the agenda ready?
- Are all the relevant documents ready?

3. Procedure

- Start on time, even if some people arrive late.

- Respect the agenda.

- Finish on time.

- Start with the easy topics.

- Deal with provocative topics last.

- Conclude by reading a résumé of the results of discussion.

4. Follow-up

- Get a written version of the meeting which includes:

o the decisions taken

o pertinent information

o resulting actions: by whom?

   how?

   when?

- Get a mailing or circulation list for this document (participants at the meeting *plus* any other people who might be concerned).

Always prepare an agenda

There's nothing more frustrating for someone than to get to a meeting and find that the agenda has not been set up in advance, realistically and precisely, as should be the case. This means that everyone is going to waste a lot of time.

I'm sure this has happened to you in the past at some point. You knew from the start that you would be wasting a lot of time, and that nothing productive would come of it. Maybe you even started asking yourself what you were doing there.

And if you were chairing the meeting, and had prepared a vague or incomplete agenda, you might have felt that you didn't have enough control over the situation. The meeting didn't go as well as you'd hoped.

Here is some advice:

1. Prepare an agenda in advance. Ideally, you should circulate the agenda two or three days before the meeting takes place. This will give the participants enough time to get together any pertinent documents.

2. Make an itemized list of the topics to be covered.

3. Draw up a questionnaire, making sure to indicate the name of the person responsible for each file or committee.

4. Place the questions in the exact order they are to be dealt with during the course of the meeting.

   Exhaust each topic before moving on to the next one.

   Tick off each point as it is settled.

5. Determine the time to be allotted to each topic, and respect this schedule down to the minute.

How to organize a super-productive meeting

Numerous studies have revealed the elements needed to organize an effective and productive meeting. These are:

1. **An effective chairperson who:**
   - can keep things moving rapidly along;
   - covers each point on the agenda in order, and in the allotted time;
   - involves each of the participants;
   - brings things to a clear conclusion, and gets the necessary decisions made.

   An excellent way of choosing a chairperson, if you haven't already done so, is the following:

   You count up to three. At three, each participant points to another. The person with the most votes is elected.

2. **Objectives are necessary**
Every meeting should have a reason behind it. Make sure that this

objective merits a meeting, and that its attainment is worthwhile.

3. A secluded space.

No telephone calls; nobody, not even your secretary, entering or even knocking (unless there's a real emergency).

The conference room should be away from office routine, and cut off from exterior noise, if possible.

4. A list of chosen participants.

- Keep the list as short as possible.
- General participation only under two conditions:
  (a) a general information meeting;
  (b) launching of a new project.
- When the meeting is called to analyse a given situation, or to make certain decisions, the *maximum number of participants should be seven.*

Be an active participant

Your role as a participant is extremely important if the meeting is to be productive.

Here's what you should do to really be a part of things:

1. Start cutting down the number of meetings you attend right away.

   Eliminate as many as possible, or find alternatives. A good way to reduce the number of meetings you have to attend is to schedule meetings with yourself!

2. Limit the time you spend in meetings. If you can't eliminate some meetings, then at least cut down on their duration. For example, ask yourself the question: 'Is it really necessary for this meeting to last two hours? Couldn't the same ground be covered in an hour? Or even in half an hour?'

3. Insist that the agenda be circulated in advance, and prepare yourself accordingly.

4. Be on time.

5. Bring a tape recorder.

6. Ask to take the minutes.

   The others will gladly appoint you minute-taker, and in this position you will be able to exercise better control over the discussions by asking pertinent questions at the right moment.

7. Study the other participants in order to get to know them better: look at their reactions, their knowledge, their strengths and weaknesses, body language, etc.

8. Don't talk unless someone asks your opinion.

9. Keep your comments brief and to the point.

10. Refuse all calls and messages until the meeting is over.

Control the meeting

If you chair the meeting, if you play the role of 'leader', then you're really in a position to make it productive.

Here's how:

1. Establish a clear objective.

2. Limit the number of participants. By doing this, you instil a sense of privilege among the participants.

3. Start on time. Here are a few methods to eliminate unnecessary lateness:
   - Don't stop to summarize what has already been covered for latecomers.
   - Insist on a fine (monetary) for each minute someone is late.
   - Lock the door after the meeting has started.
   - Make the last person to enter the room responsible for all typing and distribution of information concerning the meeting.

4. Use a stenographer, or a dictaphone if necessary. But if possible, opt for a brief summary of the main points established by each of the participants, to be written by someone designated at the start of the meeting.

5. Maintain control of the discussion.
   - Avoid all generalizations. Be clear, concise and precise.
   - Close each of the main points yourself by offering a short summary. Mention the conclusions that were reached to avoid any superfluous discussion.

- Get the conversation back to the point if it tends to digress too far, or for too long.

6. Finish on time. Never forget to end on an optimistic and encouraging note.
   Do you have trouble cutting down the length of your meetings? Here's how to do it:
   - Get rid of the chairs. When people are standing up, they tend to waste less time.
   - Cut down the allotted time. Instead of starting at 10 o'clock, start at 10.30.
   - Schedule meetings for before lunch, or before closing time.

7. Always determine the date of the next meeting immediately.

Do you know how to 'brainstorm'?

No one can deny that this technique of 'stirring up instant ideas' is surprisingly effective.

But this type of meeting can also cause considerable loss of time.

Here are a few pitfalls to avoid, in order to get the most out of brainstorming:

1. Get together in small groups of six to ten people.

2. Use a circular or U-shaped seating arrangement, with a blackboard or drawing pad facing the group.

3. Appoint someone to make notes of ideas on the board as they arise.

4. Display each new idea separately and clearly, so that the group can make a detailed analysis of each point.

5. Don't criticize, don't make any evaluations at this point.

6. Once the time limit for new ideas is up, proceed with their evaluation, and keep the three or four best ones for further study later on.

To make sure that you are getting the most out of your meetings, make use of the following checklist:

1. Only organize a meeting when there's a good reason to do so.

2. If you have to plan a series of meetings, try to group them together so as not to fragment your day completely.

3. Find a quiet place to hold your meeting.

4. Only include those people who are directly involved in the problems to be discussed.

5. Have your secretary screen all visits and calls while you're in the meeting.

6. Prepare a systematic agenda with a detailed breakdown of subjects.

7. Make sure to indicate the name of the person responsible beside each topic of discussion.

8. Start the meeting on time.

9. Make sure the participants stick to the agenda.

10. Choose a chairperson to keep the meeting going according to plan.

11. Stick to the essentials. Cut short any unnecessary discussion.

12. Only allow questions that lead to specific and not general discussion of the problem in hand.

13. If a problem cannot be resolved, appoint someone to conduct further investigations, and put it on the agenda for the next meeting.

14. At the end of each meeting, decide on the date and time for the next one.

15. If you have to attend a meeting, you can ask to be present only during the part of the discussion that concerns you directly.

16. Submit a written report, if circumstances justify it, instead of attending a meeting personally.

17. Ask others to submit written reports instead of calling them to a meeting.

18. End the meeting at the designated time.

19. Always end on a positive, stimulating, optimistic note.

Use shock tactics

We have seen how to make your meetings a success, by keeping the time allotted down to a minimum, and by exploiting the situation to the full.

But there is another kind of meeting which we haven't looked at yet, and which can be very useful.

It's called 'Master Mind'. It has been superbly analysed by Napoleon Hill in his book *Think and Grow Rich*.

Have you ever had that unpleasant feeling that you were spending hours trying to find a solution to some problem, when you could solve it in a few minutes, if you only had someone to help you?

You may waste hundreds of hours a year this way, with the answer you're looking for just out of reach ... well, actually, in somebody else's head!

Another person might find the solution right away. Not because he or she is cleverer, or more experienced than you are.

No. It's just because they're different!

Their experience is different from yours, and can complement it.

That's why most large companies use the Master Mind (or Think Tank) technique. And what is most surprising is that the people invited to participate are not necessarily specialists in the field, who are expected to give a dissertation.

Follow Henry Ford's example

Henry Ford didn't spend much time at school. Maybe that's why the *Chicago Tribune* labelled some of his statements about World War I 'ignorant raving!'

This caused a scandal. Ford sued the newspaper for libel. The newspaper's lawyers demanded to question Ford, so that they could prove their client was correct. And they asked the following question:

'How many soldiers did the British send to crush the revolt of the colonies in 1776?'

Ford answered with a mischievous smile: 'A lot more than went back to England!'

Everyone in the room started to laugh, including the lawyer who asked the question.

The interrogation continued along the same lines. The lawyers kept asking questions which were intended to ridicule Ford's knowledge and competence. Eventually Ford got pretty upset.

To conclude the discussion, he said that he had a row of buttons on his desk, and when he needed an answer to a question, he would press a button and the person who knew most about it would come into his office.

Use the knowledge of people around you

Ford went on to say that he had no need to fill his head with all kinds of information, since the people around him knew most of it already.

Do you want to do better than Henry Ford?

Do you want to have an inexhaustible reservoir of information at your disposal?

Well then, set up your Master Mind!

How to create a Master Mind

The first condition is that all the people involved must share a common and well-defined goal.

Start by establishing a common objective. This will also determine who is to be part of the group.

First invite two or three associates, whom you know pretty well, to a preliminary meeting, where you will explain your idea (setting up a Master Mind group) and then define and determine an objective. If they accept and wish to be part of the experience, proceed as follows:

To avoid running around in circles, establish these rules right from the start.

1. First, clearly explain the objective you are after.

2. Make it clear that you have no interest in forming a debating society. The purpose is to attain a specific objective.

3. Avoid all discussion of politics, religion, sport, etc.

4. These discussions should be confidential. No information should be leaked to the outside.

5. Don't hesitate to accept new members, as long as the productivity of the Master Mind group as a whole benefits.

6. Accept temporary members as well.
   You can call on the expertise of resource people, if it's in the interest of the group.
   Don't cut the group off from all exterior influences. Screen them instead, and accept them only when they coincide with the group's objectives.

7. Each member should have a turn chairing a session. Obviously, the techniques for controlling meetings should be applied even more stringently here.

8. Don't limit membership to colleagues only. Call in superiors and subordinates as well.

The only rule is: attain the objective.

Apply the principles of excellence

By creating a Master Mind group, you will be sowing the seeds of enthusiastic, creative and team spirit in your business, as well as stimulating a desire for excellence in the pursuit of a common goal.

If 'two heads are better than one', then three are better than two, and so on.

Be careful. There is one danger to avoid. As David Ogilvy said: 'I never saw anyone erect a statue to honour a committee!'

Use the Master Mind group to cultivate, criticize and clarify ideas, to make connections, etc. But don't forget that in the final analysis, you are the one who will make the final decision. You and you alone.

Having recourse to a collective brain, which is what Master Mind is, can be very useful. But you can't use it every day. So what do you do when confronted with a problem that you can't solve alone?

What do you do when you are overloaded with work, and discover that you will not be able to complete a certain job on time?

In the next chapter, I will explain not only how to save an enormous amount of time, but also how to improve noticeably the quality of the time you do spend working.

**Don't call a meeting that costs £10,000
for a decision that's worth £1000!**

17

HOW TO SUCCEED BY HELPING OTHERS SUCCEED

You can't succeed on your own

'I don't feel right unless I do it myself.'

'If you want something done properly, do it yourself!'

How many times have you heard sentiments like these expressed by people you know?

Well, what's more important? Doing the work yourself – often pushing yourself to the limit so that you have no time to enjoy life – or making sure that the work gets done?

If you're not convinced that the work could be done by someone else (and maybe even better), start by asking yourself: who did the work before you turned up?

The answer is obvious.

Nevertheless, for all sorts of reasons – excuses, I should say – you have never asked yourself this question, or you never wanted to answer it, which comes to the same thing.

You don't delegate enough

There are numerous reasons that people find not to delegate, or at least not to delegate enough.

Do you excel in what you do? Then why not take the opportunity to delegate interesting jobs to colleagues who might be less gifted than you? This is what Andrew Carnegie had carved into his tombstone:

Here lies a man who knew how to get people to work for him
that were better than he was!

Was Andrew Carnegie an incompetent? Not at all. For many years, he was considered to be the richest man in the United States. When he sold his company, US Steel, at the turn of the century he got $350 million for it, a fabulous sum at the time.

If Andrew Carnegie went to the trouble of having this eulogy to delegation carved on his gravestone, then he must have thought it was pretty important to his success.

It's really not difficult to comprehend . . .

What do empire builders do? They might start by doing things on their own. But they quickly get other people to work for them. How else could they suddenly find themselves directing a company with 10,000 employees, or even 100,000?

The equation is simple.

Delegate or stagnate

People who don't delegate at all are condemning themselves to a state of stagnation, since the number of hours available in a week is limited. Those who delegate most, make the most progress. Finally, most of their time is spent getting things done by others, motivating them and supervising them.

This is so true that highly successful managers spend as much as 40 per cent of their time doing it.

How to take the step and delegate more

The fears that prevent you from delegating more are numerous and often subtle. They can result from:

1. Lack of experience in your present position, or with your associates.

2. Lack of overall vision, or interest in your company.

3. Your personal insecurity, and your fear of losing some of your power by ceding part of it to others.

4. Your perfectionist tendencies.

5. Your need to feel constantly almost overloaded with work.

6. Lack of clear personal goals and ambitions that stimulate you always to look for challenging responsibilities.

These fears are not always conscious. And they are not (or very rarely) formalized.

30 excuses for not delegating

What are clear, on the other hand, are the excuses we come up with every day. Here is a series of 30 excuses that express a refusal to delegate, or a tendency to delegate only partially. Note the ones that apply to you:

1. 'If my associates were more mature, and had more experience, maybe I would delegate more. But at the moment I don't think I can take the risk.'

2. 'Explaining what has to be done takes as long as doing it myself. So what's the point?'

3. 'I only delegate a part of the work to be done. In this way, I know exactly what's going on and can spot any errors as they happen.'

4. 'I prefer delegating the same job to two employees at the same time. It's interesting to see how each of them does the work. In this way, I "divide and rule".'

5. 'Me? Delegate? I leave it to Number One to do all the important jobs, difficult or not.'

6. 'I really can't delegate. Can you see me giving some new job to an employee who then comes along and wants to be upgraded to a position that includes his new work? No thanks, not for me!'

7. 'Why should I even try it? Really, I mean these days, who wants more responsibility? So ... you understand ...'

8. 'Logically, I can't see why I should confer added responsibility on someone who takes orders from me and who, in the final analysis, is not the one in charge in case there's any problem anyway!'

9. 'I don't delegate because I have a large capacity for work. I like to be constantly busy, under pressure. That's how I work best.'

10. 'If I delegate something and there's a problem, then I have to explain to my superiors what really happened, and implicate my employee as well, something I really don't like to do.'

11. 'If I delegate, I might lose control. I'm not sure how I'm supposed to co-ordinate the work so I don't lose it. It's all too complicated.'

12. 'No, I do the work much faster myself.'

13. 'If I start delegating things, there won't be anything left for me to do!'

14. 'I don't want my employees to have too much power. You know what happens ... they start thinking they're indispensable.'

15. 'I must admit, I'm a perfectionist. I want things done my way. I can't accept it when they're not. So I can't delegate.'

16. 'Why should I delegate and take an unnecessary risk, when I know very well I can do the job myself?'

17. 'My boss is very concerned about this project. It's better if I do the work myself.'

18. 'I can't really delegate because my immediate superior often checks up on what I'm doing.'

19. 'I'm hesitant about delegating work, because whenever my boss needs some information about a job that is being done by one of my employees, he goes over my head and asks them directly.'

20. 'I don't really know how to delegate. I don't know where to start. I think it's safer if I just continue with my routine work.'

21. 'Delegate? So that someone can go and steal my job? No thanks!'

22. 'When I finish a job, I like to be recognized for what I've done. If I delegate a job to another employee, who do you think is going to get the credit?'

23. 'My work team is structured a little like a club. Each member has to go through an initiation. So in my case, delegating is limited to having young employees, who are new on the job, do minor tasks.'

24. 'Oh well, I've already tried delegating work, but I always seemed to choose people who couldn't get the job done. And when I

wanted to explain what had to be done, they would start joking around and asking stupid questions.'

25. 'I like to discover the real character of my staff. So sometimes I give them work to do, without telling them everything they should know about the problem. Like this, they learn the hard way, but they don't forget either!'

26. 'Here's a case in point: I had some work I wanted to delegate. I thought Elizabeth would be best for the job. But Marie was really hoping to get the added responsibility, and she's been with us much longer than Elizabeth. So I was afraid Marie would take it badly, and ask to be transferred.'

27. 'Another case in point: I hate asking Henry to do something for me. Do you know why? Because he has such a big mouth, and never stops asking me why I had to choose him for the job.'

28. 'Yes, I would like to delegate some work. But I don't have anyone available at the moment. All my personnel are so busy, you understand ...'

29. 'Helen would really like to be given the north-west service to take care of, but between you and me, I don't think she's ready for the job. And if I did give it to her, who'd take care of her own work? Too complicated ...'

30. 'Every time I delegate something for John to do, he asks for a written description of the job. Oh, I know a lot of managers are used to doing this, but I'm not so sure it's a good idea. So you see, for some time now I've been avoiding delegating anything to John.'

Adapt your delegating style to the people concerned

In his book *13 Fatal Errors Committed by Managers and How to Avoid Them*, W. Steven Brown, President of the American publishing consortium Fortune, explains:

A manager who tries to direct each member of his staff in the same way, using a single technique, can expect to be greatly let down. He will never achieve success (and will probably spend long hours asking him or herself why). An effective manager is aware of the differences in personality of his staff, and taking their strengths and weaknesses into account, directs them by above all treating them as individuals.

A little later in the chapter, he illustrates this point with a short anecdote:

> I often hear managers complaining that a certain employee is worthless because he or she doesn't respond to a certain motivational technique like the others. One day, a manager asked me if he should fire one of his employees for this reason.
>
> I asked him to show me his keychain. Surprised, he handed it to me. I held up a key. 'What does this key open?' I asked.
>
> 'The door to my car,' he answered.
>
> 'Does it also open the door to your wife's car?'
>
> 'No, obviously not.'
>
> 'Well, it's the same for your technique. It can work for one person, and not for another.'

To delegate effectively, you should always be aware of the personal element.

Why delegate?

Here are seven good reasons why:

1. Delegate to have more time for your own work.

2. Delegate to improve the skills, enlarge the field of activity, and raise the level of competence of your employees.

3. Delegate to motivate your staff, to challenge them with stimulating work.

4. Delegate to help identify employees who merit promotion.

5. Delegate to increase your company's productivity.

6. Delegate when a job could be done better and/or quicker by somebody else.

7. Delegate so that your employees will eventually be able to take over the routine parts of your work, and ensure that everything keeps running smoothly.

What not to do

- Delegate anything that is considered confidential information.
- Delegate the task of disciplining someone.
- Delegate, and then allow your employees to come back and delegate their own problems to you.
- Delegate because you don't like the work.
- Delegate responsibility that is too delicate, and that will probably come back to you anyway.

You should always:

- Accord your employees a margin of creativity and autonomy, as well as your confidence.
- Develop a sense of belonging in your employees.
- Assure your employees that while they're doing a job for you, they will always have your support if needed.
- Make sure you and your employee fully understand the objectives, the means you allow, and the criteria that will permit you both to judge the final result.

How to delegate a job to an employee

1. You must have a clear and precise vision of the task you want to delegate: exactly what do you expect from your employee? How can you evaluate his or her performance with precision and objectivity?

2. Explain exactly what you expect the employee to do for you. Go over the work to be done a few times to make sure everything is understood.

3. Explain *why* the job has to be done.

4. Personally show the employee how to do the work, and make sure everything is understood. For example, once you've finished, you can ask him or her to describe the work to be done in a few short sentences.

5. Provide all and any pertinent information related to the task that you want to delegate, as well as some information about the other people involved in the work.

6. Discuss what would constitute a reasonable time period for completion of the job with the person you delegate it to, and establish a realistic schedule for each stage of the work.

7. Set a firm date for the finished job.

8. Provide the person with whatever materials and degrees of authority are necessary to get the job done. Make sure that the person also understands the limits of his or her responsibility.

9. Ask to be presented with reports on the various stages of completion, at convenient intervals.

10. Supervise the quality of the work as it moves along. Provide your employee with a lot of feedback.

11. Evaluate the overall performance with your employee, basing your decisions on criteria established earlier.

12. Reward and encourage as the need arises.

How to delegate within a working team

1. Distribute a list to all employees: job description, time limit (overall and stage by stage), level of quality required, performance criteria.

2. Set up a strategy board, where you can, at a glance, identify who is responsible for which tasks.

3. Distribute work equitably.

4. Evaluate the work in private, you and the person who did it. Never make remarks in front of others, except in the case of an exceptionally good performance.

5. Offer a suitable reward to anyone who has accomplished their task well (e.g. a raise, a favourable report, a new title, a bonus, etc.) especially if the job was long and/or difficult.

Ten practical points

Before – During – After

Do's

Don'ts

1. Examine your employees' attitudes closely, so that you will be able to judge their capacity to execute a given task without risk to yourself.

Explain your decision to the employee: link what you consider positive attitude and abilities to the exigencies of the task.

Under no circumstances should you make excuses for having chosen such and such a person for the job. It's your responsibility, and yours alone.

Never put yourself on the defensive.

2. When you delegate some important work, it's a good idea to relieve the person of some of his or her usual duties.

Don't let yourself be manipulated by your employees. Avoid inverse delegation (work that comes back to you) except under special circumstances.

3. If your employee does a good job, let him or her know about it.

Don't flatter. Be objective, and mention weaknesses as well as strengths.

4. Plan an alternative solution in case a delegated job meets with failure.

When things don't work out, try to avoid all those interminable disputes as to what really happened. They are not constructive.

5. Be precise when giving directions, and plan for the worst. Break down the work to be done, and encourage questions.

Don't improvise with an employee. Don't keep any necessary information to yourself. This can be very destructive, and lead to failure.

6. For some people, being chosen to do a job is an honour and a challenge. But remember that for others, the same job might just represent additional, unwanted stress.

Don't blame your employee, if failure is your fault. Authority does not give you the right to blame others for your own mistakes. Doing this causes you to *lose* authority.

8. Make your employees responsible for their work. If they make mistakes, let them know, simply and directly. Use precise examples to back up your criticism.

Don't threaten, don't blackmail. It usually doesn't do any good to 'report' someone. You're better off thinking about what you did wrong.

9. When an employee tries to tell you what you think about his or her work, stop them and ask questions. What do they think of their own work? What problems are they having? Then simply restate, in your own words, what they just told you.

Any clear-cut judgement that uses the verb 'to be' destroys communication. 'You are an imbecile', for example, does nothing to help, and places future relations in jeopardy. You should rather talk about behaviour: 'You behaved in such and such a way ... what are you going to do about it in future?'

10 If you have trouble delegating, ask for the help of a colleague, a consultant or a friend. You must learn to delegate!

Don't talk badly about an employee to others. They will start asking themselves what you might be saying about them, and will start spreading rumours.

How to recruit a specialist

When you start delegating regularly, it often happens that you need to call in an outside specialist.

In general, this is an excellent practice, which often becomes indispensable. Specialists – if they are competent – can often save you enormous amounts of time. Even if their rates seem expensive, their services frequently turn out to be extremely profitable.

But you still have to know how to choose a specialist. Take the following precautions:

1. Contact a number of specialists and compare their prices with those which are currently on the market. Are they higher? If so, ask them to justify their fees.

   Are their rates a lot lower?

   This should arouse your suspicions. Bargains are not always a good thing. As they say ... 'You get what you pay for!'

If the price is very cheap, you risk getting inferior service.

Remember that good specialists are never expensive, even if they charge a lot. The only criterion for your decision should be the service's profit potential.

For my part, I've had some bad experiences with bargain specialists, and so now I only work with the best, or at least highly reputed specialists whom I sometimes, I must admit, pay very well. But I always get it back in the end.

2. If you're hiring someone for the first time, check up on their training. Where did they study? How long have they been in business? (Don't forget that there are beginners out there who offer excellent service, and whose enthusiasm can be an added plus to their performance.)

3. Essential questions:
   - What experience do they have?
   - Who have they worked for? Can you contact a referee?

Obviously, there is professional discretion to consider.

But, as much as possible, and without obliging the person to infringe the ethics of his profession (if he does you should be careful ... he'll do the same with your competitors, and might reveal confidential information) ask for precise figures.

For example: the job is an ad. What campaigns has this person designed, and for whom?

What were the results of the campaign? Was the client satisfied? Has he or she ever lost a client, or an important contract, and for what reason?

Without becoming paranoid, it's better to ask the questions *before* you hire someone, than to find yourself with a pile of unpleasant surprises to deal with later.

To delegate or not to delegate ... is that still the question?

If you're still not convinced, after reading this whole chapter, about just how important delegating work is, go back to Chapter Four.

The more your time is worth, the more you should delegate.

And so that your delegating becomes as profitable as possible, follow the golden rule, as stated by Stephanie Winston:

Delegate the task to the person lowest on the ladder, who still possesses the qualifications to get the job done. (If there's no one who fits this condition, then hire someone.)

If you're one of those managers (and there are many) who spend only half or a third of their time doing jobs which are at their optimum performance level, then you're costing your company a lot of money, and you're wasting your own time, energy and potential.

You should take immediate steps to start delegating advantageously, so that you can substantially increase the amount of time you spend at tasks that meet your performance level.

Be firm!

Delegate more!

Your employees will enjoy working with you a lot more because they will be motivated; they'll feel that they're important, that they are playing an integral role in the company's success.

Don't forget that by helping others to succeed, you're also doing a lot for yourself. It's really the only way to achieve success that is important and lasting.

We are now going to see how we can save time, and often a lot of time, by communicating well.

I beg your pardon? You communicate every day, and you don't have the impression that you're wasting any time? That's possible. But here's a way to communicate even better, and to save a lot of time . . .

18

COMMUNICATE
MORE EFFICIENTLY

In the preceding chapter, we looked at all the subtle aspects of delegating work.

One of the essential elements for delegating effectively is good communication between the parties concerned. How often do problems arise along the way, or on completion of a project, because of unclear or misinterpreted communication?

You have no doubt been the victim of aggravated misunderstandings yourself. The worst thing about this kind of situation is that, all too often, the people involved don't even realize that the problem originated from unclear communication.

They look for all kinds of other reasons, and find remedies that don't really work, because they don't deal with the true source of the problem.

I'm sure you already realize that efficient communication is not only necessary, but *indispensable* to success. People who don't know how to communicate, are incapable of motivating their associates, of giving clear instructions to employees, of receiving them from their boss, of giving presentations, introducing projects, etc.

They not only lose an enormous amount of time because of the misunderstandings and imprecisions resulting from their bad communication technique, they also let innumerable opportunities for success pass them by. This is what we'll be talking about in greater detail in this chapter.

> **'The reason why we have two ears and only one
> mouth is that we may listen more and talk less.'**
>
> *Zeno*

Learn to 'decode'

In his fascinating work *The Secrets of Fortune*, Uri Geller, the man who became famous throughout the world by bending spoons with his psychic power, tells this instructive story:

> One of my friends recently went to India, and had an especially frustrating experience trying to take a taxi to the beach in Bombay.
>
> Each time he hailed a taxi and told the driver where he wanted to go, the man would move his head from side to side, left to right, in a strange gesture which my friend took to mean an emphatic 'no!'

What was going on? Has something like this happened to you? Let's read the explanation Uri Geller offered:

> The truth is, all the drivers were expressing their willingness to take on the fare, using the local body language; a side to side movement of the head, to express their assent.
>
> My friend's frustration, therefore, arose from an incapacity to communicate properly. He didn't understand that in Bombay, moving the head from left to right means 'yes', while the occidental gesture of moving the head up and down, for them means 'no!'

How to do it

Whatever the poet may have said, every man is an island. Which means that each person has his own language. If we don't know how to decode, we can't create bridges between the islands.

This defect, this inability to decode, leads to daily problems like:

- misunderstandings;
- bad decisions;
- unattained goals;
- hiring errors;
- breakdowns in negotiation.

All these things invariably lead to loss of time and money.

A costly communication error

Bad communication can sometimes even lead to real disaster, including loss of life.

Take this tragic example: a few years ago, an American space shuttle, which cost taxpayers billions of dollars to build, exploded a few seconds after lift-off, killing everyone aboard. After a painstaking and detailed investigation, the error was identified.

Was it a technical fault? Of course, otherwise the tragedy would not have occurred.

But it went deeper than that. The important thing was why this technical error was allowed to happen.

And can you guess what the real culprit was? An error in communication! In her work *The Organized Manager*, Stephanie Winston explains:

> It is possible – and even probable – that the Three Mile Island crisis could have been avoided, if the people who constructed the nuclear reactor had organized their paperwork a little better.
>
> As troubling as this may sound, my experience as an organizational consultant leads me to believe that the Three Mile Island incident was caused by an inefficient circulation of reports!

Each time you're getting ready to launch an idea or a project, think of that American space shuttle, and never underestimate the importance of communication.

Above all ... good communication means good listening

A recent study of a large number of company presidents in France surprised the researchers, a group of management consultants.

They asked the following question:

'In your opinion, what is the most important quality of a good company president?'

Obviously, there were various responses, but do you think one of the following topped the list?

- Leadership
- The ability to make quick decisions
- Business acumen.

No! The prizewinner was:

The ability to L-I-S-T-E-N!

That's right! Not really all that surprising. Because all successful directors, as well as politicians, businessmen, negotiators, etc. pride themselves (and justifiably so) on being, above all else, excellent communicators!

They know how to communicate their ideas, their ambitions, dreams, their vision of the future, their concept of a project that might be totally new and audacious! But to do these things, to be able to boast (rightly) about being a good communicator, to have the capacity to identify the real source of a problem and know what to do about it, whether with a client or a boss, you have to start by listening!

And if you were asked the question: 'Do you know how to listen?' What would you reply?

Not sure? Not good enough! Here is a very instructive test, that will allow you to evaluate your own communication skills, and to decide immediately what corrective measures you should take to increase your effectiveness, and, as a bonus, make the people around you a lot happier.

Yes No

1. Are you attentive when others are talking to you?

2. Do you like observing other people?

3. Do you provide non-verbal feedback when someone is talking to you (nods of the head, smiles, etc.)?

4. Do you take notes when someone is giving you important instructions?

5. Do you let people finish expressing their point of view before you start talking?

6. Do you stick to the subject, or do you have a tendency to digress?

7. Are you open to other people's points of view?

8. Do you use language that other people can understand?

9. Are you interested in what other people have to say?

10. Are you patient when someone has problems expressing what they want to say?

Do you waste 13 weeks a year without realizing it?

An analysis of 18 executives selected from different American companies showed that people in these positions spend an average of $5\frac{1}{2}$ hours a day communicating verbally. It was also established that of those $5\frac{1}{2}$ hours, 2 hours were a total loss.

Two hours a day means 10 hours a week, and 520 hours a year.

If we base our calculations on a 40-hour working week, that gives us 13 wasted weeks per year.

Thirteen weeks!

People are always complaining that they don't have enough time to take holidays, while they waste 13 weeks a year on totally useless communication.

What about you? What are your communication habits like? How much time do you spend talking each week? Keep a journal of your conversations. You will be amazed. Over a one-week period, make a note of all the time you spend communicating.

Communication Journal

Monday

Tuesday

Wednesday

Thursday

Friday
Saturday
Sunday

Now that you've filled your communication journal, do some addition: you will now have a more precise idea of the time you spend communicating. Identify those aspects of your communication which waste time.

1. If someone has to communicate a lot of details, don't waste time noting them all down on the spot.

    Instead, ask for a list to be sent to your office. You will save time, and avoid possible errors due to inexact or insufficient notes.

2. Try to prepare for your conversations by having all the necessary information at hand. Establish beforehand the precise aim of the conversation, and all the points that you want to cover. All documents and files should be assembled beforehand, by you, your secretary or an assistant.

3. Avoid long introductions, repetition, and inevitable digressions. When they occur, as they invariably do, limit their duration by firmly insisting on sticking to the matter in hand.

4. Get to the point immediately. Don't beat around the bush. No superfluous details. Your time, and your associates' time, is precious.

5. Take time to explain things in depth. Better provide too many details than too few. The time you spend explaining might seem like a waste, but in the long run it doesn't add up to much.

Remember the paradox of the man in a hurry. The time you spend explaining is nothing compared to the time lost because of misunderstandings, which often result in having to start all over again.

A golden rule of communication

Always keep this golden rule of communication in mind:

What may seem obvious, clear and straightforward to you, is not necessarily so to your listener.

So don't be hesitant to explain things clearly.

Make sure that the project or task is well understood by everyone involved, in all its dimensions, by clearly defining important details, time limit and the general spirit in which it is to be carrried out.

In the next chapter we will see how to communicate effectively, and gain as much time as possible, by employing a communication tool that is often not used to full advantage.

19

TRAVEL HUNDREDS OF MILES IN A FEW SECONDS

Do you run when you're called?

One day, the British ambassador was received at the White House by President Franklin Roosevelt.

Like all presidents, the President of the United States was a very busy man.

But he also had the disturbing habit of accepting phone calls, even when he was in a meeting with someone as important as the ambassador.

And since the telephone rang continuously, the discussion between the two men made hardly any progress at all, so that the ambassador began to fear that they would never get round to the subjects he'd come to talk about.

What to do?

He couldn't slam his fist down on the table and demand that the President pay attention. He was an ambassador, and therefore much too diplomatic to do anything like that.

Then he had an idea.

While the President was absorbed on the phone, the ambassador discreetly left the office, went into the next room and called the President himself.

In this way, he was finally able to discuss the subjects that were important to him at length.

**How much time do you spend
on the telephone every day?**

**How much time do you
waste on the telephone
every day?**

Break your conditioned reflex

We're all a bit like President Roosevelt . . .

Like a faithful servant, we run when we're called. Habit or curiosity usually wins out, and we break the firm resolve we made not to be disturbed while working. This conditioned reflex is one of the most subtle and consuming ways we waste time.

What can we do?

Don't accept any calls when there's someone in your office. Instruct your secretary to take messages.

Two exceptions: if you get a call from someone really important, someone who would add to your prestige in the eyes of your visitor, then accept the call. Or if the call is directly related to the discussion or negotiation at hand, then accept it.

Danger: ten, twenty, thirty times a day, the phone rings and tears us away from what we're doing. We spend many minutes, sometimes hours, talking needlessly on the phone.

Some surprising statistics about the telephone

From anywhere in the world, at any time of the night or day, we can be reached by phone. This can be great, of course, but it can also result in certain inconveniences. For example, we don't really have any private life left.

It's extremely important to know just how long we spend on the phone every day, and what kind of conversations we have.

Statistics on the subject are surprising:

- 90% of executives spend more than an hour a day on the phone.
- 40% of executives spend more than two hours a day on the phone!

What about you? How long do you spend on the phone every day?

What are your telephone habits?

That's what we're going to discover together in this chapter. When you've finished reading and done the exercises, you will be in a position to reduce your telephone use by 25 to 50 per cent, without diminishing your productivity in the least. Not bad, wouldn't you agree?

It is very possible that you will save an hour a day, or five hours a week, or 250 hours a year. Time which you can use to concentrate on important work, or better still spend on leisure with your family or friends, learning, doing sports, travelling, etc. In short . . . living!

Here is a test which will help you discern your telephone habits.

TEST   Yes No

1. Are you the type of person who 'runs' to the phone every time it rings?

2. Does answering the phone affect your concentration? If yes, how?

_____

_____

3. If the phone keeps on ringing because no one answers:
   (a) Do you get nervous?
   (b) Do you feel you have to answer?

4. How much time do you spend on the telephone?
   per day?   number of hours _____
   per week?   number of hours _____
   per month?   number of hours _____

Daily Record

Date	Call: In/Out	Length of Call	Reason

Keep track of the number of calls you make and receive, their duration, and cause. Finished? What are the results? You're probably surprised by the amount of time you invest in the telephone. Have patience. We are going to arrange it so that your future investments will result in twice as much profit. The phone's ringing!

Stop! Why hurry? You should learn always to think before picking up the receiver. One of the best ways of saving time is to ask yourself the question: 'Who should answer the phone?' There are two possible situations: with or without a secretary.

Who should answer the phone?
1. Without a secretary

Answering the phone is an interruption, therefore a break in your activity. In addition to the time the call takes, and the energy you might waste by becoming upset, you have to account for the time it takes to regain your concentration and get back to work (not forgetting that a phone call is always more enervating than a working session, which can actually calm you down).

Do you share a work space with other people? In this case, the best solution consists of establishing a rotating system, either on a daily, weekly, or monthly basis.

Say you're six people sharing a space, and the calls come in regularly throughout the day. Set up a rotating system something like the following:

9 to 10 o'clock	Carla
10 to 11 o'clock	Phil
11 to 12 o'clock	Estelle
12 to 1 o'clock	Answering Machine
1 to 2 o'clock	George
2 to 3 o'clock	Lillian
3 to 4 o'clock	Charles
4 to 5 o'clock	Carla
5 to 7 o'clock	Answering Machine

Sound good to you? Then make it work for you!

If you're more than six, or if your daily schedules are not always the same, use a weekly rotation.

For example:

	Monday	Tuesday	Wednesday	Thursday	Friday
9 to 10					
10 to 11					
11 to 12					
12 to 1					
1 to 2					
2 to 3					
3 to 4					
4 to 5					
5 to 6					
6 to 7					

After 7 . . . Answering or Fax Machine

While we're on the subject, make sure that the messages received by the answering or fax machine are expedited quickly and correctly to their respective destinations: the person responsible for this should be aware of the importance of his or her job.

Post a sheet of instructions near the answering machine and the fax machine, listing any maintenance, tricks, idiosyncrasies, etc. of the system (how to add paper to the fax, how to erase messages, etc.).

Appoint someone to make sure the machines have enough supplies. You don't want to find yourself without paper for the fax, or tape for the answering machine, when it's too late to buy any.

Suggestions for your answering machine message? It's extremely important to be clear and concise. Make it as short as possible, taped in a warm, friendly, clear voice. Avoid being playful or eccentric.

For example:

1. General:

'This is Terma Publications. I can't answer your call at the moment, but if you leave your name, telephone number, and the reason for your call after the tone, I'll get back to you as soon as possible. Thank you.'

2. Particular:

'This is Terma Publications. Please state your name, telephone number, the person you wish to reach, and the reason for your call. Someone will get back to you within twenty-four hours. You have two minutes after the tone. Thank you.'

Delegate your calls

Do you have associates? Delegate at least some of your calls to them (and I assure you it's possible!) by naming them 'personal representatives' of clients X, Y, Z or 'responsible' for sectors X, Y, Z. They will then communicate, in résumé form, what was discussed, any problems that might have arisen, offers made, etc.

You will not take these calls except under special circumstances, where a problem calls for your personal attention, your authority and/or experience. Result? Your clients will be able to reach someone who is more available than you, while you will gain precious time which you can invest elsewhere, especially in work that is much more profitable and interesting.

Are you only two or three sharing a space? Show your colleagues how much time they could save if the task of answering the phone for one hour, two hours, or a whole day at a time, were delegated on a rotating basis. Calculate the actual time saved with them, use all the arguments cited in Chapter Thirteen about how costly inter-ruptions are ... and soon you will be enjoying long uninterrupted periods of peaceful work, where you can concentrate and so improve your creativity and effectiveness.

The 'stop' technique

You suddenly remember you have to make a phone call? Stop! Make a note of it and get back to work. Do this every time you feel like picking up the receiver: Stop!

You will soon be fusing one call into many, you will discover that some calls aren't necessary, and most importantly, you will make the calls whenever there's a lull in your schedule (or when you're a little tired, or want to do something else for a while, etc.). That's when you pull the five or ten calls off your list and make them.

Result? You will soon see the advantage of making five or ten calls at a time: you'll do each one more quickly, you'll be more concise, you'll get right to the point, you'll be in your 'phone mode' (which demands a kind of concentration that is very different from when you're studying a file, for example) and therefore at your best, ready for action.

So start making calls in blocks of five or ten, and you will soon realize just how much this technique can help you in your quest for success.

While we're on the subject, I would recommend making yourself a personal phone record. It should contain the following information:

Call _____ Date_____ Time _____

Number _____ Place_____

Notes _____

_____

_____

A last word of advice

Be prepared. Have a list of calls you have to make (written messages or computer files). Organize them in order of priority to make the task of calling easier.

Determine when you're going to call in advance, especially taking into account the schedules of the people you want to reach. This way you can plan your day better, and avoid making unnecessary calls. Some people have strange hours. Be aware of that. It might be easier to reach Mr So-and-So a few minutes after office hours, etc.

Another technique to save time:

Recently, a managing director told me he always calls people, even if he knows they aren't there. He leaves a message, asking the person to call back (with a precise date and time). And he makes a note in his diary, on the date he thinks he should try again, if the person hasn't called or been able to reach him.

Who should answer the phone?
2. With a secretary

Whether your secretary is experienced or not, take a few moments to introduce him or her to your new methods. (We will assume that your secretary is a woman, not out of any sexist bias, but to avoid having to indicate 'him or her' all the time.)

First, explain what you expect of her, that she is your representative and therefore an emanation of yourself.

She should, if possible, be pleasant, gentle, charming, attentive, professional, as much with your personal visitors as with the people who call you on the phone. This is very important: tell her that often clients only have a single clue on which to base their opinion of your business – your secretary's voice.

And if you think about the number of sales, deals, potential clients, etc. that can be lost just because of the way a secretary sounds on the phone, the figures would amaze you.

It's so easy to be nice!

But her excellent disposition should also be balanced by a sense of responsibility (sometimes to the point of being blunt) to protect your peace of mind so that you can work without unnecessary interruptions. Tell her to be diplomatic (people can lose their tempers pretty quickly, especially on the phone), but that once she's decided not to put the call through, she should never give in. It's up to the caller to make other arrangements, either to call back or leave a message.

How can you help her fulfil her responsibilities?

Tell her first to ask the caller what the reasons are for the call.

Give her your diary (as up-to-date as possible) so that she can set up an appointment with the caller.

Tell her, as well as your associates and colleagues, what you are working on, so that she will learn to transfer certain calls to the person in the best position to respond.

Discuss the best times for meetings, returning calls, updating your diary, etc. so that she can block in certain activities to suit your schedule.

Keep her regularly informed of new developments, and tell her to keep a list of all incoming and outgoing calls, as well as any following up that might be necessary (measures to be taken, problems to deal with, etc.).

Give her a 'red list' of people who should always be put through to you directly, and a 'black list' of people for whom you're always 'in a meeting'. She can consult her lists after delivering the well-known: 'Hold on a minute, I'll just see if he's in . . .'

Use your telephone even more efficiently

1. In cases where you have to answer the phone yourself, before picking up the receiver, jot down on a piece of paper the ideas that were going through your head just before the phone rang, or the work that you were doing at that moment.

2. When someone calls me at a bad time, the first thing I say, after the person has identified themselves, is 'Can I call you back . . . what's the number', or 'Could you call me back at such and such a time, at this number . . .' Precision and courtesy are primary assets.

3. When someone calls me, I let them know right away how much time I've got, so that we get straight down to business.

4. I take notes of every call. For this reason, I always keep a pad next to the phone. I make a mini-list of daily calls, which I then add to my working list. This habit is very helpful for remembering who called and why.

5. I make sure my phone has a 'redial' function.

6. When I'm not here, or if I don't want to be disturbed, I turn the answering machine on.

7. I use my answering machine as a screen, so that I only have to respond to really urgent calls right away. As for the others, I answer only if it's convenient for me.

8. When I leave for more than three days at a time, I use a special answering service to take messages. It's more personal and more efficient than a machine, and well worth the money when I compare the number of call-backs to what the machine produces.

Prepare your calls

The secret of using your telephone efficiently depends on one word: *preparation*.

How many times have you got through to an important client, only to hear yourself say:

> 'There's something else I wanted to talk about, but I can't remember what it is at the moment . . .'

or:

> 'Oh yes, just wait a moment, I know the file is around here somewhere . . .'

Or even worse, you call someone and then can't remember why you dialled the number . . .

Distractions and negligence that can be costly, very costly.

Get into the habit of always preparing your telephone calls in advance. To help you, here are two forms which I recommend using whenever possible: one to prepare your calls, the other for returning calls that you have received.

Fill in these forms carefully before making your calls, and keep them in sight while you're calling, so that you always know exactly where you are.

You can use a computer to file and display these kinds of forms, as well as your diary, and you can change them at will, print them, transfer them to self-adhesive stickers, etc.

Phone file

Caller: _____

Company: _____

Telephone: _____ Fax: _____

Date/Hour: _____

File Name: _____

Description: _____

Action Taken: _____

Details and Follow-up:_____

_____

Important ☐   Urgent ☐   Routine ☐

Call back file

Date/Hour: _____

Caller: _____

Company: _____

Telephone: _____   Fax: _____

THEY CALL – Date/Hour:_____

Message: _____

YOU CALL – Date/Hour: _____

Message: _____

_____

Important ☐   Urgent ☐   Routine ☐

Message Taken By:_____

Follow-up By: _____

The length of your calls

It is of the utmost importance to control the length of your calls –
the ones you make and the ones you get. An average telephone call
shouldn't exceed five minutes. Here are three ways to help you
develop your own personal strategy to avoid needless talk:

1. How to control call time

The director of a large New York law firm gave me this advice: keep
a stop watch next to your phone, and use it.

'I very rarely exceed the time I've allotted for the call. I communicate the essential data, and send the rest by mail.'

2. Telephone meeting

'Let's set a time to talk on the phone. How about Monday 25 September? Is the morning good for you? Say 10 to 10.15? OK, I'll be prepared, and you'll have time to get ready too.'

There are two advantages to this kind of meeting:

- Setting a date shows clients that you respect them.
- Setting a definite date shows clients that you are organized, and therefore someone to be respected.

3. Pretext: urgent business

Another way of cutting a conversation short is to use a pretext, say that you have to leave the office in five minutes to get to the airport, or an important meeting, etc.

On the other hand, there are people who use this sort of pretext, but then keep talking anyway. You have to seem in a hurry, pretend you're late, you absolutely must leave right away ... and you'll get the results you want, with no problem!

How to terminate a phone call

You're on the phone, the conversation goes on and on, and you want to end it. Here are a few techniques:

- Say that you have another meeting and that you have to leave.
- Just say: 'Before we finish this conversation, Mr Lowry, I'd like to ...' or 'I'd like to continue this conversation when we speak again, if that's all right with you ...'
- Don't hesitate to change the subject abruptly, to get right to the point, if you think the conversation is meandering.
- Knock loudly on your desk. Then say that, unfortunately, you have to go, there's someone knocking at your door.
- Centre the conversation on the most important points, and say that the details will be forthcoming, in written form (especially if they are numerous, complex, or if you have your written material all prepared).
- Keep a tape recording of a phone ringing. Play it back, and tell your caller that you're sorry, but you have another call.
- Sum up the conversation, starting with the conclusions, and

working back to the beginning. This is a discreet way of changing the subject, and bringing the conversation to an end.
- Promise to resume the conversation in a few days, or sooner if something new comes up.

How to start a telephone conversation

Receiving calls:

'Hello, this is .... What can I do for you?' This is a good way to begin, since it asks a precise question. Avoid the 'How are yous ...' which lead directly to a chat about the weather.

Making calls:

'Hello, this is .... of Globe Publishing. Have you got a few minutes? I hope I'm not disturbing you.' (It's important that the person you are calling is free.) 'I don't want to waste any of your time, so I'll get right to the point. I'd like ...'

The more precise you are, the more professional you seem, and the more effective your calls will be.

During conversations:

First time = less

When you're speaking to someone for the first time, be concise and friendly.

Many times = more

When you've already spoken to someone a few times, you should ask a few questions about their health, about how their business is going, etc. This will please the person and open the door for your own interests. But if you mention these kinds of things at the end, they tend to dilute the impact of the conversation, and you might have trouble terminating the call.

How to talk

1. Be dynamic. Avoid long silences, hemming and hawing, any kind of hesitation. Keep a list of points you want to cover handy. Be systematic, exhaustive and concise.

2. Try to use a warm and enthusiastic voice. Your ideas should be

clear, your voice should express friendliness and confidence. Don't speak in a monotone. Emphasize certain phrases, vary your rhythm and voice quality. A good way to practise this is to tape yourself, and train yourself to master:

- your tone of voice;
- the flow of your conversation;
- your diction.

3. Smile. There's a famous line by Sacha Guitry: 'How beautiful you were on the phone last night!' Smile when you speak. The person you're talking to can feel it, even on the phone.

4. Make gestures. When you're talking, gesture with your hands, or stand up. You'll be more convincing.

For points 3 and 4, use a mirror. Seeing yourself with your own eyes will help you maintain the proper tone.

On hold?

- You can refuse to be put on hold, and ask what time would be best to call back.
- You can wait. Plug your phone into a speaker, and use the time to have a coffee, read your mail, etc., in other words for tasks that don't demand a lot of attention or concentration.

You have to wait too long:

- Leave a message. It's important. Your name, phone number, the reason for your call, and the time limit for an answer. Make sure the message is understood correctly. If possible, have the secretary repeat it. Insisting on this point will add a serious note to your call.
- Never just hang up. Your wait will have been entirely useless.

Do you use all your phone's potential?

1. **Use the phone instead of a meeting.**
   This is possible thanks to:

- *Tele-conferencing*
  Use this method as often as possible. It's really fantastic when you

consider the amount of time and money you can save. Ask your phone company for information on how their tele-conferencing service works, and exploit it to the full.

● *Group calls*

Equip your phone with a loudspeaker and mike, so that anyone in the room can participate in the call. You can also be doing something else with your hands while you're on the phone.

This kind of device usually comes with a feature that allows you to listen to your callers, without their being able to hear you, or the other people in the room, unless you so desire.

2. **Electronic memory**

For a few dollars more, you can equip your phone with a memory bank of 10, 50, even 100 numbers.

Why not use it? When you've got into the habit of preparing your calls in advance, you could, like some managers, learn to use the 10 to 20 seconds it takes for the call to be automatically dialled, and the 10 to 20 seconds it takes to get through to the person you want, to prepare your call.

3. **Automatic redial**

Most phones have this feature built in, but strangely enough, few people seem to use it regularly.

But be careful! If your call is highly confidential, you'd be best to dial another number when it's finished, so as not to leave it on your phone's memory. Call your own number, for example.

Take the situation where you're in someone else's home or office and place a confidential call to an associate or client. When you're finished, your host can identify the person you called by pressing redial. Customs officials know this trick well: a dealer in stolen works of art was apprehended in this way after he placed a call to his Swiss banker.

4. **Do you move around a lot? Bring your messages along!**

Most phone companies provide a service that allows all your calls to be transferred to another number for a specified period of time. In this way, you won't miss any of your calls when you're away from home and/or the office. Ask your phone company for more information.

5. Waiting for an urgent call? Free yourself!

Another service will inform you if someone is trying to reach you when you're already on the phone. This is very handy if you're waiting for an important call, but still have to use the line. When the second call comes in, you have the choice of either calling the first person back, or putting them on hold.

6. Do you want to be interrupted? It's easy!

You can arrange for an automatic 'wake-up' call at any time of the day. It's up to you to think of different ways to exploit this service. Some directors use it to cut short interviews, to punctuate certain time slots throughout the day, to remember appointments, etc.

Even though you are equipped with the latest in telephones, computers, fax, etc. and you have a wonderful secretary, there's still nothing that can replace *the personal touch*.

How to make your appointments a success? That's what we'll be talking about in the next chapter.

The telephone is there for you:
it's up to you
to master it ... and not to be its slave!

20

HOW TO MAKE YOUR APPOINTMENTS WORK

People are what make a business successful

'I shouldn't have given him an appointment. It was a waste of time. We could have accomplished the same thing over the phone. And he just kept talking, so that I almost had to throw him out . . .'

We have these kinds of afterthoughts often enough, yet we persist in our bad habits.

Appointments – the ones you make and the ones you give – are time consumers whose real cause is frequently your own desire to move, or to occupy yourself: they reassure you by making it seem as though you're getting a lot done.

But don't forget that a three-minute phone call, or a half-page fax, can often accomplish the same thing.

But it's really people that make a business successful. So you have to meet them personally, on a regular basis, to get to know them, to exchange ideas and create new contacts.

Appointments are therefore often necessary, if not indispensable.

A new client is apt not to change his or her mind because of a personal encounter.

You never hire someone on the strength of a CV alone, however brilliant it might look. You want to meet the candidate in person.

The Complete Time Management System aims to help you make your appointments efficient and profitable in terms of time and energy.

Take stock. Were the appointments you had last month profitable? Could they have been replaced by phone calls, a fax, or a short letter? Look at your diary, review the appointments you had last month, and fill in the following form:

Appointment evaluation

Date: _____

Time: _____ With whom: _____

Description: _____

Duration: _____ Result: _____

Evaluation: _____

Appointment evaluation

Date: _____

Time: _____ With whom: _____

Description: _____

Duration: _____ Result: _____

Evaluation: _____

Appointment evaluation

Date: _____

Time: _____ With whom: _____

Description: _____

Duration: _____ Result: _____

Evaluation: _____

Appointment evaluation

Date: _____

Time: _____ With whom: _____

Description: _____

Duration: _____ Result: _____

Evaluation: _____

How many hours did you spend on appointments last month?

What proportion of your total working time was spent on appointments? If the proportion is high, pay attention. There are surely ways to improve.

What are your conclusions?

What percentage of your appointments could you have done better without?

Were you sufficiently prepared?

What could you have done to make your appointments more profitable?

Reduce the number of your appointments

You must combat your unfortunate (disguised as generous) tendency to accept all appointments without thinking.

You must:

1. Learn to say 'No'.

2. Not say 'Yes' right away.
   Start by analysing the situation, the real value of the potential appointment. Consider the time and energy it will require (especially if you have to travel) and whether or not it pays.

   Couldn't you use the time more profitably?

3. Have the person, or their secretary, call back to confirm the appointment.

4. Always ask yourself if you should or shouldn't make an appointment ... but remain open!
   When you make changes in your life, you have to be careful not to go from one extreme to the other. That would be stupid ... Being selective in your appointments is excellent, but that doesn't mean that you have to stop the appointments altogether, either with people you know, or with new individuals.
   Be discerning. When you hesitate to meet someone, or when you are worried about losing an opportunity, apply these two techniques:

1. Ask the person who wants the appointment first to send a written résumé of the project they have in mind.
   If they don't answer, then they're obviously not serious.

If they do, then you need only take a few minutes to evaluate the proposal and make a decision.

If your decision is negative, ask your secretary to write a short note, explaining that the proposal does not meet your company's guidelines.

2. Set up an appointment, but with the condition that you can only spare fifteen minutes of your time. Judge what takes place in that period, and then prolong the appointment if necessary.

Develop good reflexes

Always keep in mind that the alternatives are often preferable to an appointment itself. Instead, couldn't you:

1. **Telephone**

2. **Delegate (send someone else)**

3. **Set up a tele-conference**

4. **Send a fax**

5. **Write a letter.**

I personally force myself to stick to these rules, but when I finally do decide to opt for an appointment, I always cultivate the following attitude which, from my experience, works without exception:

'I am absolutely certain that this appointment will be profitable for me!'

How to make an appointment

1. *Make your secretary your ally.* Get her used to asking questions, and obtaining answers!

By doing this, she'll be able to answer questions you might have about a person you're supposed to meet. She should never set up an appointment without consulting you first.

If someone calls for an appointment, couldn't she answer the person's questions herself?

Try to get your secretary to develop the habit of taking a certain amount of initiative. Make it clear that, in principle, you are never available!

2. Whenever possible – and as politely as possible – *try to get the other person to do the travelling*. If they do the travelling three times in a row, then you should make the effort.

   You might want to travel, under certain precise circumstances:

   ● You want to see your client's installation and equipment.
   ● The person has documents and/or material that would be difficult to transport.
   ● The person is always late, and/or stays too long. But they're so nice, you have trouble blaming them, or kicking them out.

3. Always determine not only the time the appointment will start, but also the time it will end.

   This is a mistake most people who aren't in the know make. They forget to specify how much time they can allot to the meeting, and then complain that the appointment is dragging on.

   When necessary, and before setting up the appointment, discuss the amount of time the other person thinks the meeting should take.

   Leave nothing to chance, always remembering that if you don't know where you're going, you might end up arriving anywhere at all (or worse still . . . nowhere).

   ● If you have a number of appointments, one after the other, make sure your schedule will not suffer.
   ● If someone arrives late for an appointment, don't let this penalize the people who come after. Tell your secretary to let you know when the next person arrives, and terminate the latecomer's appointment there and then.
   ● There's nothing more disagreeable than having to wait, especially when you've been punctual yourself. On the other hand, don't hesitate to cancel or postpone an appointment if the person arrives too late.
   ● If you're the one who's doing the travelling, get your secretary to confirm the appointment before you leave. People, even the best organized, can forget to let you know if some kind of emergency comes up.
   ● If necessary, be strict with your secretary. And if you want to stay on good terms with a client, don't, except under extreme circumstances, cancel an appointment twice in a row.

- If you're doing the travelling, and if it's the first time you're going somewhere, either you or your secretary should ask for precise directions as well as an estimate of the time it takes to get there.
- Always allow yourself fifteen minutes extra. If you arrive early, have a coffee or take a short walk. Then get to the appointment exactly on time.

This creates an excellent impression. Arriving ten minutes too early, on the other hand, creates a bad impression. It places you in a weak position. It makes you look like someone who isn't very busy – and therefore not very important – or like someone who wants something very badly.

If punctuality is a mark of royalty, then arriving too early is the mark of a beggar.

Prepare yourself carefully

There's nothing more frustrating than to come out of a meeting and smack yourself on the forehead, saying 'What happened in there? I completely forgot the most important point!'

And there's nothing more embarrassing – and damaging to your reputation – than to have to make excuses while you search frantically for some file or document, with your client there in front of you.

To avoid these kinds of unpleasant situations you have to make sure that you are prepared for each appointment. Don't leave anything to chance. When you have decided that an appointment is necessary, that it can't be replaced by one or another of the alternative methods, then be logical about the whole thing and get prepared!

Ask yourself these important questions, and find the answers. Write them down, and keep them in the file you prepare for the meeting:

- What is the aim of this meeting?
- What points should I cover?
- What is the order of priority?

The order in which you cover the subjects to be discussed is very important, because you usually won't have enough time to cover all of them.

Start with what is most important

So start with the most important points. In this way, you will not have wasted any time, even if you can't get to the secondary issues.

Ask your secretary to prepare a file, with the cover title:

File No. X re: meeting with Mr Y, 13 September ....

Ask her to make an index, on the file cover, of the subjects it contains. Then you can make sure that nothing is missing.

In your diary, or on a pad, keep a list of all the points you want to cover during the course of the meeting. A separate sheet of paper is preferable, because you can place it in the file for future reference when you're planning the next meeting.

Remember: if you want to create the (reassuring) impression of someone who's organized then you have to *be* organized. And by the same token, you should suspect anyone who shows up for an appointment without being organized. This can only lead to problems.

A last bit of advice: for important meetings, make sure you're in top shape. Try to organize the night before so that you can relax, do some exercise, have a massage, get a good night's rest, etc.

Watch out for dead time

Despite the best plans and intentions, there are always delays and last-minute cancellations.

So? Be ready for them. Bring along some 'time fillers'. These are little jobs, not urgent, that you haven't had time to take care of, and that can be done in a few minutes.

What can you do in five minutes?

- Set up an appointment
- Make a list of the participants for your next weekly meeting
- Dictate a short letter
- Classify various documents
- Re-read a short report
- Outline the general ideas for a report that you will write later on
- Read a trade paper or magazine
- Evaluate your previous appointment.

In other words, there's a long list of possible 'time fillers' which can make those few minutes of waiting productive.

**Make a list of all your time fillers
and post them in full view,
so that whenever you have a few minutes to spare,
you can dispose of them in turn.**

What about business lunches?

There are those who are for, and others who are against business lunches. J. P. Getty, who at one time was one of the five richest men in the world, was totally opposed to business lunches. He insisted that a problem could be solved just as well over a cup of coffee as over a third martini. It is true that the efficiency of people who tend to imbibe a little too much at lunch is doubtful.

As for myself, I had a little experience when I was starting out that proved to be very instructive. The belief is that if we treat a client, or a potential client, to a sumptuous lunch, then that person will be more disposed to favour our product or service in the future.

This is perhaps true in certain cases. Anyway, it's what I believed to be true when I had occasion to meet one of my first important clients.

I ordered the best wine, and after the meal offered him cognac after cognac. He became very festive, and was very enthusiastic about the project I was proposing. After the third cognac, it seemed like it was in the bag.

I was ecstatic.

I hadn't skimped on anything. And it had paid off.

I should have become suspicious after he knocked over a second glass of wine, and had to be helped back to his hotel because he couldn't walk on his own.

Two days later (he'd gone back home) I called to work out some details, and had the surprise of my life when he told me that he didn't remember a thing about our discussion.

He asked me to send him all the information.

The project never got off the ground. And I learned my lesson.

A business lunch can be very costly

Business lunches are excellent occasions to establish or re-establish contacts. You can get to know your business associates better, in another context. There's time to discuss things at length, and to get into more confidential aspects of a project.

They are also a way of meeting a potential partner or client, without everyone else knowing about it.

We usually spend about an hour at midday, eating. That's a lot. The time should be put to profitable use. But we should be serious about it, because business lunches cost money and seriously diminish your afternoon's productivity, especially if alcohol is consumed.

Business lunches are useful. But you have to be discerning, and ask yourself the same question as for appointments:

'Is this lunch really necessary?'

What alternatives are there?

Instead of lunching with a client or a supplier, couldn't I meet them over a cup of coffee in my office?

Another interesting alternative is the business breakfast. Many businessmen prefer meeting over breakfast, at eight in the morning. This leaves their day entirely free. The time limit is already established. People usually have to be in their offices by nine, while business lunches can go on until three in the afternoon!

Some people even have two light breakfasts, over which business is discussed, the first at seven-thirty, another at eight-thirty. And then off to the office at nine-thirty.

Don't you think that's a great way to start the day?

There are two other advantages: breakfasts don't cost much, and alcohol isn't (usually) served.

If, after thinking about it, you opt for the business lunch, here is some advice that you might find useful:

1. Choose the restaurant that is closest to your office, if possible a place where you're known, and where the service is good. Eat simple food. Save your gastronomic adventures for another time.

   If the other party thinks the restaurant is too far, try to find one half-way between your offices, so that everyone is satisfied.

2. Ask your secretary to make a reservation.

3. Try to avoid peak restaurant hours. If you can manage to take lunch at twelve-thirty or one-thirty or even two, then the discussion will be more relaxed, and the service faster.

4. Eat lightly, drink little or no alcohol, and get used to ordering things which are easy and fast to prepare.

   When you arrive, let the waiter or the *maitre d'* know that you're in a hurry (especially if you really are!).

   Ask for the bill when the waiter brings you coffee. Then you won't have to sit there waiting, or go looking for him. If you're picking up the tab, give the waiter your credit card as soon as he brings the bill. Then you won't have to stand around waiting for change.

5. Don't forget to ask for a receipt for your expense accounts.

Appointment checklist

1. Is this appointment (or business lunch) really necessary?

2. Can the person you're meeting do the travelling?

3. Couldn't you delegate someone to take care of the appointment?

4. Could you obtain the same result over the phone?

5. Does the appointment have a precise objective?

6. Have you planned to group your appointments?

7. Before leaving, have you obtained the following information:
   - appointment confirmed;
   - precise directions on how to get there;
   - estimated travel time.

8. Have you planned to travel by taxi, car, or public transport? Couldn't you get someone to drive you?

9. Have you checked to make sure that you have all the necessary documents?

10. Have you checked the contents of your briefcase?

11. Have you brought along a few 'time fillers' or some relevant reading, in case there's some kind of delay?

Appointments lead us to another problem area which merits some attention: travel time.

This problem is encountered not only when you have to go to an appointment, but also in getting to and from work (unless you work at home) which takes half an hour, or an hour, or sometimes even an hour-and-a-half each way.

If you spend an average of an hour a day travelling (which is very conservative, when you consider appointments, commuting to and from the office, getting to restaurants, etc.) you can end up wasting 5 hours a week, or 250 hours a year.

Are you aware of the fact that 250 hours represents *5 full weeks*? If you waste one little hour a day, you waste 5 weeks a year! Something to think about, isn't it?

Of course, driving your car requires all your attention. That's true. But there are still a number of things that you can do, without compromising your attention or your safety.

For example, you can:

- Dictate a letter which your secretary will type later.
- Dictate instructions for the day.
- Use your micro-cassette to note any ideas you might have.

Pascal once made a note in his journal:

'I had an interesting idea. I forgot it. So I wrote down that I'd forgotten it.'

This won't happen to you if you use a micro-cassette.

Do you have a cellular phone in your car?
If your hourly rate is high enough, each minute
you lose can be very costly. So if you spend
an hour a day in your car, why not make use
of that important time?

Get informed! Competition is stiff, and prices are falling every day. A cellular phone allows you to contact your secretary or a client at any time, from anywhere on the road. You can conduct important business negotiations while getting from one place to another.

And on top of all that, a cellular phone will add to your prestige.

Car or public transport?

Your car isn't the only way to get around. Many people forget that. If you have to make long trips on a regular basis, think about taking a bus, a train, or a plane.

You have a lot more freedom when someone else is doing the driving. You can read, for example.

Hiring a chauffeur

If your salary is high enough, and you have to do a lot of moving around, a chauffeur might be the solution. Too expensive? A chauffeur doesn't have to wear a uniform and gloves. I know one company director who made a deal with a taxi driver so that he would be at his disposal whenever necessary.

Spend the best hours of the day working. Half, or even two-thirds of your working time can be saved if you don't travel during rush hours. And you'll be saving not only time, but energy as well, since driving in rush hour engenders a lot of tension and stress.

Why not ask your boss if you could start work an hour earlier each morning, and finish an hour before everyone else? A system of flexible hours has already been adopted by many companies, and has been proved effective, since a better quality of life makes employees more productive.

Your employer will probably be open to such a suggestion, especially if you demonstrate how cost-effective a flexible system can be. If you arrive earlier, you could start the day without interruptions from the telephone, colleagues, etc.

'Go slowly, I'm in a hurry'

Note that it isn't obligatory to use your travelling time in a systematic way. For many people, driving somewhere is the only time they have to be alone (relatively speaking, if you consider sitting in a traffic jam being alone!) and they like to use it to think, to review, to prepare for the day, or to listen to some pleasant music and relax.

I'm lucky enough to live very close to my office, and often go to work on foot. For me, those few minutes are among the most pleasant in the entire day. Instead of mentally preparing myself for the day that lies ahead, I try to stop thinking about anything in particular. I look at the trees and the sky, listen to the birds, feel the changing seasons, etc.

I walk very slowly, feeling my body, breathing deeply, looking at everything around me.

Even when I'm overloaded with work, I walk slowly, following the advice of Talleyrand who said, 'Go slowly, I'm in a hurry!'

Slow movements of the body calm the mind. That's why, whenever I get the chance, I walk to the restaurant for lunch, very slowly, forcing myself to think of nothing, a little like a Zen Buddhist monk. These few minutes of inner silence are like an oasis in the burning desert of a busy day. In any case, they do me a lot of good, and help me stay connected to that source of calm and strength inside myself.

I think it's important to have something like this, because you can easily get lost, submerged in the many tasks you have to accomplish each day, especially if you're a busy person.

Don't forget that your inner balance is the key to your success. Anything that threatens to upset it, even momentarily, must be combated.

Apart from commuting to and from work, and getting to appointments, there's a type of moving around that's more important, and usually much more pleasant: taking trips. To discover how to make them tools for success, turn to the next chapter.

Prepare your appointments:
– what is the objective?
– what points should be covered?
– in what order?

21

HOW TO TAKE PROFITABLE AND EFFECTIVE TRIPS

An adventure with London cabbies

On my first visit to London I had a little adventure – or mis-adventure – which was very instructive.

You have probably been in the famous London taxis. They are black, spacious, a little like mini limousines. There's something quaint and poetic about them. And there are so many!

At least that's what I thought as I left my hotel on Baker Street. I was going to a very important meeting with a literary agent. It was a Thursday, six o'clock in the evening. My appointment was for six-thirty. The agent had informed me that the drive from my hotel to his office would take twenty minutes maximum ...

I was early, which is the way I like it. I hate arriving late. I didn't take the trouble to ask the hotel to call a cab for me. Not necessary, I thought. There were hundreds, thousands of cabs in the streets, especially at rush hour ...

I hailed the first cab that drove by. It didn't stop. I hailed a second, and a third. Not one was free. Finally I saw an empty one coming, but just then a beautiful woman stepped off the kerb in front of me and hailed it. I couldn't argue ... She was so elegant as she took her place in the back seat!

So I started to walk. 'Maybe I'm not on the right corner,' I thought. I saw the Ritz. Saved! (At least that's what I thought.) There are always taxis waiting in front of a large hotel like the Ritz.

Wrong again.

There were a dozen people waiting already. I couldn't wait. I started walking faster, away from the hotel. Finally I found an empty cab. But he refused to take me because he didn't know the street I wanted to go to. I was desperate.

It took me fifteen minutes to find another free taxi, and that one refused to take me as well. My destination was too far out of his way. I was already half an hour late.

When I found another free cab and told him where I wanted to go, he too started to make excuses. But this time I thought of a solution. The Number One solution around the world – money.

I took out a wad and offered it to the cabbie.

He smiled. He wasn't a materialist, but he was understanding. I finally got to my appointment, almost an hour late. If travelling is an education, it is also a test of character.

The agent welcomed me without blame. He had begun to worry about me a little, and explained that it was almost impossible to find a free cab in London during the rush hour.

I understood. It had been a mistake to trust in my common sense. Just because I saw a lot of taxis didn't mean that it would be easy to find one. My problem was the result of a lack of experience and planning, which led to a considerable loss of time, and could have had a disastrous effect on the success of my meeting.

In this chapter you will find advice that will help you limit as much as possible the inconveniences you are apt to encounter on all your trips abroad. It will also help you make all your trips extremely productive and, even more than that, fun!

To go or not to go

The first question you should ask yourself before undertaking any journey is:

'Is this trip really necessary?'

Most specialists will recommend asking yourself this question. I think it is also a matter of attitude. Personally, I believe that every trip can have significant benefits, so it won't surprise you to hear that I travel a lot. Nevertheless, I have often hesitated to embark on a journey:

'Can I really spare the time to travel for a week, or even for a few days?'

'This trip will be expensive. Is it worth it?'

Yes, I've often hesitated before taking a trip, but I've never regretted going either.

Why? For numerous reasons. Travelling allows you to:

1. Discover new horizons, different ways of thinking.

2. Take a beneficial, and often necessary break from your usual routine.

3. Make new contacts, or renew old ones.

4. Force yourself to delegate or terminate certain important jobs before leaving.

5. Reward yourself, since in general, even though a trip might be exhausting, it is also usually enriching and stimulating.

On the other hand, if you are a buyer and have to spend a hundred days every year out of the country, then travelling doesn't hold the same attraction.

Don't forget the first question:

'Is this trip *really necessary?*'

Instead, couldn't I:

1. Make a phone call, even a long and costly overseas call. A £500 telephone bill is cheap compared to what travelling there yourself would cost, in terms of time and money.

2. Organize a tele-conference.

3. Send a detailed letter.

4. Send someone in my place.

Once your decision to leave has been made, there are a number of things you can do to make your trip as pleasant as possible.

Plan your journey

This is one of the first things to do. Before going out and buying your ticket, think of all the people you could or should meet on your trip. Will they be available on the dates you plan to be there? Make it a veritable battle plan: exhaustive, detailed, precise, where everything is taken into account (each minute you spend out of the country costs five, even ten times as much as at home).

It's easy to find yourself caught without a plan, and to realize, too late, that the people you wanted to meet are not there, or cannot see you because of their heavy schedules.

Group your appointments as much as possible. And if you think it's useful or necessary, plan to see people in a specific order, which you have thought out beforehand. Keep in mind that a person in his own country is usually more flexible towards visitors than to his compatriots.

Plan for the unpredictable

Good planning means leaving not a single moment of dead time. With intercontinental flights (longer than six hours) it is advisable, because of the jet lag factor, to plan nothing for the day you arrive except a long bath or a sauna, or something of that nature, to relax you and get yourself into top shape. Take a siesta, or do some sightseeing if you have the energy. Or look over your files. Even after many years of travelling, long flights still have a tiring effect, both physically and mentally. Take this into account and never meet a client the day you arrive, except under special circumstances – for example if you're only in the country for a couple of days, or a few hours.

How to fight jet lag

Some experts suggest going to bed an hour early during the week before the trip. Others say an hour later is better. Both theories are debatable.

One thing is certain: everyone suffers from jet lag. So plan for it. The best advice I can give is to get a good night's sleep during the week before leaving, and don't indulge in excesses of any kind.

Sleeping a few hours in the plane helps enormously. Bring earplugs and ask the flight attendant for a sleeping mask. If reading a novel helps you sleep, bring one along. A mild sedative can produce the desired effect. You can also take it when you arrive, depending on the time of day or night. A glass of wine may help you sleep, or certain foods (especially ones rich in tryptophane, a natural sedative found in dairy products, eggs and poultry) or tea. Whatever it is, make sure you have some on your flight.

Your travel agent

Choose a dynamic agency, one that offers good and competent service. They will get you better prices, and they'll know about the most practical and fastest routes to take.

It's best to travel light, ideally only with hand luggage. If, for some reason, you have to bring a lot of bags along, tell the travel agent. Most airlines accept two pieces of luggage with no extra charge, and will ask for a small supplement if you have more than two (excluding what you carry on to the plane). But some companies, even well-known ones, demand exorbitant amounts of money for extra baggage. I know this from first-hand experience, so be very, very careful.

Reserve your hotel at the same time as your flight

Unless you decide to go for adventure, always ask your travel agent to reserve your hotel room at the same time as the flight. Travellers can be disagreeably surprised upon arriving in a large city with no reservation, even though there are many hotels. If you are attending a conference or a convention, try to book a room at the same hotel, even if it costs a little more. You will save on taxis and on time, and you can freshen up in your room whenever you want to.

You usually get a better hotel rate through the travel agent than if you walk up to the front desk on your own.

Rent a car or take cabs?

It's always better to decide in advance. If you want to rent, consult your travel agent. There might be some interesting package deals available. A reservation should be made for a car before your departure.

But renting a car isn't always necessary. In most large cities – Paris, Rome, London, New York, etc. – taxis are much more practical. On the other hand, if you have to get out of town, then rent a car. This detail is important. Tell your travel agent. Plan to get an international licence, and take an international credit card with you.

Travel light

Take only what is essential and if possible travel with hand luggage only. You will save a lot of time, especially those long waits for the luggage to come off the plane. You won't have to worry about your bags getting lost, either.

In order not to leave anything indispensable behind, always use a checklist. Use the one below, or write one up yourself, suited to your particular needs.

Travel checklist

1. Transport

Travel Agency: Address:

Telephone:

Contact:

Reservation: Date:

Reference:

Telex/Fax:

Confirmation: Date:

Reference:

Telephone:

Telex/Fax:

Airport:

Terminal: Zone:

Seat: Smoking/Non-smoking:

Tickets: Numbers:

Date of Issue:

Connecting flights:

2. Accommodation

Hotel:
_____

Address:
_____

Telephone:
_____

Contact:
_____

Room: Number:
_____

Single/Double:
_____

Outlook:
_____

Confirmation: Date:
_____

Reference:
_____

Telephone:
_____

Telex/Fax:
_____

Car: Company:
_____

Type:
_____

Insurance:
_____

Rate:
_____

Credit card:
_____

Maps:
_____

Restaurants: Names: Addresses: Telephone numbers:
_____

_____

_____

_____

Cultural Activities: Names: Addresses: Telephone numbers:
_____

_____

_____

Cultural Activities: Names: Addresses: Telephone numbers:

_____

_____

_____

3. Various

Medication:
_____

_____

Emergency telephone numbers:
_____

_____

Bank and credit cards: Numbers:
_____

_____

Associated bank: Address:
_____

Telephone:
_____

Telephone credit card:
_____

Traveller's cheques: Currency:
_____

Denominations:
_____

Numbers:
_____

Passport:
_____

Number:
_____

Dates of issue and expiry:
_____

_____

Visa:
_____

Dates of issue and expiry:
_____

Vaccination: Reference:
_____

Type:
_____

Date:
_____

Earplugs: Micro-cassette:
_____

Calculator: Business cards:
_____

Notebook and papers:
_____

Itinerary (including appointments, addresses and telephone
numbers)
_____

_____

_____

_____

_____

_____

_____

Make copies of the list and give them to whoever you think should
have one, in case problems arise. With this information they should
be able to take the appropriate (often urgent) measures.

Another advantage: using this list, you can organize your packing
in minutes rather than hours.

Distribute your itinerary

Have your secretary make a few copies of your itinerary. Include
dates, names and telephone numbers of hotels where you'll be
staying, as well as those of the people you'll be meeting. Leave one
copy of this itinerary at the office, and one at home, in case of
emergency, sudden developments, important clients, etc.

To make your itinerary really complete, add your working time-
table to it.

Plan for delays and postponements

Despite all your precautions, you will, at some point, experience delays of one kind or another. The plane might not be ready, a connecting flight might be late, your luggage misplaced, etc.

Take along a few 'time fillers'. You might want to do some shopping, or take the opportunity to write a few postcards to your clients or colleagues at the office – an excellent way to improve your public relations.

Travel with your portable office

In your briefcase, which you have with you at all times, always carry important documents or reports related to your trip, a micro-cassette, calculator, etc. Use any dead time to review your itinerary, or to finish some job that you've been wanting to do for months.

I always bring along my portable computer (a Sinclair Z88, weighing two pounds) which allows me to work anywhere, any time, even in the plane.

Train or plane

You don't always have to take the plane, especially in Europe or Japan. Consider the alternative: train travel.

There are many advantages to taking trains. They are slower than planes, but if you count an hour to get to the airport, baggage check, security, waiting, delays, etc., then the train becomes a more viable alternative.

The advantage of a long train journey is that you can travel at night in a sleeper. You sleep all night, and arrive at your destination in the morning, fresh and relaxed, without wasting any time.

You don't have to arrive at the departure point as far ahead of time, as with air travel. And the train is less expensive.

A last factor to consider is the distance from the airport to the place where your appointment is taking place. It could take an hour-and-a-half to get there from the airport, whereas the train usually brings you right to the centre of town.

How much did you spend?

Bring along a special envelope for all your receipts: hotels, restaurants, taxis, etc.

When you get home, draw up your list of expenses and attach the receipts. Give this to your immediate superior as soon as possible. Don't forget to include your money exchange receipts (you will be reimbursed at the rate you paid, not at the new rate).

Prepare your return. On the last night of your trip, or on the return journey, or after you get home, bring everything up to date.

Which files should be dealt with first?

Which decisions have to be made first?

Prepare the letters and a list of documents that you should expedite when you return, and then follow them up. Many trips could have been profitable if the person hadn't waited two months before following up on the contacts they made. If you can't get all the documentation together right away, send a note or a fax anyway, just to remind the people you met that you haven't forgotten them, and that the information they require is forthcoming.

Write an appraisal of your trip

- Who did you meet?
- What resulted from your discussions?
- Did you make any new clients/contacts?

Note the names, addresses and telephone numbers of these people. Keep a file which includes what they do, their positions, and what you discussed with them.

- Was your trip positive?
- Was it worth the effort? What were the negative aspects?
- What can you do to avoid them in future?
- What projects or ideas are worth developing? Ignoring? Which are top priority?

A last word of advice: do a *written appraisal* of your trip. If you don't, you'll forget a multitude of details and your efforts will not be profitable. Don't wait. After a week, you will have forgotten half of what you did, and you will be caught up once again in the flow of events around you.

22

HOW TO AVOID DROWNING IN PAPERWORK

In the last few chapters we have examined different kinds of time consumers: interruptions, meetings, telephone, travel, etc. But there's one more, especially subtle and efficient time consumer that we have to deal with every day, something we can drown in: paperwork.

How can we handle all the paperwork that comes our way daily? Most people fall behind, put it off, answer their post a month late. If you are one of those people and would like to make a change, then this chapter will be of special interest to you.

80 per cent of your papers will never be useful.

Did you know that studies have shown that 80 per cent of the papers on your desk, in your filing cabinets and safes, are useless (excluding legal and other important documents)?

Before going any further, have you ever asked yourself *why* you neglect your paperwork? There are many reasons. Maybe paperwork bores you or upsets you, or seems futile. Nevertheless, paperwork is important, and can be done efficiently if you follow a few simple rules.

How to deal with your paperwork

The basic rule for dealing with paperwork is quite simple, yet many people don't adhere to it:

**Managing paperwork means being able to classify
any document, important or not.**

We continually neglect to do this, so confusion quickly sets in and numerous important files get lost in the pile, causing delays and lost opportunities.

There are four main classes for your papers. Try to train your secretary so that she becomes familiar with these categories and is able to classify most of the paperwork herself. She should only submit documents to you that demand your personal attention and she should file all the others herself. Alternatively she should organize them so that your verification can be done in a minimum of time.

These are the four categories:

1. File

Have a tray at your disposal for documents to be filed, either by you or your secretary (we will discuss filing systems a little later on).

2. Pass on

Have another tray for documents that should be expedited to your secretary (she hasn't been doing her job properly if these find their way to your desk), to your boss, colleagues, assistants, etc.

3. Rubbish

This is one of the most important, yet underestimated categories of your filing system. Always ask yourself the question: 'What would happen if I threw this away?'

We have the tendency not to throw away enough, so that our files and shelves are stuffed with useless documents that make sorting and filing what is important a lot more difficult.

4. Read

Any document that requires more than five or ten minutes to read should be filed separately. Have a drawer for lengthy reports, professional publications, newsletters, etc. Obviously, your READ file should be thinned out from time to time.

I've got into the habit of devoting at least one afternoon a week to reading, usually a Thursday or Friday when things slow down in the office and when there are fewer phone calls. And I also ask my secretary to screen the calls and visitors.

In the chapter on speed-reading, we learned how important it was to increase the speed of our reading (without compromising our comprehension). But we shouldn't fall into the trap of reading everything, just because we read quickly. You have to make a strict selection of what you will and won't read.

More advice for greater efficiency

W. J. Redding, author of *Effective Management by Objectives,* showed that there is a direct relation between management by objectives and the amount of paperwork.

In what sense?

Well, contrary to the opinions of many people, who take an office littered with all kinds of paper as a sign of activity and efficiency, *the more efficient management by objectives is, the less paper there is.*

We live in the photocopy age. Memos, reports, correspondence, multiply and pollute our offices. And it's not only other people's fault, it's our own fault as well. By writing a report instead of making a phone call or having a five-minute meeting, we get the impression that we're working, we're *doing* something. But, in fact, what we are doing, according to Parkinson, is *creating* work, for ourselves and for our colleagues: reading documents that are completely useless and unnecessary. Instead of spending our time on really productive things, on effective tasks, we create time consumers.

Handling paperwork (especially handling it badly) results in the wasting of large amounts of precious time. How much time have you wasted trying to locate a document, only to realize that it was filed somewhere else, under another title?

14 ways to win the war against paperwork

1. Before writing anything, whatever it is, even a short memo, STOP! Ask yourself: 'Is this indispensable?' If yes, then go ahead. If not, then remember: 'Anything that is not indispensable is useless.'

2. Get into the habit of never writing more than one page for a report, and one paragraph for a memo.

   Short reports and memos take up less space, less paper, less reading time, and create fewer problems.

3. Finished writing? Who will you send it to? No, not to everyone: keep the number of recipients down to a minimum.

4. If the memo or report you have to write isn't urgent, then plan a space for it in your diary: not only might it become unnecessary, but you might be able to integrate it into one of your colleague's reports or memos, which means an increase in efficiency and productivity.

5. Avoid writing regular reports (weekly, monthly or daily): only new and important facts and developments merit a report. Reduce the frequency of regular reports if there is nothing of importance to communicate: daily becomes bi-monthly, etc.

   Instead, you can use a graph on your computer system (all you have to do is press a button), or a kind of warning device on your computer that goes off when certain thresholds are reached concerning variations in sales, inventory, credits/debits, etc. These will merit a written report.

6. Find out what mailing lists you're on and get your name deleted from any that regularly supply you with useless information.

   Be ruthless! Delegate as much reading as possible of reports, publications, etc. that you think *might* be interesting, and keep only what you *know* is interesting for yourself.

   A technique: to know whether you should leave your name on such and such a list, ask yourself: 'Could I not obtain this information somewhere else, in some other way which is faster and less cumbersome?'

7. Make up checklists, ready-to-use forms for all your correspondence. You will save time because information and questions that you frequently repeat will already be formulated. You will avoid forgetting a different detail each time.

8. Get it right the first time. Force yourself to write your ideas without making mistakes, without having to go back and correct, delete, refine, etc. Never go back and start a report or a memo twice. You will soon learn to write fast and well.

9. Train yourself to write well, so that people can understand you easily and completely. Readable and good-looking handwriting is a sign of a sane personality, someone with clear and precise ideas.

10. Whenever possible, use a graphic, a photograph or a drawing: this can save you whole pages of text. You know the saying: 'A picture is worth a thousand words.'

11. You might get into the habit (this is becoming more and more popular) of writing your replies on the back of the letter you receive, and then making a copy of both for yourself. This saves time in writing and filing.

    You (or your secretary) can write the reply by hand.

12. Get used to 'not respecting' the publications you receive: tear pages out that interest you and throw away or pass on the rest. File these pages immediately so that they don't get misplaced in the shuffle.

13. Get into the habit of removing a drawer, a tray, a cabinet or a shelf, etc. from your office now and then. The less storage space you have, the less you will keep, and the less encumbered you'll be.

    While we're on the subject of space, you've seen pictures in newspapers or magazines of big bosses in their offices. Did they have 15 filing cabinets, 50 drawers and 2000 shelves behind them? Not at all! The opposite, in fact. One large table with one or two phones, a computer, paper, pen, that's all. Almost empty space!

14. Plan reading sessions to take care of your post. Choose those times of day or week when you're at your worst. Use this task as a 'filler' whenever possible.

Resist the tendency to jump on a memo as soon as you get it. Also don't open the post as soon as it comes, or worse, go and look for it.

Again ... be careful! Don't take things to the other extreme and start getting rid of so much that the only things left in the room are you and me!

Techniques for drawing up personal checklists and forms

1. Analyse all messages that resemble each other, all requests, pro-positions, tasks that appear often, etc.

   This might take some time to organize, but the more exhaustive and methodical you are, the more efficient your checklists and forms will be.

2. Subdivide each category into sub-categories (for example: stages, sub-tasks, logical progressions, etc.). Study these sub-categories, asking yourself appropriate questions about them, such as: Was the artwork sent to the printer? By whom? When? Did the printer confirm receipt? etc.

3. Try to make all your checklists and forms at the same time so that they'll be as standardized as possible. Establish a maximum number of lines, paper size, etc. to keep everything uniform.

4. Keep a good supply. Don't waste time having to look for them, or photocopy new ones.

5. Force yourself to use them as much as possible, and for memos always include a personal touch at the end, your signature or initials, or a salutation like 'Thanks!' or 'Best Wishes!'

Sample memo

Memo

from: _____ date: _____

to: _____

subject: _____

_____

- urgent
- information
- in response to your letter/memo
- waiting for your reply
- other _____

_____

Example of written memo

Memo

from: *A. Martin*   date: *21/11/95*

to: *all personnel*

subject: *Personal photocopies*

- urgent
- information
- in response to your letter/memo
- waiting for your reply

- other: *The photocopy machines installed on each floor are strictly for office use. Photocopy staff **do not have time** to make copies of personal documents. Since there are occasions when personal photocopies are necessary, a machine will be made available for this purpose between the hours of 8 and 9 in the morning, and after office hours, on the first floor. There will be a charge of, say, 5p per page, to defray operating costs.*

Publication form

Title:

Date/Issue Number:

Mailing List: Date of next shipping:

Library Return Date:

Your filing system can increase your productivity

A good filing system should meet the four following requirements:

1. Group information into simple categories, reflecting your real needs.

2. Allow rapid access of information (maximum three minutes).

3. Facilitate addition of new material.

4. Include a simple method for eliminating outdated documents

How do you know if your present filing system is efficient? Just take the following test:

1. Does it often take you more than a minute to retrieve a document from your files?

2. Do members of your team (secretary and employees) have trouble locating documents when you're not there?

3. Have you left certain tasks unfinished because you weren't able to locate the necessary documents?

4. Do you keep documents longer than two years?

5. Are documents pertaining to a single report filed in different places?

6. Can the same document be found under different headings?

7. Have you forgotten to subdivide large categories? For example, to break the Travel file into: Travel Agencies; Hotels; Restaurants; Client Addresses; Car Rental, etc.?

All right, how many 'yeses'? Here's how to update your filing system so that your productivity will improve considerably, and your life will be a lot simpler.

1. Don't file your press cuttings under 'Newspaper Articles' but according to theme. So, when you look up your Marketing file, you'll find a documentation sub-file with articles, graphics, news-letters, etc.

2. Arrange the contents of your files chronologically, with the most recent at the front of the file. Staple documents together. Paper-clips fall off and are clumsy. Always unfold letters before filing

them, they'll be easier to read. Always leave some space in each section. Use colour codes: they're pleasant, and make your files more visible.

3. Don't accumulate files. Ask your secretary to thin them out regularly. You should do a major inspection every three months.

4. Keep your confidential and legal documents in a fireproof safe.

5. Separate current files: obviously, you should keep the files you're working on at the moment handy, or at least all together in a special category.

6. Make an index: ask your secretary to make a second copy of every heading, sub-heading and title in your files, and to use these to compile an index, so that you can locate any file easily and quickly. Delegate this task entirely to your secretary.

Checklist: Document Organization

Filing

1. Easy access

2. Arranged alphabetically or by subject

3. Easy retrieval

4. Understood by colleagues

5. Method for eliminating useless documents

6. Periodical revision of the system

Processing

1. Screening by your secretary of incoming and outgoing material.

2. Removal of your name from useless mailing lists.

Post: in

1. Priority

2. Delegate to someone else

3. Hold: not important

4. Useless: eliminate immediately

N.B. Don't let documents 'on hold' accumulate. Study them regularly. Use moments when you're not overly productive.

Post: out

1. Demand a reply by phone rather than by post.

2. If possible, reply directly on the letter.

3. Reply by memorandum or business card.

4. Reply on form (standard reply letter).

5. Reply on dictaphone tape for your secretary.

6. Concise, precise and polite reply.

7. Mailing: list prepared in advance and stored on computer.

You can reproduce this checklist for your personal use, and post it in your office, to help you organize all your documents efficiently.

Practical techniques for making your filing system even more productive

1. Use your wastepaper basket! Filing is above all eliminating.

2. Never accumulate files. Deal with them rapidly, in small blocks.

3. Always place the most recent information in front.

4. Attach replies to letters with a stapler.

5. Mark the files clearly so that they can easily be identified and retrieved (index, colours, graphs, etc.).

6. Don't over-stuff your drawers. Always leave some empty space so you can get to the files easily.

7. Don't file your post according to date, but subject.

8. Consult your solicitor, accountant, bank manager, etc. to find out which documents you must keep.

9. Don't make your files too thick: more than 15 items justifies opening a second file on the subject.

10. Always label a file with the date it was started as well as the expiration date.

11. Fold large pages so that you can see the contents.

12. When you pull out a file, leave a note in its place, or a form like this:

Out

Title of Document: _____

Borrower's Name: _____

Date Out: _____

Return Date: _____

13. To reduce retrieval time, practise saying the alphabet backwards, from Z to A.

14. Remember: everything in its place, and a place for everything! Don't let documents accumulate on your desk or in your files.

Don't pile up, file up!

Accumulate nothing, file everything! What you've learned in this chapter will help you and your secretary to eliminate documents, articles, memos and reports that are not really useful to your business.

Now we're going to confront a topic that will make you or break you: decision-making.

This step is of capital importance. Some people who are used to responsibility and success seem to do it with no effort at all. Others have so much trouble. (It's paradoxical that a person can work a hundred times longer and harder trying to prepare for a decision ... and still make the wrong one!)

If you want to learn how to make decisions like a successful, high-performance company director, the next chapter will tell you everything you need to know.

23

MAKING THE RIGHT DECISION FAST

Increase your percentage of success

At the beginning of Part Two, we looked at the main consumers of time in your professional, social and family life. The method wouldn't be complete without in-depth coverage of one of the most important aspects of time management: *decision-making*.

We spend hours every week making decisions. For some this function is simple and doesn't take a great deal of time. But for others, making decisions – especially complex and important ones, with numerous factors and implications – can be a long, difficult and even painful process. If you find yourself spending hours weighing the pros and cons of a given situation, trying to come to a positive decision, then the next two chapters will be of enormous benefit to you.

Even those people who find decision-making easy will find some useful advice in these chapters. They will refine their methods, compare their own techniques with the experts, and increase their percentage of successful decisions.

Six weeks a year spent making decisions

You have to make dozens of decisions daily, in your professional, social and family life.

Some decisions are of secondary importance. For example, where you're going to have lunch. On the other hand, if your time management system is finely tuned, and you're applying what you read in Chapter Twenty about appointments, then even this won't be left to chance.

Some decisions are very important. Should you accept a job offer that looks attractive at first glance? Should you hire someone on the basis of an impressive curriculum vitae?

Some decisions can have a profound determining effect on your life. Even though, as Alvin Toffler demonstrated in his book *Future Shock,* we are called upon to change careers an average of five or six times within one lifetime, which is very different from previous generations, nevertheless the decision a young person makes when choosing a career will have repercussions for the rest of his or her life.

Whether you decide to become a doctor, an engineer, an accountant, a computer analyst or a lawyer, your choice will affect an important part of your life. The same is true of the decision to marry, or have children.

All day, throughout your lifetime, you are continually confronted by a variety of important choices to make – about a hundred per day, sometimes more. Each of these decisions takes time. Some take a lot of time, others less, but in total you generally spend over an hour a day considering what decisions to make. If you string all those hours together, you get six weeks a year spent on decision-making!

Maybe you call it something else: reflection, hesitation, cogitation, musing, problem-solving, consulting, meditating, weighing pros and cons, planning.

You might procrastinate sometimes: put a decision off for later. Setting a time limit is sometimes wise. But it can also be costly. And if you get into the habit of putting decisions off for later, it can be catastrophic.

Here is some advice that will help you with the decision-making process.

Should you make decisions?

The popular image of a successful person is someone who has the ability to make fast decisions.

But fast decisions don't necessarily mean *right decisions!*

To fully understand this important distinction, consider the case of a chess champion. If he is playing against you (or even against a few people of your calibre), he'll make every move – every decision – with amazing rapidity.

Try to do the same.

What do you think would happen?

That's right, you'd lose faster! Your game would suffer, you'd play worse.

So trying to make decisions as quickly as the chess champion is an error. The champion can make rapid decisions because he already knows, through experience, all the situations that will occur in the match with you. He knows thousands of moves, hundreds of systems by heart, so he needs only a minimum of reflection time. His real reflection can be found in the years of study and preparation behind his experience.

So don't be duped.

Obviously, it's a different story if the champion plays against another chess master. He might then take hours, even days, to make a single move.

Speed is not the most important criterion

Speed is therefore not the most important criterion, despite its reputation. It usually takes time to make an important decision.

Sometimes we have to make too many decisions. We hesitate, procrastinate, and these decisions become sources of anxiety. Why? Because decision-making – even at high levels – is a vague and intuitive process.

The Complete Time Management System offers a method for decision-making that will help you refine your own techniques so that you can make the right decision more quickly. You will save time and avoid the anxiety associated with having to make last-minute decisions.

You'll also be saving time for the people around you, since they won't have to wait for you to make your decisions.

Your success depends on your ability to make decisions

Of course you can't expect yourself always to make the right decision.

Even the best of us make mistakes. However, it is within your ability to make the right decision as frequently as possible, something your entire success depends on. It's that ability that TMS hopes to develop in you.

Whether you decided to hire the wrong executive, an inefficient consultant, or an expert who isn't one, you were forced into a situation where you had to make decisions. If you don't want to go under, you must learn to make the right ones in future.

You may think that you don't need to read this chapter because you can already handle decision-making pretty well. How do you know if your decision-making ability is already developed? Read a little further, and do the following test.

1. Do you reflect about a decision even after it's made?

2. Do other people's opinions have an exaggerated influence on your decisions?

3. Do you procrastinate when faced with decisions?

4. Do you tend to take too much time to make difficult decisions?

5. Do you have the troublesome tendency of according too much importance to details when you make decisions?

6. Do you put too much energy into making a decision that really isn't all that important?

7. Do you often let others decide for you?

8. Have you missed opportunities, or a promotion, because you weren't able to make a decision?

9. Do you always want all the facts, all the information, before making a decision, even if you know that it is realistically impossible to get them all?

If your answers were mostly 'yes', then it's very important that you read these two chapters on decision-making attentively.

If you only ticked off a few, don't skip to Part Three just yet! Don't forget that successful people are always looking for ways to refine their methods, and never think they know everything. Their success is certainly not based on chance.

Get rid of mental blocks

Often, when we put off making a decision or we are bothered by the fear of making the wrong decision, the reason, without our knowing it, is because we suffer from certain mental blocks. By becoming aware of your blocks, you take an important step toward getting rid of them. The enemy is identified. It has a name and a face. You can then crush it much more easily. (See Chapter Eleven.)

Before analysing your mental blocks, and each time you have difficulty making a decision, ask yourself the following three questions:

1. Do you really want to make a decision?

2. Do you have the resources (financial, technical, personnel) to resolve this problem?

3. Are you really responsible for making this decision?

Ten main blocks to decision-making

1. You have trouble listening to your feelings, your intuition.

2. You lack real priorities. You don't exactly know why you make certain decisions, since they don't seem to fit (or fit badly) into the larger scheme, or flow of events.

3. You lack self-confidence.

4. You are over-extended, maybe even depressed.

5. You are overly afraid of failure and criticism, and/or other people's judgement.

6. You're a perfectionist. You never finish getting all your data together, data you think is 'necessary' to make the right decision.

7. You feel that you don't have enough time to make decisions.

8. You think that things will work out by themselves, whether you make a decision or not. You are a 'super-optimist'!

9. You feel you should consult everybody you know before making an important decision. You are afraid of making unpopular decisions, which will fail to please everyone.

10. You think that, since you've already put off a decision and have a number of others which are running late, you won't be able to regain control of the situation and so you let things go entirely.

Take a clear and objective look at yourself and make a written list of your main blocks. How honest you are about yourself is your primary tool for self-development.

Don't forget that the exercises in this book concern you and you alone: no one else will have access to them. Play seriously. You have everything to gain, and nothing to lose.

Be aware that blocks often appear in groups, as if they were really related to each other. Don't be ashamed of your mental blocks. Usually, you're not even responsible for them. They come from your childhood, when you experienced so many things without having the slightest control over what happened. And don't forget that the nobility of the human race lies in its perfectibility and not in its perfection!

The best cure for mental blocks

What is the best way to get rid of these mental blocks, however varied they may be?

Is there a remedy?

Fortunately, yes! And this universal and extremely effective remedy is simply ACTION.

That's right: ACTION!

To stop hemming and having, to get rid of mental blocks, you have to act as if you didn't have any. Conquer your fear! Act as if you had no fear and you'll end up not having any. You will develop new habits and improve the power of your decision-making faculties.

Stop the thought machine

Maybe you have the upsetting habit, as many of your colleagues surely do, of incessantly mulling things over in your mind, of reflecting for long hours before putting anything down on paper.

I know that Mozart composed whole movements of symphonies

in his head before writing them down faultlessly, as though taking dictation. But we're not all Mozarts. Most of our abstract thinking remains sterile and useless until we take the trouble to put things down on paper.

Sometimes that's all you need to do to avoid enormous waste of time and terrible anxiety. By writing things down, at least in outline form, by examining the real aspects of a given decision, we can avoid spending hours on a choice that perhaps isn't that important after all.

As we've said before, you don't spend a thousand pounds (in time) on a decision worth ten!

To help prevent you wasting time on long and futile reflection, we have drawn up some guidelines to help you evaluate a situation before making a decision.

Questionnaire: Decision No. 1

	Yes	No
Will this decision:		
1. Generate income	☐	☐
2. Increase productivity	☐	☐
3. Improve quality	☐	☐
4. Utilize my and/or my colleagues' skills	☐	☐
5. Utilize equipment and/or resources efffectively	☐	☐
6. Improve security	☐	☐
7. Reduce costs	☐	☐
8. Reduce waste	☐	☐
9. Improve employee morale	☐	☐
10. Justify company working procedures	☐	☐

In the light of your responses, what will you:

Do yourself? _____

Delegate? _____

Ignore? _____

Questionnaire: Decision No. 2

● What will I gain by opting for this choice_____

_____

● What will I lose? _____

_____

● When will I recover my investment?_____

● What are the realistic chances of profit or savings?_____

● How will this decision affect employee morale?_____

● How will this decision affect productivity?_____

● Will this decision have an effect on the company's cash flow?__

How can this decision have a negative effect on my company's
image? _____

● What positive effect will this decision have on my company's
image and/or prestige? _____

_____

● Compare the consequences of a positive with a negative decision.
Sum up the situation. _____

_____

Conclusion

My decision is:_____

I hope that you will now be able to make decisions more easily:
faster, more rationally, and with a high percentage of success. How
can you become a really 'great' decision-maker, someone who exudes
success? You'll soon find out ...

24

THE SECRETS OF GREAT DECISION-MAKERS

Secrets/tricks/personal techniques

Now I'll tell you how I, as a professional, make my decisions. All my secrets, tricks and personal techniques are largely inspired by great decision-makers.

1. I always ask myself a question which is, in appearance, obvious, but on closer analysis isn't always so:
    'What is the subject – or object – of my decision?'

    I force myself to state the problem as clearly as possible.
    I try to identify the determining factors with precision. To do this, I always have my priorities in mind, and I ask myself, even for secondary decisions:
    'How does this get me closer to my goal?'
    'Does this fit in with my priorities, my objectives?'
    If a certain choice doesn't bring me any closer to attaining my objectives (or not close enough to justify my investment in time and energy), my decision will not be long in coming:

    **My time is too precious and my goals too important
    for me to do anything useless!**

2. I systematically keep notes of everything that is material for reflection (things that have passed the test of the first question). I use a special notebook for this, and write only on the right-hand page. I reserve the left-hand pages for thoughts and ideas that occur later. I never note two subjects for reflection on the same page, except on the first three pages, which I use as an index.

These subjects for thought will be dealt with later on. But I always keep in mind what Pascal said: 'I had an idea. I forgot it. So I wrote down that I'd forgotten it.'

I forget just as much as anyone else. Thoughts pass, but the written word remains ...

3. I try to define the problem as clearly as possible, in order to know what I have to think about. Keep in mind that a well-formulated question is already half the solution.

In this definition, I establish an order of importance and urgency. I use three categories of importance:

A Very important
B Somewhat important
C Secondary importance.

I have discovered that more numerous categories, a more specific breakdown, only results in loss of time.

For important problems there are two categories:

(a) Urgent
(b) Can wait.

If some external factor prevents me from making a decision, I note it down. If I've set a time limit for my decision, I note that down as well. If there's no date limit imposed from outside, I set one myself.

I spread things out: I set one date for getting all the data I need together (including the process of consultation) and another for making the decision.

If I discover that a decision isn't worth making within a set time, I conclude that it simply isn't worth the effort at all, and eliminate it from my notebook.

This procedure is very helpful. If you are not capable of deciding, or if you spend months, even years, thinking something over, if it doesn't really matter whether you have a time limit for making the decision or not, it might be because the decision is not really all that important, even though you may have thought it was.

4. I know that quick decisions are desirable, but that haste can also make waste.

In the past, I've acted spontaneously, trusting my impulses. I made a lot of mistakes.

I try not to suppress my bursts of spontaneity, but I am careful. I include this spontaneous energy as just one factor on the positive side of the scale. I no longer accept it as the deciding factor.

I also want facts, reflection and analysis.

To combat my natural impatience when confronted with certain very interesting propositions, I oblige myself to accept a period of maturation. I know things shouldn't be put off. But before giving my final decision, I prefer to 'sleep on it'. Doing this has worked for me over and over again, especially for important decisions.

During the maturation period, and as my deadline approaches, I try to nourish my subconscious as much as possible, through frequent consultation and gathering of data.

I know that ultimately it will be my intuition, my feeling, that decides, because facts and figures rarely speak for themselves, and can often be interpreted in different ways.

It's my interpretation, my judgement that counts, unless the decision is being made jointly with my boss, or a board of directors.

5. I get personally involved in a decision. If I have the final word, I don't ask for others to approve, and I don't try to hide behind a façade of neutrality until my final decision is made.

   I assume responsibility right from the start, and I want my associates to do the same. At the same time, I always cover for my subordinates in front of my superiors, knowing that I am fully responsible for the success or failure of the team working under my direction.

6. I accept the fact that conditions are never ideal for making a decision, and I also accept that I can never get *all* the data together for making my decision.

   If I wait too long, I know that conditions will change anyway, and that much of my information will no longer be valid.

7. I don't like failure, but I know that it's part of the job. So I try to be ready for failure ahead of time, by salvaging as much as possible in the way of positive feedback from the experience.

8. I know that no decisions are made on a completely rational basis. Feelings always play a role in the decision-making process. I don't try to deny it. I accept my feelings. But when they begin to take over, I postpone the decision.

   I re-evaluate the data objectively later on. I try to *act* and not *react* to situations.

9. As long as I still have doubts, I wait.

   At the same time I try not to fall into the trap of procrastination.
   I respect my feelings, my personal intuition. I don't hurry myself. I know that a decision made prematurely will usually turn out to be a bad one.
   If I still have doubts, I will not be able to motivate myself, and others, as I should.

10. When a decision seems complex, when there are numerous factors pro and con, I have learned to make cuts with a facility that surprises even myself at times!

    I simply ask myself: 'If I had to give a simple yes or no answer, without taking any subtleties, any unusual circumstances into account, if I absolutely had to say yes or no, what would I do?'

    And I don't give myself more than five seconds to make up my mind.
    A simple yes or no.
    This is an effective way of seeing through complex situations. Sometimes details can assume exaggerated importance, and blind us to the really important issues.

11. I play the 'devil's advocate' to help my thinking. I pretend to be violently opposed to a certain opinion, and build a case to support that position.

    I try to be as convincing as possible. If I can't convince myself, then the chances are good that the opposite position is the right one.

12. I am always aware of my personal rhythm. If I'm tired, if I feel that my intellectual faculties are low, or just not at their best, I systematically postpone any important decision because I know that those are the times when most bad decisions are made.

If I go ahead and make a decision in such a state anyway, I will be plagued by uncertainty, knowing that my choice was not made under optimum conditions.

13. I learn from other people's experience. But I do try to distinguish between opinions and facts.

   I take pleasure in consulting specialists from different backgrounds, cultures and professions in order to sample a large variety of opinions. I systematically keep notes of these opinions, and in time, and as events proceed, I assign them to one side or another of the issue.

   I have more confidence in people who have given me sound advice on numerous occasions, and I am careful of, or avoid completely, people who have offered bad advice (even if I didn't take it).

   I do the same thing with references. I note down the name of the person who referred such and such an individual, and in time I can evaluate the reference.

14. Whenever possible, and especially if I have to make the same kinds of decisions often, I use a checklist. I ask myself the same basic questions: Who? What? Where? When? How? Why? How much does it cost? How much will it earn?

15. If I suffer from a mental block about a certain decision for too long, I ask myself certain questions:

   (a) Do I lack any essential data?
   (b) Should I consult a specialist in the field?
   (c) Is my hesitation a warning? Should I opt for a negative decision?

16. I know that 'perfect and logical certainty' can never be attained, and that even though a decision might be a good one, there is still some risk involved. It's just something you have to live with. However, this doesn't prevent me from looking ahead, and accepting the risk factor as something very real that must be considered.

17. I try to evaluate a situation before I get involved, and determine

what kind of investment, in terms of energy, money, time, worry and problems, it represents.

From past experience I have learned that there are usually more worries and problems than expected, in any kind of business (remember Murphy's Law!). On the other hand, I'm neither pessimistic nor a defeatist.

I am not lacking in energy or resources, but there is a kind of natural inertia, a resistance that objects and people have to new projects.

I also know that although I may have a lot of energy, it's limited, and has to be managed to avoid ineffective dispersion, spreading myself too thin.

So I try to see just what a given decision is going to cost, and take that into account before saying 'yes'.

Often I say 'no'. I'm not afraid of hurting people or losing their esteem.

18. Last but not least (perhaps I put this last because it is most important!) I want to talk about my intuition.

Intuition isn't useful in every situation. But each time there's an ambiguity, each time I could say 'yes' or 'no', I call on my intuition for help.

I have observed that my intuition is rarely wrong. I have very often gone wrong by doing the opposite of what it suggested.

Why didn't I listen to my intuition?

Because I didn't recognize its worth. Because sometimes, even though my intuition tells me to do one thing, I do the other so as not to hurt people, not to let them down, because I'm afraid to say what I really think. Because sometimes the facts and figures are in conflict with my intuition, because of my 'rational' education, which suppresses all irrational action.

Maybe you don't trust your intuition. Don't worry. That doesn't mean you can't or shouldn't use it.

Intuition can prevent many errors

What should you do?

Each time you have a decision to make, take a few minutes. Close your eyes, relax, try to put aside all thoughts related to the decision, and concentrate on an inner image of yourself, walking into the largest and the best equipped conference room in the world, programmed with a vast memory bank of information.

Don't forget that your subconscious mind forgets nothing, that it records everything you've ever read, learned, experienced and heard since the beginning of your existence. That's no small feat! And it has probably also recorded information of which you are totally unaware, subconsciously ...

Calm your mind for a few moments, and ask yourself if you're making the right decision, yes or no.

You'll always get an answer. If not at that very instant, then the next day, or a week later, often at the most unexpected moments.

What should you do with this answer?

At first you're not obliged to trust your intuition every time; simply include it as one of the factors to be considered. Make a note in your decision book: Intuition suggests doing this. In time, you'll be able to see whether your intuition has been right or wrong.

Calculate actual statistics. If the percentages are good, then learn to trust it more often, without ignoring the other factors of course.

Intuition can save you a lot of time, and it will prove to you again and again that pure rationality rarely pays. Personally, I trust my intuition implicitly. And if I had followed its advice more often in the past, I could have avoided a lot of mistakes.

Now, what about you? How do you make decisions? It's worth taking some time to analyse your decision-making process, because if you can learn to make the *right* decisions, then you can also become a *great* decision-maker.

Almost everyone follows a precise pattern (even if it's unconscious) when making decisions. Do the following exercises. Try to discover what method you are already applying to make your decisions.

Imagine that you have to teach someone else exactly what your method is when faced with a decision. Often, teaching something is the best way to learn it. By imagining that you're teaching, you will learn how you make your own decisions.

Exercise No. 1

● How I make decisions

_____

_____

_____

Exercise No. 2

● A recent example of a bad decision

_____

_____

_____

(Describe the situation, and try to identify the errors that you made. Take at least fifteen minutes to do this exercise.)

Do you often make these kinds of errors?

If so, what conclusions can you draw about your decision-making process? What corrective measures can you take?

Exercise No. 3

● Recent examples of right decisions

_____

_____

_____

(You've heard the saying 'learn from your mistakes'. But we also have to learn from our successes. Success can be very instructive. So analyse the correct decisions you've made recently. How did it happen that you made the right decision? Did you think enough about the factors involved? Did you consult the right people? Ask yourself these kinds of questions, and draw your own conclusions.)

And if you still can't decide . . .

It happens rarely enough, but there are times when you think you've tried everything, when you've consulted all the specialists you could find, and weighed all the pros and cons exhaustively, and still don't know what the right decision is.

You're at a dead end, a black hole! You're lost in the forest, and it looks as though you'll never get out . . .

What do you do? Here are some techniques that can help you:

1. Don't force yourself, you'll only make things worse. Time can clarify many things, revealing precisely that missing factor which prevented you from knowing what to do.

2. Give yourself some rest. Maybe you're overworked. Why not take a few days off, a long weekend or even a whole week? Very often, just finding yourself in a different environment, surrounded by different people, gives the perspective you need to resolve your problem.

3. Review your objectives and priorities. Maybe the decision seems so tough because you've lost sight of your goals. If the problem is of a professional nature, ask yourself:
   (a) Why are you getting paid?
   (b) What can you do to make your company more profitable?

4. Review your list of mental blocks. Is one of them hindering you without your knowing?

5. Promise yourself a reward once the decision is made.

The best decision is to make a decision, in extreme cases ANY decision, and most importantly, to act on it.

It's completely useless to decide that you want to learn speed-reading, increase your income by 20 per cent, and take two more weeks of holiday every year, if you do nothing to realize these objectives. You won't become a great decision-maker like that, only a great procrastinator. There are millions of those in the world already.

So make decisions, and act on them!

The great decision-maker's guide

Take the time, day after day (ideally after every decision you make) to verify whether or not you've followed the correct procedure. The following checklist, which is a true guide for making great decisions, will help you:

1. Have you been exhaustive in your examination of the different options available to you?

2. Have you made a list of them?

3. Have you listened to your feelings, your inner thoughts, your intuition?

4. Have you incorporated these thoughts and different options in your decision?

5. Have you written down all the factors involved?

6. Have you considered these factors in the light of your priorities?

7. Have you opted for a plan of action?

8. Have you written this decision down?

9. Have you considered and eliminated all other possibilities?

10. Have you examined this choice in the light of your inner feelings?

11. Have you transformed this decision into positive action?

Once you've made a decision concerning an important project, you want to see it materialize as efficiently as possible, with every chance of success. The next chapter shows you how.

Develop your intuition and follow its advice.

PART THREE

HOW TO STAY ON THE SUCCESS TRAIN

25

APPLY THE SCIENTIFIC METHOD

To be a master of the art of time management, it's not enough to know the method and its techniques, however excellent they may be. You must also *apply them*, integrate them into your daily life. You must experience a real *inner transformation* – a transformation that lasts, that's durable, solid and strong. To do this, you must adopt a new attitude.

In this third section, you will discover how you can develop this lasting attitude which will allow you to become a master – and so *have more time*.

A long approach for a steep hill

We have seen how astute and profitable it is to make long, complex jobs manageable by dividing them into sub-tasks, even sub-sub-tasks, and considering each one as an essential part of the whole. In this way, each task seems much more attainable, and the progression towards the final objective is a lot simpler to understand. We 'feel', in a very real way, that we are advancing, that we're approaching the objective with each step, with each victory, conquest, success along the way.

Remember that in this process, it is of the utmost importance *to reward yourself* at every stage.

Why?

First, confirm each achievement; after reaching each objective, take the time to note the date and engrave this message of success on your subconscious.

When faced with a very difficult obstacle, when you're in doubt or when the risks are high, or when you're discouraged or lack motivation, you can look back on your storehouse of success, on your conquests, on all those objectives you've set for yourself and were able to attain.

It's important to reward yourself because it helps you savour your success, take pleasure in your prowess, which is something you deny yourself all too often. You should congratulate yourself, encourage yourself, bask in the tangible proof that you can achieve what you set out to do, when you are motivated.

Result?

The next step will be a lot easier, with your morale high, bursting with optimism and self-confidence.

How to reward yourself

How should you reward yourself? It's up to you. In this area, your imagination is all that counts. Some people give themselves a few minutes of complete freedom, or an afternoon of sport, a good bottle of wine or champagne, some extra time with the family, a book or magazine, an article of clothing, a seminar, a weekend at the seaside, a long walk, a drive in the country, a new record ... it doesn't matter what it is.

Choose something you want. But there's one essential and strict condition: take the time and means to give yourself pleasure, and to savour this pleasure well. That's all.

You'll see how effective this is. By applying this technique every step of the way, stone by stone, you can move mountains.

It is always a good idea to take a long run at a steep hill, especially if you have a lot of fun doing it.

Analyse your projects scientifically

You are raring to go, and decide to undertake a huge project.

Rule number one: *invest the time to do an in-depth analysis of your project*. Napoleon said that battles are won first on the drawing-board, and then on the field.

The first advantage is that you will be able to save a lot of time by integrating different tasks, and accomplishing them together.

Here's an example of three very simple tasks: you have to post a letter, pick up some photographs and buy some theatre tickets. The first task is urgent, the second can wait a few days, and the third can wait a couple of weeks. If you can do them all at the same time, why not?

The second advantage is that some tasks will be rendered unnecessary or obsolete by the completion of others.

For example: you want to get a driving licence, and you decide to obtain a guide to prepare for the test, so you go to the appropriate office and pick up all the necessary forms, etc.

All that becomes unnecessary if you opt for the following alternative: find an organization that offers a course of driving lessons and have them do all the paperwork. They're familiar with the procedure, know all the ins and outs of the bureaucratic labyrinth, and can do everything in a lot less time.

The third advantage is that you will be able to predict 'bottlenecks' and take the appropriate measures to avoid them.

For example: you tell a client that the work will be finished by the end of the month, without fail. Horror of horrors! You forget another obligation, or a colleague goes sick and you have to cover, or a supplier is late, etc. You have 20 days to do the work if you want to meet your deadline.

Bottlenecks are most numerous in the area of building. If the carpenters are available, as well as the electricians and plumbers, there shouldn't be any problem. The house will be finished on time!

Mistake! How can you expect twelve people to work together in the same room? Steps, often quite simple ones, must be taken. For example, when the roofers have finished, the plumbers come in, followed a week later by the carpenters and the electricians.

You might even have to operate shifts. But the work will get done!

The fourth advantage is that you will be able to shorten delays and/or make optimum use of your budget.

For example: say that to construct the same house, you need a crane for ten days, and that it will cost £2000 per day. But you find that you can save three days on the complete job by renting two cranes at £3500 per day (you get a reduction for taking two, even though it's for a shorter time) for three of those days, since they can work very well together.

Calculate: three days less for the foreman, for the construction crew etc. all for a small supplement, an assistant crane operator, for example.

Not only do you save three days' time, but a large amount of money as well: money that you can surely put to good use.

You will realize, from your own experience, that there are very frequent opportunities for optimizing your budget, shortening delays, etc.

The fifth advantage is that you will always know what the most efficient remedy is for unexpected problems, unpredictable events, even catastrophes.

Why?

Because you'll be able to see the repercussions of each event, each new decision on the project as a whole, clearly and quickly. You'll have it all at your fingertips, and be familiar with the whole progression, the files and sub-files, of your project.

You'll be able to react quickly, after having weighed the alternatives carefully (like in chess: 'If I move this pawn, what will happen?') and you'll be aware of the causes of a given situation.

In this way, you can minimize the negative effects of unpredictable events on your project.

The sixth advantage is by no means the least important: after having put down on paper all factors concerning a given project, you might conclude that it's too hazardous, unrealistic, in other words impossible.

It's always wiser to abandon a project in time, than to spend months of enthusiastic time and energy on something that is bound to fail.

Especially, and here's *the seventh advantage*, if you do 'block simulations'. As far as you can see, your project doesn't stand up. All right! Now isolate each of the blocks of tasks which you know to be perfectly achievable.

Result?

First you will be able to simulate real events, seeing what happens if you make such and such an investment, integrate tasks, cancel, delay, divide, accelerate, etc. What's more, you will be able to attack the real problems head on: each stage, task, sub-project, etc. that poses a problem and endangers the project. Your analysis of the problems will therefore be as astute as possible, and you can concentrate all your energy, your creativity, all your resources on any remaining obstructions to your success and your self-fulfilment.

These seven advantages make the scientific analysis of a project the most effective tool there is for realizing your goal.

Scientific analysis in action

Convinced? All right. Let's get to work! Step 1 is defining, as precisely as possible, your primary objective, the reason behind your project, the reason you're willing to invest so much time and energy.

An American friend of mine, a trained scientist, recently confided: 'For my last business venture, I spent nearly three weeks on this stage: I analysed all my different motivating factors, my needs, desires, expectations, etc. It was good work, which turned out to be an excellent investment in terms of simplifying and speeding up what had to be done, and easing any worries I had about the success or failure of the project.'

For Step 2, subdivide your project into as many sub-projects, tasks, sub-tasks, etc. as possible. Ideally, each of the subdivisions will be easy to understand and achieve, and take about a day's work.

For example, my friend had found premises for his new office. He had the funds, the product, the distribution network, etc. All he had to do was register his company. In the United States this can be a very time-consuming operation . . .

Exercise

Do a written breakdown, in any order, of what this task entails:

- Make phone calls to find out which department, at which levels of government, you have to deal with.

- Order the required documents. Will you have them sent by mail? Courier? Or will you pick them up? Open a file for all these documents.

- Get a copy of your birth certificate, and your civil status.

- Go down to the courthouse, to the Business Registration Office, and ask for any necessary information.

- What are the opening hours of the offices you will have to visit?

- How much will it cost?

- Get the money (cash or certified cheque) at the bank.

- Make copies of your lease.

- Contact the phone company to discuss the phone system.

Now you can group tasks: if you have to go to the bank, why not make the photocopies while you are out? And what would happen if you hired someone to do everything for you, at the right price? And so on...

Step 3: arrange the steps in order of priority. To do this, take a separate sheet of paper and write the first sub-task you noted – in this case calling government information (look up the number in the special section of your phone directory, or ask information) – in a box, as follows:

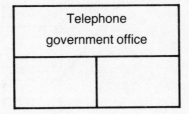

... and cross this item off your original list.

Second item (unless you reached the right department immediately) is to call the various offices.

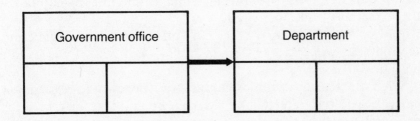

The steps follow each other one after the other; their development is sequential.

Cross 'Call Registration Department For Documents' off your list. When you make this call, you will ask for a number of things at the same time:

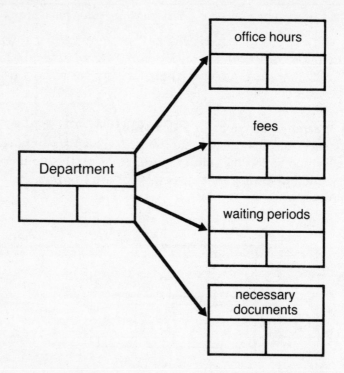

Cross these four items off your list. This brings you to the next step, which, in graphic form, looks like the chart opposite:

Did you notice that you have to add new tasks, ones you forgot, but which become apparent as you work on the plan? It's the same for sequences of tasks, which are grouped into parallel, more efficient blocks of activity that save precious time (combining bank, photocopies, stamps, envelopes, etc.).

And now you can cross everything off the first list. Registering the company will take a few hours at most. But what if you hadn't been prepared?

When the friend who told me this story went to the registration office, he was congratulated by a clerk, who said that the record for the number of times someone had to return to the office to register a company was twelve. Wish that person luck. If he needs so much time to do a simple task like registering a company, how will he cope later on, when the company is in business?

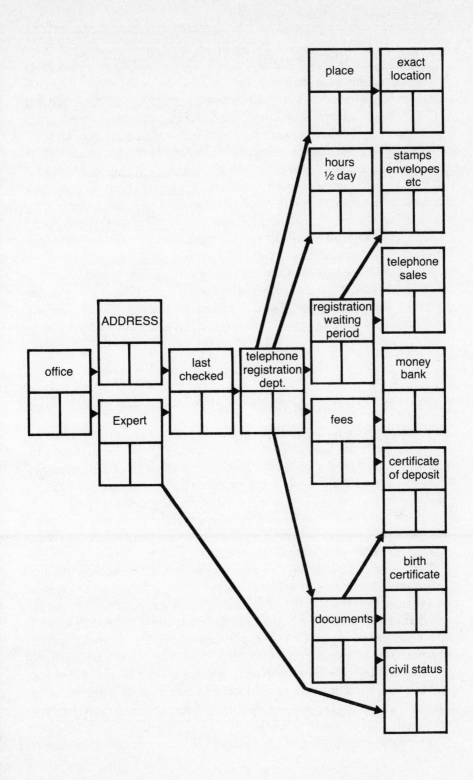

How to manage your projects scientifically

Are you asking yourself why the little boxes in the chart had two smaller boxes underneath? The answer is simple. In this example, all the tasks (except maybe getting hold of your birth certificate) were short and easily organized; you could do them all in a day.

If each task itself takes a day, or a few days of work, then it would be useful to know, based on previous experience, the *'earliest date'* and the *'latest date'* for completion. You can then determine a schedule and find ways to save time and money, for example by delegating a task or cancelling, or merging etc. This will be not only a strategic tool, but an aid to making optimum use of your time and budget.

Some managers go further, and add more spaces to each box, for data like total cost and/or rate, daily, hourly, etc. Their diagrams are covered with red marks: corrections, arrows, notes: £500 sacrificed for two days' time saved ... two days' delay for £2000 saved somewhere else, etc.

Look for the critical path

A last technique for optimizing your plan: look for the critical path. Starting from the first task on the left-hand side of the diagram, to the last task on the right, it's the shortest route, in terms of time, that you can use to complete the project. That's the Critical Path.

At each step of the way, try to shorten any delays: the path is scientific, and will provide plenty of opportunities as you go along. So you understand that these little squares are very precious tools, with their dates and price estimates ...

You can make your diagram more sophisticated by asking all your colleagues, associates, employees, suppliers, etc. to tell you as much as possible about what they're doing (deadlines, possible advances, at what price), and by delegating as much as possible at each step of the way, reserving only the supervisory role for yourself, you'll always come out on top!

What's the difference between someone who's just following orders, and someone with a mission to accomplish – someone who feels part of a larger project that mobilizes a whole crew of professionals, out to move mountains?

The difference is that in the second case, the person understands the place his or her work plays in the larger whole, its usefulness and importance; while in the first case, the person was nothing more than a pawn, doing a job, following orders without asking any questions, nothing more.

And believe me when I say that a team's motivation can make all the difference between success and failure.

What about you?

Follow your critical path and you will keep winning. You will be fulfilled and repay those around you a hundredfold. A strong feeling will grow inside you: that each day you are moving inexorably forward towards your goal.

Finally, your diagram will be concrete proof of your success. You feel that at last you are going to attain your number one objective, for which you've been striving for so long...

**Take time to think about the problem
and organize a scientific approach.**

26

How to Conquer Your Bad Habits

Three almost infallible ways to be inefficient

There are three types of eternal losers: perfectionists, tortured workers (workaholics) and people who are always in a state of crisis.
Do you, at least at times, belong to one of these types?

To find out, and learn how to get out of this trap, study the following questions:

Yes No

1. Are you worried about what other people think of you?

2. Do you put off making important calls because you're afraid of being rejected?

3. Do you do work over and over, until it meets with your complete satisfaction?

4. Do you take a long time to do simple things?

5. When something is finished, do you always think you should have done better?

6. Do you feel good about yourself only when you're satisfied with your work, and depressed at other times?

7. Does your self-esteem depend only on what you accomplish at work?

Did you answer 'yes' to any of these questions? Then accept it, you're a perfectionist!

Why always try to be more perfect than others?

Are you aware of the real effect this attitude has on your creativity? It produces tensions between you and your colleagues. It results in enormous loss of time. And the secondary effects are countless. Is it worth it?

Perfectionists are people who live – and cause those around them to live – in a constant state of tension, which is very unpleasant. And contrary to popular opinion – especially the opinion of those who suffer from this failing – perfectionism is not a quality but *a fault*.

Perfectionists might work longer hours than others, and are concerned about details that others ignore. They never want to delegate, preferring to do everything themselves because they are certain that they – and they alone – can do the work correctly.

But in the final analysis, their results are never superior. In reality, their work is often inferior to that of people who are demanding, certainly, but who are tempered by such factors as balance and being realistic.

Most perfectionists forget the principle formulated by Peter Drucker: they *do things right* instead of *doing the right thing*.

And they also forget about the Pareto Principle, that 20 per cent of our efforts produce 80 per cent of our results.

Get rid of it once and for all

In addition to the suggestions offered in Chapter Three, what techniques exist to help you rid yourself of this mania for perfection, which saps your energy and your morale?

Here are a few:

Accept the fact that the notion 'below average' for a perfectionist is, in reality, perfectly acceptable to most other people.

The Pareto Principle states that 20 per cent of our effort produces 80 per cent of our results. Ask yourself: what is the minimum amount of work I can put in, to get the same results?

Determine the amount of time you should invest in a job in relation to the objective. For example: a memo designed to communicate only essential information does not justify three hours of writing.

Know how to delegate. Don't ask if others can do the work as well as you, but only *if they can do the job well*!

Put things in their proper perspective. The question to ask is: 'Will this still be important in 100 years?'

Don't be afraid of making mistakes. Remember the attitude of the IBM management team: 'Learn from your errors!'

And finally, repeat to yourself day after day: 'The "best" is the enemy of the "good"!'

Perfectionists often exhibit another characteristic – or fault – which is a direct result of their uncontrollable mania to have everything done to perfection, despite the number of hours it might take: they are tortured workers.

Are you a tortured worker?

Do you recognize yourself in this portrait?

- You love working very hard
- You live for your work
- You set goals for yourself which are too ambitious
- You can't stand being inactive
- You are overflowing with energy
- You get tired quickly with routine work
- You feed on challenge and competition
- You try to do more than one thing at a time
- You have trouble reconciling your personal and professional lives
- You bring your office stress home at night
- You feel guilty if you relax, or slow down in your work
- You accept more work than you can handle
- You're often behind in your work
- You suffer from excessive stress
- You demand too much of yourself
- You often bring work home from the office.

Did you have to answer 'yes' to many of these questions? If so, you are a tortured worker. You're a workaholic.

Unfortunately we can affirm, with studies and statistics to back us up, that this seriously reduces your chances of success. This attitude by no means signifies that you will do better than someone else who works less.

Paradoxical? Unjust?

It doesn't matter! It's a trap, the same as being a perfectionist. It has its roots deep in your mind, often going back to childhood. How many times have your parents and teachers repeated that you have to work to succeed?

On the other hand, how many people have told you that you have to *work intelligently*? Maybe you've heard the saying, 'Don't work harder, work smarter!'

It might seem that there is a large variety of tortured workers, almost as large as there are individuals who fit the mould. But on closer inspection, we find that, despite minor differences, these people fall into two categories. Do you belong to one?

Tortured worker type 1: 'I can do it myself!'

In the first category (which produces most coronary patients) we find those people who don't want to delegate. They find it impossible to say 'no' (there's a little voice in their heads always telling them to be nice). This means that they accumulate job upon job and they end up doing everyone's work, even the work of their subordinates, in whom they have no confidence whatsoever.

Fortunately, there's still hope, as long as the person *wants* to get better. Here is the treatment:

1. Sit down and don't do anything until you've figured out who should do what.
2. Only work on *important* things, and forget about the rest.
3. Group your phone calls.

Resist the temptation to call at any time without a good reason.

Tortured worker type 2: The procrastinator

What characterizes the second type of tortured worker? This is the person who procrastinates all the time, and whose office is littered with a ton of paperwork. This person is also absolutely incapable of respecting a schedule.

Ring a bell? Even a small one? Here's how to eliminate the problem:

1. Sit down and keep on working, despite any distractions.
2. Set deadlines for each stage of the work, and not for the work as a whole.
3. Force yourself to meet the deadlines for each stage.

4. Delegate as much routine paperwork as possible, starting with the least important tasks.
5. Schedule a daily 'hour of solitude', and make sure you take it.
6. Make a critical path diagram for 80 per cent of the things you have to do, and don't alter it except in case of emergency.

Learn to limit yourself

An average executive should work 50 hours a week. If you can't get your work done in less than 60 or 70 hours, then you should re-evaluate your working methods.

How many hours a week do you now work?

Number of hours _____

Calculate the number of hours you could eliminate, if you had to: _____

Ask the same question another way:

Don't you think you could accomplish as much while working 10 hours less a week? 20 hours less? _____

Exercise

Write down at least five ways in which you could reduce the number of hours you work a week.

1. _____

2. _____

3. _____

4. _____

5. _____

Learn to recognize the causes of an emergency

Even the most astute manager is sometimes faced with a crisis situation.

One of the best ways to prevent a crisis is to be able to recognize the signs before it actually happens, signs which are almost invariably present. A crisis which is caught in time is much easier to arrest. In fact, when steps are taken early enough, it usually stops being a crisis altogether. By recognizing the warning signs, you will be able to stamp out the fire before it grows.

What are the four main causes of a crisis?

1. **Bad planning**.
   You ignore the warning signals which precede the real problem.
   Your work schedule is overloaded.
   You only plan a few days in advance.

2. **Inaccurate estimation of deadlines.**

3. **Pleasure from playing the 'saviour'.**
   Are you one of those people who enjoy working 'under pressure'? Or who takes pleasure in the challenge of a crisis situation? Well, stop! Because you are the one who is producing the crisis.

4. **Ignoring the facts.**
   When a crisis occurs, hiding your head in the sand will only aggravate the situation. Face the situation head-on, and do something about it.

How to stay on top of things during a crisis

You've surely experienced one of those days when just everything goes wrong. These crisis situations unfortunately happen more often than we'd like: work delays, boss calls with some emergency, bad time estimates, etc. It seems that Murphy's Law is often the way of the world:

Whatever can go wrong will go wrong!

Haven't you sometimes felt this?
There are ways, however, to avoid panic in such situations.

12 effective ways to dominate a crisis situation

1. You must take five minutes to be alone and regain your calm.

2. Review the list of things to be done, and the deadlines you have to meet.

3. Re-evaluate the deadlines for certain jobs to alleviate the pressure of the emergency: do you need more time? Find it, whatever it costs! There's always a way. Push back deadlines, if necessary, and inform the people involved. Above all, notify the people concerned. They will usually show more understanding than you expected.

4. Practise selective procrastination. Instead of uselessly wearing yourself out by working two hours more that day, plan to work half an hour longer for the rest of the week.

5. Look for alternatives.

6. Delegate a representative.

7. Create conditions which optimize your concentration.

8. Re-evaluate your priorities.

9. Shorten your breaks.

10. Call on all those who can, or could, help you.

11. Ask for 'payment' of past favours. Don't hesitate to ask colleagues, whom you've helped out in the past to repay the favour now. But make sure that you're faced with a real emergency! Of course you must do the same for them, when the occasion arises.

12. Prepare yourself for future crises. At the end of the day, take time to evaluate what happened and look for ways to prevent the same kind of thing from happening again.

Know how to prevent crises

There are effective ways to prevent a crises. Here are three:

1. Keep a list of possible solutions handy.
2. Appoint different people to take charge of different kinds of crises.
3. Know how to prepare alternative plans of action.

To help you, here are 15 ways to prevent the appearance and development of potential problems, and therefore of crises. Read each of the suggestions carefully, and tick off each of the techniques that you think you should put into practice:

1. Try to predict any problems that might occur. Try also to find ways to prevent or solve them.

2. Always try to keep in mind your plans for the future, your projects and objectives. This will keep problems in perspective, by placing them in the context of your overall goals.

3. Include controls in your planning diagrams for each important phase in the development of your projects.

4. Allot yourself enough time to finish your projects.

5. Learn to face problems as soon as they occur. The more you wait, the larger the problem becomes.

6. Never play ostrich and hide your head in the sand. If there's absolutely nothing you can do about a problem, then put it out of your mind completely.

7. Try to predict changes in larger trends, and prepare yourself for them.

8. Always take the time to think, even during a crisis, in order to regain control of yourself, and to be able to look at the facts objectively.

9. Write the problem down.

10. Try to evaluate the real seriousness of the situation, in order to decide whether drastic measures like changing your priorities are necessary.

11. Inform your superiors about the problem.

12. Inform other members of the staff about the problem, if necessary.

13. Try to remember whether you've been faced with a similar problem in the past. If so, apply the same measures as before if they were successful, and if they failed, don't repeat your mistakes.

14. Once you've found a solution, either through consultation or analysis, draw up a plan of attack to put the solution into practice: Who? What? How? When?

15. Carefully evaluate the results of this plan of action, and use it to prevent other problems from developing before or as they occur.

So now you're ready to face a crisis, and to deal with the problems it entails. Is everything clear? Here's a checklist, in five questions:

How to deal with a crisis

When a difficult situation arises, instead of avoiding or trying to ignore it, face it positively, without panicking or getting discouraged. Here are two key questions which will help you think clearly and creatively:

1. What is it about the situation that makes me afraid?

2. What past situations does this one remind me of?

It's important to identify these factors, to bring out the important aspects. Read over your answers, and pick out what is essential. You must never minimize or ignore the negative aspects of a situation, because instead of disappearing it will only grow. In other words, you have to understand a problem perfectly in order to be able to fight it.

Now examine the situation again:

3. What are the risks involved in confronting the problem?

4. Does this problem represent a stimulating challenge for me? If yes, how? If no, why not?

5. In case of failure, what will I do?

For any given situation, you must be able to examine all the angles objectively and thoroughly, including the possibility of failure. You must be ready to assume full responsibility for your decisions, and this with full awareness of what that means.

In this way, whatever you do will result not from fear or desperation but from a full awareness of the causes of your actions.

An ideally productive day

To conclude, let's study the following checklist carefully. It includes the optimum conditions for a productive and effective day, where crises are not impossible, but at least not probable. If one occurs, you are ready to deal with it and so they're really not crises any more but unexpected challenges which give you the opportunity to put your planning and time management system to the test.

If most of the items on this checklist correspond to what you're already doing, then you are a highly organized person. You are master of your own time and most of your days resemble this ideal working day. If there are still some snags, you can identify them and take the appropriate steps to eliminate them.

Keep in mind that the ideal day described below is not the figment of someone's imagination but is based on the real events in the working day of someone who has mastered time organization.

May this soon be your case as well!

Checklist for an ideal day

1. When you get up, you are alert, relaxed and in a positive frame of mind.

2. Your agenda for the day is already planned out when you arrive at work.

3. You have brief meetings with colleagues, superiors and subordinates to find out about any instructions or questions they might have.

4. You spend an hour working alone.

5. You take care of interruptions efficiently and quickly.

6. You use your break times to relax, always respecting your schedule.

7. You have a light, nutritious lunch.

8. You sort your post to reduce your paperwork.

9. Your meetings are well prepared and run smoothly.

10. Your appointments are well prepared.

11. Before leaving the office, you plan the next day.

12. At home, you take full advantage of the time you have to spend with family and/or friends, separating your professional from your personal life.

In this chapter, we've looked at ways to get rid of the image of the eternal loser. In the next chapter we'll find out – in ways that might surprise you – that the aim of TMS isn't to get rid of all your faults. Far from it!

Don't work harder, work smarter!

27

YOUR FAULTS
ARE YOUR BEST FRIENDS

'It's so good to do nothing...'

The aim of The Complete Time Management System is not to turn
you into a machine. On the contrary.

You must not become a slave to your time management system.
The system should be there to serve you, transform your life by
giving you more time for leisure, and helping you to be more creative
and perform to your best advantage.

In the same way, you should be aware that your business is there
to serve you, and not the other way around.

You should always be sensitive to your inner rhythm, your
intuition and your desires. You should also be aware of your faults,
of your weaknesses, of your ignorance of certain matters and of your
mistakes.

Of course, organizing your time efficiently includes a process of
self-transformation. The Complete Time Management System in
no way pretends to make you into a 'perfect being', even if such a
thing existed, and even if it were something to be desired. Thanks
to TMS, you learn how to live with your faults.

Live with ignorance?

That's right. Just like Henry Ford, who knew that all he had to
do when he didn't know something was to press a button and ask a
specialist. You can do the same.

Because of your ignorance, you can delegate and consult, two
activities which are indispensable to a healthy organization of time,
and which are, unfortunately, repellent to perfectionists and 'tortured workers'.

Celebrate each day

I don't congratulate myself for having faults, but I do exploit them, and I try to learn from my mistakes. I force myself to respect my inner rhythm at all times because I know from experience that my equilibrium is fundamental to my very existence, and that anything that threatens it must be combated.

As soon as I feel overloaded, as soon as I feel hemmed in on all sides by my obligations, I take a step back, I know it's time to let go. Not possible, you say? Your boss wouldn't appreciate it?

First I tell myself that if I let myself drown in my problems, if my days are filled with nothing but worries and tension, then what's the point of living?

And I always, always keep in mind that such a situation is the result of nothing else but my own deficient organization, my bad management of time. In short, a step back is necessary to determine what measures need to be taken.

And then . . . action!

Maybe I'm at a critical point in my career seeking to attain the next level and therefore move a step closer to my objective. Maybe I have to readjust my strategy, eliminate certain activities, etc. Whatever the situation, I take the necessary action.

I always keep in mind the epitaph that I will have inscribed on my tombstone:

**Here lies a man who tried to be content
with each day of his life.**

What about you? Would you merit this inscription on your tombstone?

If you died tonight, could you say that you were happy on the last day of your life? Who says that you are not in the process of living out the last year, the last month, or even the last day of your life? It's not the most pleasant thing to think about, is it?

There have been times, when I needed to motivate myself very strongly, that this thought sent shockwaves of electricity through my being. And like the dawn smiling on the world, a big confident smile spread across my face: I was recharged! Don't you think that you should start today to organize your time so that each day of your life becomes a triumph, a celebration, a success?

Small paradoxes with great benefits

Peter Nicolas, in his work on time management, reveals some 'paradoxical principles for more effective action'.

Read them carefully. Which of these principles are you presently applying in your life, and which would you like to apply? Do they upset your conception of how time should be organized?

Here are the four main paradoxes:

'I give myself the right to make mistakes.'
'I repeat to myself regularly: you don't have to know everything, you just have to know where to find what you need.'
'I never miss an occasion to do nothing.'
'I count on my faults.'

And he expounds on this last point:

Neither a genius nor an idiot, but full of faults, I am a business, in other words an organization with the objective of attaining positive results on a regular basis from a group of people who, on average, and if left to themselves, are not positive.

My faults will not change: *I work on that basis.*

So I do all kinds of things, with full confidence in my failings: I write because I have confidence in my lack of memory; I organize myself because I have confidence in my sloth, etc.

Your faults are your fortune

You have just seen how you can transform your weak points, your deficiencies and your faults into strengths and attributes. The secret is honesty.

First and foremost, be honest with yourself. You must accept your weaknesses, your deficiencies, your shortcomings. In fact, when you think about it for a moment, who, in your opinion, is the person most likely to succeed?

1. The people who admit none of their weaknesses or faults, who prefer to do everything themselves, and always refuse advice?

or

2. People who are aware of their limitations (while not falling into

the trap of self-denigration) and develop their strong points by delegating everything for which they have no talent?

They say that a good question is half the answer.

When formulated in this way, the question elicits an obvious answer. Nevertheless, we often persist in hiding our faults, and not taking our weaknesses into consideration.

The following checklist will allow you to verify whether you have this tendency or not, and to take appropriate measures to combat it.

1. Are you able to take responsibility for your mistakes?

2. Do you feel guilty after making a mistake?

   Can you recall an instance when, because of a past error or a feeling of guilt, you have been unable to make a decision? Write the details down, and examine them carefully.

3. Do you analyse your mistakes in order to learn from them? Note two examples of mistakes that you've made, which have resulted in improvements in your work.

   At work, what errors do you most frequently commit which, if eliminated, would increase your effectiveness and productivity? Note the most frequent, and the ways to resolve them.

4. Do you re-examine your decisions in the light of new information? If not, write down an example of a bad decision which could have been transformed into positive results had you adopted this procedure.

5. Do you feel the need to know everything? If yes, note the time you spend on various kinds of reading.

   Then ask yourself how this time could be put to better use.

6. If this isn't one of your faults, do you know where to find the information you need? Write down your potential sources of information, and the frequency with which you call on them.

7. Do you have a list of priority reading, which is related to your work priorities?

8. Do you allow yourself to do nothing?

9. Do you feel guilty doing nothing?

10. Do you give yourself time to do nothing?

11. During these times, do you give yourself over to creative thinking?

12. Are you aware of which of your faults could lead to self-improvements? Identify two, and define the ways in which they could help you mature and gain experience.

13. In order of priority, what decisions are you going to make, following completion of this questionnaire, that will improve your habits in your professional and personal life?

14. Carry them out!

**Use your faults to motivate yourself
and gain precious time.**

28

THE KEYS TO CONCENTRATION

In the preceding chapter we saw that it is necessary to learn to live with certain of our faults and weaknesses. We have to account for them in our organization of time if we want to be happy and efficient. More than that, they can actually help us if we use these faults correctly.

But there are, nevertheless, certain faults which are difficult to accept – for us as well as others!

One of them is distraction, which is one of the greatest time consumers. I could have included it in the previous chapter, but since its causes are usually psychological, I prefer to cover it in this chapter on concentration.

The problem of distraction

How many times have you spent ten minutes looking for your keys, only to find that you left them in the door?

What about the name of an important new client – it's on the tip of your tongue but impossible to recall?

Or a document that you and your secretary spend half an hour looking for – only to remember that it hasn't been written yet?

These are a few examples of distraction. There are obviously many, many more. What is upsetting about distraction – and the reason why it must be located and eliminated – is that it not only results in a waste of time but usually causes a lot of stress as well.

What about you? Are you distracted?

Test

1. Do you forget where you parked your car?
   often _____ sometimes _____ never _____

2. Do you change plans already made?
   often _____ sometimes _____ never _____

3. Do you forget birthdays, appointments and other special occasions?
   often _____ sometimes _____ never _____

4. Do you sometimes go on a long shopping trip and spend hours looking around, only to return without the article you wanted in the first place?
   often _____ sometimes _____ never _____

5. Do you forget why you've called a client or a friend?
   often _____ sometimes _____ never _____

6. Do you hang up the phone and then remember that you've forgotten to mention something important?
   often _____ sometimes _____ never _____

7. Do you do things while thinking about something else?
   often _____ sometimes _____ never _____

8. Have you found yourself locked out of your car or house?
   often _____ sometimes _____ never _____

9. Do you leave home, only to remember that you've forgotten something important?
   often _____ sometimes _____ never _____

10. Do you put things in the wrong place? For example, your keys in the fridge, and the butter in the cupboard?
    often _____ sometimes _____ never _____

11. Do you miss planes, trains, buses?
    often _____ sometimes _____ never _____

12. Do you leave your keys in the lock, or forget to do the zip on your coat?
    often _____ sometimes _____ never _____

13. Do you repeat an action because you forget that you've already done it?
    often _____ sometimes _____ never _____

14. Do you forget to do things on your agenda?
    often _____ sometimes _____ never _____

15. Do you find yourself suddenly lost, because you've kept on walking or driving, completely absorbed in your thoughts?
    often _____ sometimes _____ never _____

16. Do you lock or unlock your door when it's already done?
    often _____ sometimes _____ never _____

17. Do you slip, or bump into objects when you walk?
    often _____ sometimes _____ never _____

If you have more than five 'often' or 'sometimes' answers, here's what to do...

Some advice on how to combat distraction

There are many causes of distraction, often deep-seated, insidious and subtle. It can be the result of overwork, boredom, a lack of motivation, a fear of being wrong or of an obsessional desire to please, which makes us incapable of concentrating.

Fortunately, distraction is not incurable. Here are techniques to lessen or eliminate the effects of distraction, and advice on how to cure, or at least treat, this infirmity.

1. Try to establish a place for each object. Don't place anything randomly, or at least do so as seldom as possible.

2. Place the things that absolutely must be done so that they are easily visible, with some kind of memory aid. Better still, associate one thing with another that has to be done.

   For example, if I have to post an extremely important letter, I put it with my car keys. I know I will need my keys when I go out, so I won't forget the letter either.
   If I'm not sure I have to go out, I put the letter on the office floor, in front of the door: either I'll step on it, or deal with it.

3. Force yourself to be more conscious of what you're doing by practising concentration. Ask youself if you're not over-extended. We often don't realize it, even though we exhibit all the symptoms.

4. Make checklists. It is without a doubt the best way (and unfortunately the least applied) to remember things.

   This book contains numerous checklists. Don't hesitate to draft more, as the need arises.

5. Systematically keep notes or recordings of things you don't want to forget.

6. Why not take a course or read a book on how to improve your memory? It will be of immense service to you.

To conclude, a last piece of advice, perhaps the most important. Learn to live *in the present*. It's the only thing that really belongs to you.

**The past will never return, the future doesn't exist,
only the present counts!**

Worrying doesn't solve anything

Stop and think a minute. Has any of the worrying you've done about everything and nothing ever helped to solve your problems? Has it ever accomplished anything positive to further a project?

The answer is clearly: no.

Yet how often do we let ourselves get carried away by a tide of worries, fears and anxieties, which, in certain cases, render us completely inneffective? I'm not suggesting by this that you should be completely careless. What I'm saying is that *worrying is always useless*.

What should be done instead is to look calmly and energetically for solutions. That's how progress can be made.

Analyse your worries carefully. They usually take the form of an incessant internal monologue, something like: 'I wonder if the client's going to like the new product...' (Will worrying whether or not the client likes the product, while you're at the other end of town, have any effect on the final decision? No! And yet you continue to worry...)

'My boss might want me to resign when he sees the report of this month's catastrophic sales...' (Is your boss going to like the report any more because you're worried about it?)

'I wonder when I'm going to get that cheque. I've been waiting two weeks!' (Is your worrying going to speed up the cheque?)

Analyse the situation lucidly

Try to understand just how useless worry and anxiety are (except as alarm signals in certain situations, which might lead to urgent, sometimes radical preventive measures). What you have to do is *take steps to resolve the situation.* That's all! Nothing else!

For example, you're waiting for a cheque: why not call the client right away to find out what's causing the delay?

Sincerity can often be a disarmingly effective tool. Explain that you're in a difficult position, that you really need the money, etc. You might be surprised at how quickly the cheque arrives after that.

Or you can ask when, exactly, the cheque will be sent. What the latest date will be? When you know that you'll be receiving the cheque on a certain date, you have nothing more to worry about.

If the particular client is not reliable, and has caused unreasonably long delays in the past, look right away for alternative methods of recovering your money: a lawyer's letter perhaps, or engaging a collection agency (which will take a small percentage of the total amount).

Isn't there anyone else, another client, who owes you money? Could you ask a friend, or your bank manager? Banks will sometimes accept the debt as collateral, and advance the money you need right away.

If a single solution is not enough to allay your fears, then find a back-up, or a few alternatives. From these, you can choose the best one.

Also ask yourself what you would do if the worst were to happen. Find a super-solution in case of extreme need.

Most worries never materialize.

This principle belongs to the great Dale Carnegie. When I discovered it I was a little surprised. But since I have a systematic nature (and a certain amount of scepticism, which I consider healthy), I decided to do a little verification.

I reviewed all the causes I had for worry over the past few months and I realized, to my great shame, that nine times out of ten my worries were completely groundless. The things I was afraid would happen didn't happen, or didn't have the negative effects I thought they would.

So worries are not only useless, they can be positively *harmful*.

Make your worries disappear like magic

Here's an 'anti-worry' technique which can be applied to any upsetting situation. There are only five, extremely simple steps:

1. First conduct an analysis of the situation, without leaving anything out. Then determine what the most negative consequences of the situation could be.

2. Resign yourself to accepting these consequences, if they ever materialized.

3. Next, devote all your time and energy to finding a solution which is likely to ease the negative repercussions of your mistake.

4. Act!

5. Do something else: clear the air.

Always keep in mind the famous statement made by Charles Kettering:

> 'A well formulated problem is half the solution!'

How to formulate a problem well

Here's Dale Carnegie's method. It's simple, and it has helped millions of people solve their problems.

- Take two pieces of paper.

- On the first write: '*What exactly am I afraid of?*'

- Define your apprehensions as exhaustively as possible.

- On the second sheet write: '*What can I do about it?*'

- Note any and all solutions that come to mind.

- Break each solution down into step-by-step activities.

- Finally, make a decision.

Once your decision is made, follow the advice of William James: 'Once a decision has been made, and the time for action is at hand, you must deliberately put aside all apprehension about the final result!'

And never forget Alexis Carrel's maxim: 'Businessmen who don't know how to fight off their fears die young!'

Life and happiness is a state of mind

All authors, psychologists, philosophers, etc. would agree with the statement: 'Life and happiness is a state of mind!'

If you cultivate positive thoughts, if you develop a dynamic way of thinking, thoughts of prosperity, etc., you will attract energy and situations favourable to achieving your objectives.

Life will become the game that it was always meant to be. You will know the rules, and apply them to your advantage, like those who belong to the élite class of winners and achievers.

Success and mastery of time are the results of a lasting and profound process of self-transformation.

By deepening your understanding of yourself, you will realize that there are two types of individuals: some are programmed for success, others for failure.

This mechanism can be translated into what psychologists call self-image. To learn more about the subject, I recommend the best-seller by Dr M. Maltz entitled *Psychocybernetics*.

The mysterious self-image

What is a self-image?

Briefly, it is the product of all your past experiences, of your successes and failures, and the sum of all the thoughts you've accumulated throughout your lifetime. Some people are deeply convinced that they will never be able to attain the post of director of their company. That's their self-image.

Result?

They don't get the job, because, strange as this might seem at first, reality conforms to the image we have of ourselves.

As the philosopher William James said:

'We lead our lives as it is imagined in our minds.'

One of the best, simplest and most rapid ways to transform your self-image is to use auto-suggestion. I have personally recommended it to hundreds of people, and all those who tried it have undergone a rapid transformation, surprising even to themselves.

Change your inner attitude

Re-read this method. Underline phrases, sentences and paragraphs that mean something to you, that you would like to incorporate in your thoughts and behaviour. By repeating them in your mind, by reading them over often, you will become more and more positive. And at the same time, you will realize just how negative you've been up to now. Your sense of time organization will change. All the mental blocks, which have been preventing you from putting the techniques you've learned here into practice, despite the fact that you are rationally convinced of their value, will disappear one by one. Your inner being will assimilate them, and they will become part of your life.

You will understand why you procrastinate. It's often because you have a negative self-image. Because you lack confidence. Because you're afraid of failure. All these things are simply the result of negative programming, which you can change in the twinkling of an eye.

You will understand why you've been a perfectionist.

You will understand why you've been a tortured worker or workaholic who can never stop to enjoy life. You will understand why you never seem able to attain your objectives.

And you will immediately be able to start putting all the positive aspects of time management into practice.

What are you going to do ... starting now!

Start right now by writing down the measures you are going to apply.

What are you going to do, starting tonight?

From the moment you get up tomorrow, what are you going to do to make your day more dynamic, and more in keeping with the principles we have studied together?

Make your evenings power sources for the following day

An evening at home is too often spent brooding over the day's problems, worrying about what has to be done tomorrow, in short wallowing in negativity.

Put a stop to all that: think positive!

Keeping in mind the principles you've just read, how can you transform your evenings into sources of positive power? Note down five ways you can think of to pass a free evening pleasantly (Family? Going out? Cinema? Theatre? Concert? etc.)

You now have all the elements you need to make positive thinking a fact of your life. It's up to you to take advantage of them.

**The only limits on tomorrow's accomplishments
are the doubts we have today.**

CONCLUSION: YOUR MOST IMPORTANT ASSET

You're getting older ... The time you have is limited ... If you let unexpected disturbances distract you, if you don't use your time intelligently, each time you hesitate to apply the techniques of The Complete Time Management System remember the story of the fisherman, which demonstrates the maxim: 'Time is money ... and fun!'

'There was once an old fisherman, living on a deserted island off the coast of Ireland. One day he found a shining object on the beach, something he'd never seen before – a mirror.

'He looked at himself and exclaimed, 'My God, it's my father!'

'He brought the mirror home in secret, and hid it in the attic. And every night, without his wife knowing, he went up to look at it.

'She became worried by his strange behaviour, and one day, while he was fishing far out at sea, she went up to the attic to see what was going on.

'She ended up finding the mysterious object, and was immediately reassured. "Heaven be praised," she said, "it's only an old woman!"'

Tick tock ... each second counts

We are all a little like the people in this story. We are not aware of the fact that time is passing, and we're getting older. Or more accurately, we're not aware of how quickly time goes by.

Thanks to TMS, you have learned how to organize your time so that you have more freedom to enjoy life, and more time for your leisure.

And when you come down to it, isn't that what's most important?

The more you master your time, the freer you will become, and the better you can savour each passing second.

The art of regularly asking the right questions

I've had occasion to think a lot about time organization these last few years. Thinking about time is a process that demands constant revison. It's not something you acquire, once and for all.

What you *can* acquire is the right attitude towards the organization of your time. And this attitude consists of regularly questioning the efficiency of your methods. You have to ask yourself decisive questions:

● How much is each hour of my time worth?
● How can I make better use of my time today? Am I using my time to the best advantage right now?
● Do I delegate sufficiently? The right tasks? To the right people?
● Am I master of my use of time, or a slave?

I got into the habit of asking myself a series of ten key questions once a year – usually in January, which is a good time to make adjustments and resolutions. I won't tell you what these questions are because they depend on the individual and you should find *your own*.

I answer these questions as honestly as possible.

And I check to see if I've kept the resolutions I made the year before.

Few people take the trouble to do this. However, I can state that since I started this practice, which only takes one afternoon a year – very little if I compare it to the benefits it brings – I have made enormous progress.

If you think about it, how are you supposed to know where you're going if you don't regularly measure the progress you've made? On the other hand, it's much easier to stagnate, to let yourself go, if you don't take stock. The precision of your objectives and progress go hand in hand.

As we come to the end of this method, I suggest doing a very important exercise. You've had the opportunity to think about your time organization for a number of hours now. Write down the ten questions you think you should ask yourself each year.

Notice that the simple fact of having chosen these ten questions instead of any others is very significant. You didn't choose these questions by chance. (And that's why I didn't try to influence you by revealing my own personal questions.) The choice of these ten questions – and you could have chosen a thousand others, completely different – reflects your personal preoccupations, your weaknesses, your strong points, things you want to improve, as well as your objectives for the year to come.

Now that you've asked yourself the right questions, determine ten objectives that you would like to attain in the year to come (objectives, or things to improve).

What is your personal philosophy of time?

You have just assimilated the method of The Complete Time Management System. Even if you do nothing else in the immediate future, even if you have no intention of systematically putting into practice the things you've learned, you're already a better person.

First, you have become aware of the quantity of faults you have, and errors that you – and the majority of people around you – commit. It's often enough simply to become aware of a fault to correct it. In any case, it's a first, and very necessary step.

You have also learned a multitude of techniques and secrets.

I would like to suggest another exercise. If you had to sum up your philosophy of time management in 25 points, how would you do it? Write it down.

To help you, imagine that you want to pass on to your children, or to your best friend, the main points of your personal philosophy of time.

This is very important because you now understand that if you are not the master of your time, then neither are you the master of your life.

Next, write down what you'd like as your epitaph – your ultimate thought on the subject of time.

Congratulations!

That took a lot of thought!

My 55 personal techniques

Allow me now to reveal to you my 55 secrets, or personal techniques, for organizing time. They are the fruit of more than twenty years' experience, reflection and discussion with some of the most successful directors around the world. Many points have been covered in this method; others are more personal. Here they are, for you to use:

1. I exploit 'free' time: time spent in waiting rooms, airports, taxis etc. Key: visualize the day ahead, estimate the probabilities of any dead time, and prepare yourself with simple tasks: reading, correspondence, writing letters, etc.

2. I have a good idea of what an hour of my time is worth. I calculate the figure each year, and based on this I determine whether it's profitable – or not – to have work done by someone else.

3. When I work I'm careful that my time investment is not out of proportion to the profits I expect to make – in money or in satisfaction.

   Possible trap: if you don't separate work/leisure/family, you might end up being one of those 'tortured workers' or work-aholics.

4. I realize that life is short, and that 'you can't take it with you!' I therefore try to make it as pleasant as possible, here and now, and not tomorrow.

5. At the beginning of a meeting, I tell the other person how much time I can spend.

6. Not only do I make daily and monthly lists of things that have to be done, I keep the completed lists and analyse them closely.

7. I have a list of telephone numbers I use frequently, and an index of 'Companies', 'Hotels/Restaurants', and 'Health' in my address book as well as listing names alphabetically. (This list is also on my computer. I use a program that will store the information, and print out a series of address labels of the people I correspond with most frequently, every three months, in alphabetical order.)

8. I tell myself that the time we usually allot to do a task is

based on our mental limitations, which should be re-evaluated regularly.

9. I do not let outside opinions limit my activity.

10. When I write, I keep it short: letters of three lines, notes of one sentence. I don't feel obliged to make things longer.

11. I answer my mail – or throw it out – or delegate it – each day, so that it doesn't pile up.

12. I make photocopies of important sections of books, magazines and documents and file them according to subject.

13. I have a very large wastepaper basket, and I don't worry about how much it weighs at the end of the day! I throw everything away that isn't useful, even books, thick files, etc.

14. I have a watch with an alarm, an ultra-light portable computer, a fax machine, a telephone with programmable memory, a telephone answering machine (with remote message retrieval), a micro-cassette; in short, all the gadgets that can really help me, and which are indispensable to my work.

15. I take 1 gram of Vitamin C per day.
I eat light meals.
I avoid 'dead' food (meat, fast food, etc.)
I fast one day a week.

16. I systematically avoid negative people, people who always have problems and people who give me headaches.
I seek out the opposite: positive contacts, dynamic, stimulating, creative, original people.

17. I allot myself numerous periods to relax, refresh myself, enjoy myself, etc. every day, as a way of rewarding myself for objectives I have attained.

18. I ask people who come to me with *problems* to propose their own *solutions*.

19. Before answering 'yes', I ask myself if I really want to get involved.

20. I'm not afraid of making drastic changes in my life. I act according to the principle: *If you don't like it, change it!*

21. I am honest, and start by being honest with myself. I accept my faults, weaknesses, errors, etc. as much as possible. This saves me a lot of time.

22. I sometimes go against the flow: never drive during rush hours (if possible), get some writing done when I can't sleep, etc.

23. I have ready-made checklists for everything.

24. I have my baggage prepared in advance for all my trips.

25. I consult the best specialists I can find. If they're really good, they can save me a lot of money.

26. I tell my employees that they have to 'pay their own way', by bringing in more income than their salary.

27. I put each thing in its place.

28. I empty my wastepaper basket each night – and I put whatever worries I have down on paper, which is another way of emptying the rubbish.

29. I keep notebooks, with all the information I can find on various subjects of interest. (A notebook is better than separate sheets because it's easier to manage.)

    I only write on the right-hand side: I reserve the left side for later observations.

30. I try to predict any snags that might occur, and work out what I would do in each case. I consider the possibility of failure – and plan my reactions as if I were playing a game of chess.

31. When a mistake is made, I look for its cause and make sure that it doesn't happen again.

32. I take frequent vacations. This forces me to finish a job – or to delegate it – before leaving. Holidays are a source of new ideas. They help recharge my batteries, providing renewed energy. They motivate me to really get things moving, add fresh perspective and enthusiasm, etc.

33. My business works for me, and not the other way around. Organizing time is supposed to help me, give me pleasure. I am not its slave. I am always sensitive to my inner rhythm, my intuition, my desires.

34. Everything that isn't indispensable is useless! This is what I tell myself when tasks, obligations, etc. start hemming me in.

  The beauty of a flower, the smells of spring, the joy of a beautiful countryside . . . these are things which I consider indispensable to life.

  I know what I need to function well.

35. What epitaph do I want on my tombstone?
Each day I take a step closer towards this goal.
I try to live so that I could die each day, and be content with my life.

36. I eliminate worries as much as possible: they are the main negative consumers of time. I have confidence in my subconscious.

37. I telephone – or send a fax – instead of meeting someone personally. I call instead of writing. I inform people, instead of keeping things to myself. I always call before going to a shop or meeting, to see if they have what I want, if the appointment still stands.

38. I write memos with:
  ● points
  ● numbers
  ● CAPITALS
  ● underlining
  ● destination: . . .
  ● copies to: . . .

39. I subscribe to newsletters and magazines. I cut out interesting sections, and throw away the rest.

40. I take time for personal hygiene (bath, sauna, massage, etc.) which is a source of pleasure.

  I take the time to have a good breakfast, which is a source of pleasure. I try to start the day with pleasure!

41. I buy myself gifts as rewards for my performance.

42. I limit my needs to the pleasure I get out of things I do, give, ask for, receive, etc.

43. I always keep my word.

44. I refuse to be disturbed by other people's opinions.

45. I learn to make the distinction between what's important and minor details.

46. I learn to group things I have to do. I try to be as astute as possible in my organization of time.

47. I use abbreviations when I write: prgm instead of program; commtn instead of communication; tm instead of time, etc.

48. When I'm walking in the country, I consider the resting periods as important as the walk. I rejoice in the splendour of nature ... mountains, the sea, etc. I engrave these positive moments on my mind. They are storehouses of serenity.

49. I listen to my body, I respect it, care for it, make deals with it.

50. I make deals with myself and with others about anything that might recur, and that I – or the other person – wants to change.

51. I apply the Pareto Principle to the full: 80 per cent of results are obtained from 20 per cent of the work.

52. I train myself each day to increase my powers of concentration. I know that it is possible, with practice, to be totally concentrated, with no distraction, for periods up to three hours (and even longer for people who are more gifted).

A study conducted by Executime, publishers of an executive newsletter, shows that the average executive spends 10 minutes getting into a file, stays concentrated for 20 minutes, and then uses another 10 minutes to relax. This makes a total of 40 minutes, half of which is unproductive.

So I train myself to gain a minute more at a time of extended concentration, with these statistics in mind. (My record is four hours, but I regularly remain totally concentrated for $2\frac{1}{2}$ hours.)

53. Whenever possible, I apply the rule: *Whatever is not indispensable is useless.*

54. I pay as little attention as possible to value judgements. If I am sure of what I'm doing, others can think what they like while I continue to progress.

55. I always verify my sources of information when I decide to get involved in a project or solve a problem. (Amazing how much time this saves!)

Monthly checklist

To be sure that you're making progress, get into the habit of making regular checks of your performance. Do this each month. This checklist covers all the important aspects of The Complete Time Management System. Make 12 copies, one for each month of the year.

If you notice, when filling in this checklist, that you're repeatedly confronted with the same kinds of problems, read the relevant chapters in the method.

Don't forget that honesty, common sense and perseverance will help you overcome all your difficulties. In this way, you can master your organization of time.

Yes No

1. Do you plan different kinds of tasks in your daily schedule, in order to revitalize yourself?

2. Do you purposely limit the number of hours you work a week, and stick to this schedule?

3. Do you work with a flexible schedule, as often as the situation permits? For example: have lunch a little early or late, to avoid the big rush.

4. Do you get to your appointments on time? Do you include getting to and from appointments when calculating your time expenditure?

5. Is there only one project at a time on your desk (the one you're working on at the moment)?

6. Are you reluctant to ask for supplementary information about a particular question or problem?

7. Do you plan regular contact sessions with members of your staff?

8. Do you train your employees so that they can accomplish new tasks easily and efficiently?

9. Do you anticipate changes, prepare for them, and adapt yourself to suit the new situation?

10. Do you avoid accentuating personal conflicts and treat their resolution as an objective to be attained?

11. Do you allot yourself the time to plan your activities better, and determine your objectives?

12. Have you identified the time of day during which you are most productive?

13. Have you eliminated all forms of interruption during those hours?

14. Have you scheduled top priority work for those hours?

15. Do you use those hours to do difficult or unpleasant work, that demands a lot of concentration?

16. Do you assign easier tasks for the rest of the day?

17. Do you accord a minimum of attention to non-priority tasks?

18. Do you eliminate all useless activity?

19. When you make decisions, do you act on them immediately or very soon after?

20. Do you evaluate tasks to be done in a realistic way? (Earliest completion date ... Latest completion date, etc.)

21. Do you prepare a daily agenda of things to be done?

22. Do you subdivide a job into numerous sub-tasks?

23. Do you set deadlines for each of these tasks?

24. Do you finish one job before going on to the next?

25. Do you delegate as much as possible?

26. Do you delegate or eliminate the maximum number of reports?

27. Do you stick to the essentials in your conversations?

28. Do you manage your work so as to get results in a reasonable amount of time?

29. Do you provide your colleagues with *precise instructions*?

30. Do you try to improve channels of communication?

**Revise this checklist regularly and add items
that are relevant to your personal situation.**

Rejoice in the present and in life

You are now equipped with the practical tools to *have more time*.
How are you going to use it?

● Invest your time harmoniously in work, family life and leisure.
That's how you will remain *balanced*, self-confident, and be a
source of constant satisfaction to yourself and those around you.

● Spend time on your health, keep yourself in good physical shape:
you'll feel better and live longer.

● Joy and happiness are also children of time. You need contacts,
friends, intimate relationships and love to be happy: and all these
things take time.

As the Greek physician Hippocrates said, life is short. It must be
lived and enjoyed to the full while it lasts. Let TMS help you stop
procrastinating about your own happiness. I wish you success and
joy, with all my heart.

APPENDIX
MODELS AND CHECKLISTS

Checklist: change your attitude

Make lasting changes in your attitude to manage your time better.

1. Observe yourself: make regular appointments with yourself and evaluate your progress, your strong points, your weaknesses, the things you should correct as quickly as possible. Set yourself new objectives, with figures and dates, to be attained before your next observation session.

2. Observe others: identify those who are causing you to waste time, who are preventing you from managing your time well, or obstructing certain of your efforts. Take concrete measures. If necessary, meet them to discuss ways of solving the problem.

3. Improve your understanding: time management is a technique which must be practised vigilantly. Always try to refresh your understanding by reading the method over regularly, and by writing down each of your personal discoveries; read other books on time management and personal development, to expand your understanding; take part in seminars or conferences on the same subjects.

4. Help others: discreetly, and as much as possible in private, help others to get rid of their bad habits concerning time management; teach them your favourite techniques; recommend publications and methods that can help them.

This will not only be easy to do, and make the person you help feel indebted to you, it will also permit you to co-ordinate your own time management with theirs, so that if you work together, you will improve your chances of becoming the leader of a successful team.

5. Be reasonable: use common sense, and don't try to revolutionize your use of time and your working methods all at once. On the contrary, you should proceed in a steady, open manner. Be patient, and don't adopt new techniques or habits until you've mastered and implemented the most important ones. In this way, you can measure the results of each of your efforts step by step.

List of priorities

Time period: from: _____ to: _____ 19___

Objectives _____

_____

_____

_____

Priorities for this period

Estimated time _____

Description _____

_____

Priority _____

Person in charge _____

Deadline _____

Estimated time _____

Description _____

_____

Priority _____

Person in charge _____

Deadline _____

Estimated time _____

Description _____

_____

Priority _____

Person in charge _____

Deadline _____

Estimated time _____

Description _____

_____

Priority _____

Person in charge _____

Deadline _____

Estimated time _____

Description _____

_____

Priority _____

Person in charge _____

Deadline _____

Estimated time _____

Description _____

_____

Priority _____

Person in charge _____

Deadline _____

Long-term goals or objectives

Name: _____ Date: _____

In the space below write the list of your objectives in order of priority

Objective No. 1: _____

Steps necessary to attain it: _____

_____

_____

Date limit: _____

Objective No. 2: _____

Steps necessary to attain it: _____

_____

_____

Date limit: _____

Objective No. 3: _____

Steps necessary to attain it: _____

_____

_____

Date limit: _____

Objective No. 4: _____

Steps necessary to attain it: _____

_____

_____

Date limit: _____

Objective No. 5: _____

Steps necessary to attain it: _____

_____

_____

Date limit: _____

Objective No. 6: _____

Steps necessary to attain it: _____

_____

_____

Date limit: _____

Annual goals or objectives

Name: _____ Date: _____

In the space below write the list of your goals in order of priority

Objective No. 1: _____

Steps necessary to attain it: _____

_____

_____

Date limit: _____

Objective No. 2: _____

Steps necessary to attain it: _____

_____

_____

Date limit: _____

Objective No. 3: _____

Steps necessary to attain it: _____

_____

_____

Date limit: _____

Objective No. 4: _____

Steps necessary to attain it: _____

_____

_____

Date limit: _____

Objective No. 5: _____

Steps necessary to attain it: _____

_____

_____

Date limit: _____

Objective No. 6: _____

Steps necessary to attain it: _____

_____

_____

Date limit: _____

Quarterly goals or objectives

Name: _____ Date: _____

In the space below write the list of your goals in order of priority

Objective No. 1: _____

Steps necessary to attain it: _____

_____

_____

Date limit: _____

Objective No. 2: _____

Steps necessary to attain it: _____

_____

_____

Date limit: _____

Objective No. 3: _____

Steps necessary to attain it: _____

_____

_____

Date limit: _____

Objective No. 4: _____

Steps necessary to attain it: _____

_____

_____

Date limit: _____

Objective No. 5: _____

Steps necessary to attain it: _____

_____

_____

Date limit: _____

Objective No. 6: _____

Steps necessary to attain it: _____

_____

_____

Date limit: _____

Monthly goals or objectives

Name: _____   Date: _____

In the space below write the list of your goals in order of priority

Objective No. 1: _____

Steps necessary to attain it: _____

_____

_____

Date limit: _____

Objective No. 2: _____

Steps necessary to attain it: _____

_____

_____

Date limit: _____

Objective No. 3: _____

Steps necessary to attain it: _____

_____

_____

Date limit: _____

Objective No. 4: _____

Steps necessary to attain it: _____

_____

_____

Date limit: _____

Objective No. 5: _____

Steps necessary to attain it: _____

_____

_____

Date limit: _____

Objective No. 6: _____

Steps necessary to attain it: _____

_____

_____

Date limit: _____

Weekly goals or objectives

Name: _____ Date: _____

In the space below write the list of your goals in order of priority

Objective No. 1: _____

Steps necessary to attain it: _____

_____

_____

Date limit: _____

Objective No. 2: _____

Steps necessary to attain it: _____

_____

_____

Date limit: _____

Objective No. 3: _____

Steps necessary to attain it: _____

_____

_____

Date limit: _____

Objective No 4: _____

Steps necessary to attain it: _____

_____

_____

Date limit: _____

Objective No. 5: _____

Steps necessary to attain it: _____

_____

_____

Date limit: _____

Objective No. 6: _____

Steps necessary to attain it: _____

_____

_____

Date limit: _____

Problem sheet

The problem:

Causes:

internal _____   external _____

Ways to resolve the problem:

Solution No. 1 _____

_____

_____

_____

Solution No. 2 _____

_____

_____

_____

Solution No. 3 _____

_____

_____

_____

Time limit: _____

Objective: Number of weeks _____

Starting dates to apply measures: _____

Control dates

1: _____ 19____   2: _____ 19____

3: _____ 19____   4: _____ 19____

Comments: How have I attained my goal? _____

_____

Suggestion: ask your colleagues or the directors of other companies how they deal with similar problems.

Project management

Project Name:

Stage

1. Exact goal: _____

_____

2. Expiry date: _____

3. Division of sub-tasks: _____

_____

_____

_____

_____

4. Order of execution: _____

_____

_____

_____

5. Dates/deadlines and indicators: _____

_____

_____

6. Description of tasks: _____

_____

_____

_____

_____

7. Follow-up: _____

_____

_____

Note down deadlines, personnel and resources.

Your level of coherence

Establishing priorities means directing our thoughts so that there is a coherent relation between *who we want to be* and *what we do*. First determine, as honestly as possible, the following priorities. Be concise and precise.

1. Lifetime priorities

1. _____
2. _____
3. _____
4. _____

2. Professional priorities

1. _____
2. _____
3. _____
4. _____

3. Reasons for your function (job)

1. _____
2. _____
3. _____
4. _____

4. Priorities of your function (job)

1. _____
2. _____
3. _____
4. _____

When your priorities are established, try to see if there are convergences, contradictions or flaws in the answers you provided.

It is important to establish priorities, to avoid trying to do too many things at the same time, which leads directly to a dispersal of energy. We must also make sure that our priorities don't contradict each other, which is a sure sign of an incoherent strategy.

Lines of thought

1. Did you notice that some of your answers are not related? Is there a way to make your priorities more compatible? If yes, how?

2. You have raised certain contradictions. Are they real contradictions, or only apparent ones? Can you reformulate them so that the contradictions are eliminated?

If the contradictions are real and deep-seated, don't try to eliminate them just yet. Keep them in mind, and look for medium- and long-term solutions so that they are dealt with in the context of a larger perspective.

Also get into the habit of periodically reviewing your objectives, to make sure that they're in line with your development.

General comments

What is your level of coherence?

- Very good
- Average
- Nil.

What are the remedies?

Do these exercises again in three months, once you have digested the material in this method and started putting it into practice.

The ideal division of your time

Here is a technique used successfully by Louis Robert, a friend of mine, who is a management consultant. The principle is based on first structuring the long term, and working progressively down to the day by day.

1. Yearly
- Determine optimum periods for vacations, long weekends, days off, etc.
- Determine optimum periods for training, business trips, visits, etc.
- Determine optimum periods for work, project development, etc.

2. Monthly
- Determine the number of days of rest.
- Calculate the number of working days for important jobs.
- Determine the days for meetings, important appointments, seminars, etc. when everything should be 'under control'.

3. Weekly
- Determine the days off.
- Calculate the total number of working hours.
- Determine which working days will be used for important business.

4. Daily
- Establish the number of working hours.
- Calculate the hours spent travelling/commuting.
- Determine the number of hours with your family.
- Determine the number of hours for yourself.
- Determine the work sequence. For example:

Study: 2 hours
Negotiations: 1 hour
Planning: 1 hour
Management: 3 hours.

Bibliography

Bliss, Edwin, *Getting Things Done: A.B.Cs of Time Management*, Futura

Carnegie, Dale, *How to Win Friends and Influence People*, Heinemann

Crosby, Philip B., *Running Things: The Art of Making Things Happen*, McGraw

Ferner, J. D., *Successful Time Management*, (Self-teaching Guides), Wiley

Hill, Napoleon, *Think and Grow Rich*, Wilshire Book Co., L.A.

Hobbs, Charles, *Time, Power: The Revolutionary Time Management System That Can Change your Professional and Personal Life*, Harper and Row

Peters, Thomas J. and Waterman, Robert H., *In Search of Excellence*, Harper and Row

Seiwert, Lothar J., *Time Management*, Kogan Page

Turla, Peter and Hawkins, Kathleen, *Time Management Made Easy*, Panther Books

Winston, Stephanie, *Organised Executive: New Ways to Manage Time, Paper and People*, Kogan Page

Business Books for Successful Managers

PIATKUS BUSINESS BOOKS have been created for people like you, busy executives and managers who need expert knowledge readily available in a clear and easy-to-follow format. All the books are written by specialists in their field. They will help you improve your skills quickly and effortlessly in the workplace and on a personal level.

Each book is packed with ideas and good advice which can be put into practice immediately. Titles include:

The Best Person for the Job Malcolm Bird

The Complete Time Management System Christian H. Godefroy and John Clark

How to Collect the Money You are Owed Malcolm Bird

How to Develop and Profit from Your Creative Powers Michael LeBoeuf

How to Win Customers and Keep Them for Life Michael LeBoeuf

Leadership Skills for Every Manager Jim Clemmer and Art McNeil

Powerspeak: The Complete Guide to Public Speaking and Communication Dorothy Leeds

Smart Questions for Successful Managers Dorothy Leeds

The Strategy of Meetings George David Kieffer

Your Memory Kenneth L. Higbee

You too can benefit from expert advice. Just look out for our distinctive Piatkus silver business book jackets in the shops. For a free brochure with further information on our complete range of business titles, please write to:

Business Books Department
Piatkus Books
5 Windmill Street
London, W1P 1HF

PIATKUS

LEADERSHIP SKILLS FOR EVERY MANAGER
by Jim Clemmer and Art McNeil

Here is a book which offers managers new techniques to improve organisational effectiveness. It shows how, by developing leadership skills throughout a company, the right ideas can be transformed into profitable, bottom line results. With practical examples, highlighted discussions, charts and quotations, managers, executives and supervisors will find *Leadership Skills for Every Manager* an invaluable catalyst for effective action.

Jim Clemmer and Art McNeil are founders and operating executives of The Achieve Group, a Canadian company dedicated to helping organisations improve quality, customer service, innovation and productivity.

THE STRATEGY OF MEETINGS
by George David Kieffer

Meetings are central to business and professional life. They are where you reach decisions, make deals and manage people, and they give you prime opportunities to boost your own career. Using a wide range of strategies, lawyer and businessman George David Kieffer shows you how you can make any meeting work for you.

'Kieffer shows how meetings are central to your own career success and effective management. His book will change forever the way you conduct yourself in meetings.' – *Kenneth Blanchard PhD, co-author of 'The One-Minute Manager'*

'His book is must reading for anyone who participates in meetings, from novice to chairman of the board.' – *Harold M. Williams, president and Chief Executive Officer of the J. Paul Getty Trust*

'. . . full of sound conventional advice, as relevant to schools and colleges as to corporations . . .' – *The Times Educational Supplement*

HOW TO DEVELOP AND PROFIT FROM YOUR CREATIVE POWERS
by Michael LeBoeuf

People who know how to create good ideas and turn them into reality will always do well, whatever the future may bring.

- Learn how to get in touch with your creative self
- Strengthen your imagination with 9 simple exercises
- Focus your creative energies on goals that work for you
- Break out of habitual thinking patterns
- Learn simple techniques for creating new ideas at will
- Discover how to present your ideas to other people and turn them into a profitable reality

Michael LeBoeuf PhD is professor of management, organisational behaviour and communications at the University of New Orleans.

HOW TO WIN CUSTOMERS AND KEEP THEM FOR LIFE
by Michael LeBoeuf

How to Win Customers and Keep Them for Life will be the most important sales aid you will ever have. It will tell you:

- How to provide the best quality customer service
- The reasons which makes customers buy and come back
- How to be the kind of person customers like to buy from
- How to find more customers
- How to make customers recognise the fine service you give them
- The five best ways to keep customers coming back
- How to keep your customers happy

How to Win Customers and Keep Them for Life is a hard-hitting, action-ready, rewards and incentive programme for creating a winning sales team. Written by Michael LeBoeuf, one of America's foremost business consultants, this practical no-nonsense guide tells you everything you need to know about successful selling.

POWERSPEAK:
THE COMPLETE GUIDE TO PUBLIC SPEAKING AND COMMUNICATION
by Dorothy Leeds

Excellent speaking and presentation skills are the key to success. In *Powerspeak*, Dorothy Leeds shows you how to:

- Control fear – and use it to your advantage
- Get attention and hold it
- Learn techniques and strategies known only to top professional speakers
- Avoid being boring
- Handle difficult questions confidently
- Make every presentation a winner

Dorothy Leeds runs a management consultancy firm in the United States. She is an experienced public speaker and runs seminars and workshops on public speaking and communication skills.

YOUR MEMORY
by Kenneth L. Higbee

Your Memory explains how the memory works and shows how to learn simple recall systems which will enable you to perform seemingly miraculous feats of memory in your daily routine. This practical guide will tell you:

- What you can expect from your memory
- How to remember almost anything
- How to develop strategies for effective learning
- How to work miracles with your memory
- How to create mental filing systems
- How to use mnemonics

Kenneth Higbee PhD teaches memory improvement at Brigham Young University in the United States.

'. . . most undergraduates would save themselves a great deal of wasted time and energy if they put Higbee's precepts into practice.'
– *The Independent*